C

PREFACE

The goal of Creative Retirement for Women is to provide an overview of the most common retirement concerns for women and couples combined with wisdom and common sense solutions. Retirement for the current generation will be more individualized and less reliant on prior models. This book is about creatively designed retirement and how women are in control of its success.

The reason I wrote this book for women began about 10 year ago when my male friends began to retire. Almost every one of them destroyed the retirement for themselves and their wives. One panicked when he had to care for his wife and ran away to South America leaving her destitute. She now resides in a budget nursing home for the rest of her life. Another guy day traded the couple's life savings away. They lost their house and now live in a trailer park. This pattern of the male accidentally sabotaging the retirement causes an increase in divorce that has been ignored.

I decided to write a book to help keep couples together through the adjustments of retirement. But, the male does not see his behavior as a problem and won't plan or read about it. So, I had to appeal to the better judgment of women to save their retirement. The better social and organizations skills of women are needed to successfully plan and manage their partner. This puts the women in control, reduces the confusion for men and ensures a happier second half.

The author wants to thank the many female consultants who helped make this work relevant and insightful. Besides empowering women, a unique aspect of the book is that by revealing motivations of male behavior that are understandable to women, it becomes useful for couples planning. If you have some idea of what to expect from your partner when he confronts age milestones, you'll be better prepared and have solutions rather than be undermined in retirement.

The author's background of a psychotherapist, hospice therapist, a stockbroker, insurance agent, and real estate investor are all combined to yield a comprehensive analysis of retirement. With the use of female based research, female consultants, and as a male therapist, I provide unique viewpoints of both genders in a factual and supportive manner with a future orientation. L. J.

Copyright 2014 by Lee Johnson, LCSW   All rights reserved. No part of this book may be reproduced in any form or by any electronic or mechanical means, including information storage and retrial systems, without permission in writing except by a reviewer who may quote brief passages in a review

Cover Illustration courtesy of dreamtime.com. Cover by Jolene Naylor

1 THE POWER OF NETWORKING

© Randy Glasbergen
glasbergen.com

"Here's our new retirement plan: at age 65,
we'll get divorced then marry other
people who planned better."

This book was written for the millions of female baby boomers who are in the process of redefining retirement. Due to progressive medicine and preventative healthcare, this generation will achieve greater longevity and live longer in retirement than all prior generations. This promising and wonderful news of increased life is tempered with the challenges and expenses of long-term retirement.

According to the U. S. Census Bureau, baby boomers were born from 1946 through 1964, and are retiring at more than 10,000 people a day. Seventy-eight million boomers turned 65 years old in 2011, and this trend will continue through 2029.

In separating male and female retirement plans, some issues overlap while others are gender-specific. Funding retirements and maintaining good health are clearly important for both sexes. The differences between men and women become noticeable in the personal, social, and planning parts of retirement. In discussing these differences, I'll use studies involving only women when available, and studies of combined genders when not.

One of the most powerful traits for a woman's longevity is certainly a solid and diverse social network. It's natural that our networks change as we evolve. The group of friends we have when younger may be quite different than the network of friends we have now.

Networking is part of our social health, a measure of how deeply involved and emotionally connected we are with other people. Since seniors are more likely to become isolated than our younger colleagues, our social network becomes an important topic to address and manage. Our social network often begins with the type of relationship we have with our existing or potential partner. If you're single at this time, you may want to prepare for both scenarios as our relationships often change in retirement.

YOUR PARTNER

The first issue you are likely to confront upon retirement is the amount of time you spend with your partner. When this balance changes, it can be disruptive at first. If you continue working part-time, you can preview and prepare for future changes. You'll face a bigger adjustment to your relationship, of course, upon full retirement.

If you're in a traditional marriage where you are at home while your husband works, you need to consider a few things. First, I guarantee you that you will feel invaded if you are used to having the house to yourself all day. Just as your husband has his space at work, you have your space at home. Your husband will not understand this at first. You may have to explain this to him a few times.

The husband who is not aware of this will be surprised that he's not always welcome in his own home. He gave up some of his personal space from work and there is a need to replace that in a different arena. This situation can happen if you both retire at the same time, since you both give up your work environments and involvements. Cooperative planning for personal space is important to avoid this most common of problems.

You may need to encourage your partner to take this opportunity to expand his social network, since many will discover they have too few friends outside of work. To help set expectations and prevent this conflict before it starts, I strongly recommend having your partner (or you) arrange some out-of-the-house time for him before he retires. During this time, don't be surprised if your relationship goes through an adjustment period.

I know a traditional couple where the husband was an administrator and the wife was a homemaker who raised five children. When the husband turned 65, he felt it was time to retire full time. He did not have a reason to quit working other than that he turned a certain age. He never even considered planning for retirement and just thought it would be like the weekends he'd spent at home. Like so many traditional men, he headed for the couch and TV, and ended up drinking more and going to bed earlier in the day.

The wife, who is an excellent caretaker, still continued to do all the housework, shopping, and cooking. She tried to engage him in helping her around the house, but because of his old-fashioned roots, he rebelled. He wanted her to continue doing all the "women's work;" he felt entitled to it after working all those years.

The idea that they could be a team, working together, never got through to him. She began to feel more resentful and angry as time went on. They started arguing about it almost daily, but he just would not adapt. In his second year of retirement, she became completely exasperated, and filed for divorce.

So, as this example illustrates, the second most common problem is the husband's failure to adapt to domestic life. You don't want to be surprised or upset by your husband's stubbornness. Of course, you'll know what to expect by how he has acted in the past. It's not a secret that the best predictor of future behavior is past behavior. Changing his well-established behavior won't come easily, unless he gets a dramatic wake-up call. If he never helped around the house, don't expect him to change much without some negotiating.

Most women would know intuitively that his past behavior is a preview of his care-taking intent and abilities. You might question whether he will accept a more involved role of caring for you if you become sick or disabled. He needs to know what you expect of him around the house, and how to act when illness occurs. If you have these discussions early on, then you set the tone for cooperation.

Because the third common problem for husbands is lack of direction and purpose, I believe it's useful if you set parameters for your partner before he retires. By parameters, I mean to set expectations for him so he has some idea of what you expect. Most men will appreciate some direction, since few plan their own. By direction, I mean to set some social or personal goals for him that's in his area of interest. I'll get into more detail about goal setting in the next chapter. An initial discussion will determine how cooperative he intends to be in these areas. Some men reluctantly help out to keep the peace that I believe you can build on.

Personal space, domestic cooperation, and life direction and purpose tend to be the three most common relationship adjustments in retirement for both of you. In the next chapter, I'll discuss how life review and bucket items determine how we arrange for space with time out of the house. I'll also discuss how to facilitate domestic life and establish future goals based on your personality. Once you complete these exercises, you'll have creative plans for your future.

In terms of determining the actual benefits of having a partner, we look at studies of marriage and longevity. The problem with most of these studies is two-fold: they don't account for non-married couples who live together, and they rarely address the quality of the relationship. Traditional thought is that men benefit more in marriage because the wife takes care of them. She takes him to the doctor, gets him medicine, and addresses his needs. If this sounds like your relationship, then he will certainly look to you for direction.

My experience confirms that a caring relationship is beneficial to all parties. If men suffer more without a partner, it appears to be due to the narrower social circle that men have compared to women. The man's partner often becomes his best friend as well, while the woman most likely has a female best friend. The male partner often become more dependent on the relationship, and will react more to the loss of its stability. Consequently, while female networks are larger and emotionally deeper, male networks tend to be smaller and less diverse, rendering it less supportive.

Survey studies are often unreliable because the results are based on self-report rather than objective factors. A study(1) that involved people ages 57 to 75 focused on biological factors for measurement instead. The study tested blood pressure, resting heart rate, waist circumference, risk of diabetes, and inflammation.

The results showed that "Women came out best over all on these measures. The longer their marriage, the fewer their cardiovascular risk factors: a 13% decrease for every 10 years of continuous marriage." It seems that research shows women benefit more from marriage than men. However, they found this advantage for continuous marriage only; with two instances of divorce or widowhood, the benefit did not exist. They found no biological benefit for men.

As more attention becomes focused on this area, the positive effects of long-term relationships will be measured. Of course, a woman in a dysfunctional relationship involving mental illness or substance abuse would no doubt be an exception to the findings so far -- but it's unlikely that a dysfunctional couple would continue to be married long-term. We've known for a long time that women reap rewards from social networking, and a fulfilling, romantic relationship is simply part of that network.

So, if you are a woman with a relationship of average to poor quality, you don't want to pull out the axe right away. Don't get divorced if your partner isn't' adjusting well to retirement the first year, because we know it takes up to three years for the adjustment to work out satisfactorily.

Considering how to manage our relationships obviously depends on many factors, and involves many very personal decisions. If we do have a connected and supportive relationship that benefits us, we want to pull out all our problem-solving skills before we become so frustrated that we give up on it.

I always recommend building on what you already have. After we put in years of time and effort, we don't want to see the relationship end. Besides that, we don't know if the next relationship will be any better. Also, seeking out a new relationship takes more time and has different criteria when we're older. Our first priority is to maintain and improve our current personal involvement as long as we find it beneficial.

When women step back to view their relationships, they may feel they have given up too much or received too little. Prior generations of women have accepted giving up part of life to give to a man. In this phase of your life, however, it's the involvement and direction provided by you that makes all the difference. You can design your husband's retirement along with yours, and become the "manager" of the relationship. Retiring together becomes a natural time to re-evaluate your relationship and nurture it as needed.

Common Sense Conclusion: Becoming actively involved in planning the retirement relationship with your partner promotes cooperation and reduces adjustment time.

We all want to know the secret of a long and happy relationship. In the Aging Well study(2), the task of generativity was the best predictor of an enduring and happy marriage in old age. Generativity is basically how involved we have been as parents. We generate and raise our children with a varying degree of involvement. The top four traits from the study for a long and happy marriage are generativity, commitment, tolerance and humor.

This is a measure of our caretaker abilities extended into retirement. This usually involves raising children, but can apply to any caretaker position. The skills we use in the child-rearing role certainly include dedicated caretaking, especially when children are young. We make a long-term commitment to our children as a matter of course, and we all know how much tolerance we need when they become adolescents. Humor is a good coping mechanism that helps relieve stress and lighten the intensity of the situation.

You don't necessarily need children to develop these skills. Good caretaking appears to start with an attitude of embracing the importance of relationships in general. Those who had a positive and supportive role model from their parents tend to emulate those behaviors. But, those who did not develop basic trust with their primary caretaker tend not to be good caretakers themselves. Relationship skills learned in childhood are usually transferred to marriage and other friendships as well.

The study mentioned above may suggest that if your partner was not involved with child-rearing, did not bond in childhood, or is not involved in a caretaking role at work, he may not be involved with the caretaking demands of your relationship going forward.

If you do have a partner who wavers on these skills and you want to keep the relationship intact, you might consider managing his retirement plan by adding caretaker development goals. Caretaking skills can be learned, of course, as long as there is motivation. It's important to develop his caretaker skills for future times when you may need to depend on him.

MANAGING HIS RETIREMENT

"The woman's mission is not to enhance the masculine spirit, but to express the feminine; hers is not to preserve a man-made world, but to create a human world by the infusion of the feminine element into all of its activities." --- Margaret Thatcher

There are various examples throughout this book describing how men fail to plan for or adjust to retirement. They can end up sabotaging the retirement for both themselves and their wives. Since these men often don't recognize this as a problem, they have no need to resolve it. This is my primary reason for writing a book for women. So, in order to save the retirement for yourself and as a couple, you will need to become more involved and become the manager of the relationship.

It's probably no surprise that most men will not have a thought-out retirement plan. They have trouble asking for driving directions; so asking for retirement directions is even less likely. This appears to be a need for them to feel self-sufficient and knowledgeable even when they are not--a form of denial. It may be a survival instinct, like a cat that hides his wounds so as not to appear helpless. The instinct may be a need to hunt rather than gather. Regardless of the reason, if you have a male partner, you may want to initiate a discussion of retirement goals, rather than wait for him to do so.

We know that having your partner at home all day means some compromise from both of you. Rather risk conflict by telling him just to get out of the house, it's more productive to help him plan activities. If he spends two hours out of the house per day and you do the same, that's four hours of personal space each day for both of you. Tell him this outside time is not only good for the relationship, but benefits his health through social involvement.

Most of us will establish our out-of-the-house time with a routine activity such as part-time work, volunteering, exercising, visiting friends, going to the bookstore or library, and so forth. Others will prefer to use their free time for a variety of non-routine activities they find interesting. Whatever arrangement you choose, be sure both of you have enough to do to fill your time away from home.

Since employment provides a great sense of personal value and social importance, your husband will sorely miss it. Replacing these benefits will be a challenge unless you've pre-planned a satisfactory substitute. In order to reduce the stress of his confusion and the risk of him going astray, you can organize some interesting plans for you both.

He just needs a little direction and to feel involved. You can give him important things to do inside and outside the house. He can go grocery shopping and start planning the meals. Putting him to work around the house and encouraging him to venture out socially will suffice until this becomes routine for him. Give him a lot of praise to reinforce his new behaviors, until they become habitual.

Some men have a loss of motivation right after retirement, and are sometimes confused, because they have never done this kind of planning before. You may need to provide him with a little more effort and encouragement than in the past. Some people appreciate being able to follow a predetermined program, even if they don't admit it.

You probably have a good idea of his interests and his friends, and can plan his activities around them. Even if he complains about your micro-management, you can just tell him you have to take care of your man and be sure he's happy. Men generally like being mothered, since it allows them to regress a bit.

As you draft your own retirement plan, write a suggested plan for him in the next column. This way, he can view how well organized and thoughtful your plan is, and how it relates to him. This will give him ideas and get him involved with his own planning. I'll give more details and show how to design these plans in the Getting Organized chapter.

If you need a certain amount of time alone at home, be sure to work that time into the plan, and encourage him to do the same. If this doesn't make sense to him at first, be open about your feelings and need for space. Tell him he has the same needs, but they were taken care of at work; now these needs must be replaced in a different setting – your home.

If you or he moved from full-time work into full retirement, expect a desire to return to work for the first couple of years. Some women and most men are so over-involved with their careers that it takes them a long time to adjust. It's not unusual to miss work at first, but it's often our co-workers that we miss. This reaction reveals a need for more social involvement that we must work into our plans.

Depending on how you feel about retiring together, you can encourage a return to work or better planning at home. I know men who fail to make the adjustment and only think about being at work. If he really is not adjusting, it's okay to encourage him to return to work. The goal is to get him involved in something interesting so he won't fail to thrive and bring down your retirement in the process. Extending his longevity actually helps extend your own.

If your partner cannot return to work due to advanced age or illness, you will need to be more actively involved with his plan. Remember you are both in the retirement boat together and it only takes one person to sink it. In this case, your involvement may need to be managing his health and personal affairs. I'll discuss the many resources available for this situation in the next chapters.

Some men think sitting on the couch watching the game is ideal retirement. This is maladaptive thinking based on old models. If at first your husband shows resistance about your ideas, he may be feeling a loss of control and need reminding that he is in control. He wanted an enjoyable retirement and planning it is the way to get there. Becoming the manager of the retirement is really nothing new to most women, who have often managed the kids and home for years anyway.

Common Sense Conclusion: Since most men have difficulty designing their retirement plan, you can be a source of encouragement with ideas and directions for blending their plans together.

DIVORCE AND SEPARATION

Unfortunately, relationships do run their course. We are witnessing an increased rate of divorce among the retired. This worries me because it can lead to isolation and depression if not properly managed. If you have tolerated a mediocre marriage for many years, you may be considering what it would be like on your own. Remaining in a frustrating marriage can have negative health consequences. Since we don't want our golden years tainted with conflict, some of us may be looking for a way out.

Even if you want this change, there are still emotional and lifestyle adjustments. If conflict in a marriage is prolonged, some people spend a surprising sum on its dissolution. I know people who spent over $100,000 in attorney's fees. So, you certainly don't want to create any negative feelings that motivate legal activity.

There are many reasons for an increase in the divorce rate, and I have mentioned a couple of them. Unfortunately, divorce always creates a substantial change in lifestyle. There is a dramatic change financially, whether you are working or not, because you now have two rents or mortgages, two sets of utility bills, and so forth. Plus your social security checks are split into two different locations.

Some studies show that a divorced woman suffers a larger setback and is more likely to end up in poverty. If the woman has been married for less than ten years, she won't qualify for the spousal social security benefit. Obviously, your decision should carefully weigh all the factors with an eye to future impact.

I find that an abrupt announcement that the relationship is over can be devastating. Remember, divorce is a personal rejection and a perceived social failure. It can produce resentment and downright anger. This is especially true if one partner is taken by surprise. So, you first want to talk to your partner over and over again to discuss how things are not as good as they have been and you may be growing apart.

Couples who separate before going directly into divorce proceedings seem better prepared and less upset. Many people separate for years without getting divorced, and I find that very understandable. Separation implies hope. Since you are still married, you are less likely to feel a social failure. You are also less likely to suffer intense personal rejection, since separation still leaves some chance of reconciliation. Therefore, the concept of trial separation gives each partner perspective and time to prepare for a divorce that may follow.

I've noticed that men are more predisposed to acting out their anger and wanting revenge. This is partly due to a greater personal and social loss for a man. Remember, if he has a narrow social network, his dependency on his wife will be greater than hers on him. The greater this dependency, the greater his emotional reaction upon dissolution of the marriage.

I've seen men create terrible misery for their ex-spouses for many years, and it can be horribly emotionally destructive. To avoid this situation, the wife should gradually introduce the idea that things are not working, and even emphasize the freedom that he could have if they divorce. That is, she should focus on the positive aspects for him, and make it seem that it's his idea. This will greatly reduce the anger and resentment he'll feel from being rejected.

Separation also allows some adjustment and healing to occur. People actually begin the grieving process at this time that allows some of the emotional volatility and intensity to drain out of the situation. This makes it a lot easier to negotiate the final settlement in the divorce with a level head.

If the kids are old enough to be out of the house, they can be a support if needed. Even though you may be angry at and frustrated by your spouse, and are dying to express it, being diplomatic with him will result in the best outcome for you. It's better to rely on your friends and family to vent your frustrations once you know the relationship is over.

If some of you are a little numb after a separation or divorce, you will not be alone. It's a significant life-changing event even if you desire it. Hopefully, your separation and your retirement don't come at the same time, since those are two life changes to deal with.

After you are alone in you new place, it may seem as if you are starting a new life. Some of you will feel exhilarated because the troubled relationship is over and you can move on with your life. Of course, there will be some loneliness and boredom at first, but that just takes you back to your plan.

A woman I know was married for about 20 years when she decided to divorce at the age of 58. She complained that she and her husband would argue all the time. She is still working full time and finds support from her friends. She was also able to maintain a friendship with her ex-spouse. In fact, to my surprise, their relationship improved after divorce. They get together on most weekends and visit each other for the holidays--they have become best friends. The pressure of living together and getting along has dissipated, and they can now focus on the common interests that originally brought them together.

Divorce must have been the correct decision for them, since their relationship improved as a result of it. She can now move on with her life and plan for a new future. But, when I asked her about dating, she said, "Who wants to date a 60-year -old woman?" My response was a 60-year-old man would. But, guess what, men think the same way. We are all dealing with declining confidence levels as we age and see our bodies go through changes.

Common Sense Conclusion: The decision to separate or divorce can dramatically change your emotional stability and your financial situation, so careful and thoughtful consideration is needed to determine the best future outcome.

MARRIAGE COUNSELING

Many of us will go to marriage counseling in times of marital discord. As a marriage counselor for a number of years, I've noticed that most couples come with one of two agendas. The first is that they really want to figure out the relationship and are motivated for the work ahead. The second agenda is that they come to prove to themselves that the relationship can't work; they are looking for some confirmation of this idea, so they can move on.

Many people think the only goal of marriage counseling is to reconcile the relationship. But, when the therapist recognizes that the marriage really cannot work, or that one partner is toxic to the other, he or she feels an obligation to be honest, and to identify problems that are in the best interest of both parties to address.

The therapist often assumes a dual mandate of addressing the issues and goals you want, as well as uncovering the festering problems that are under the surface. However, I never make a recommendation of separation or divorce, because that decision must be up to the couple. My job is to guide them on their efforts to resolve issues and to discover the information they need to make their own decisions.

Some couples become frustrated with this approach because they are looking for outside advice. But, as the Chinese proverb says, rather than giving a boy a fish, it's better to teach the boy to fish so he can sustain his life. I try to teach couples to be responsible decision-makers going forward. If couples come out of therapy without an answer about what to do, they haven't weighed all the information yet. Sometimes the therapist might feel one partner needs a bit more work than the other, and can schedule individual sessions for that person.

If you decide to try marriage counseling, keep in mind that childhood issues can surface. That's because we tend to react to all caretakers in similar ways. Thus we transfer feelings from our childhood caretaker to our adult caretaker in marriage. If your father rejected you in your childhood, then you may have feelings of frustration and anger toward your husband in certain situations, since he plays the same caretaker role in your life now. One way you might express this is by being overly sensitive to rejection when your husband is too busy to pay attention to you.

As childhood issues lead you into repressed feelings of the past, you have an opportunity to become aware of your tendencies and their impact upon your life. Some therapists may conduct inner-child work to recover and address past memories. You can revisit your childhood and have different conversations with your caretakers to alter the dynamics of the past.

Therapy can open up or uncover problems that you were never aware of that effect you today. Patients will often see these problems as an extra issue, but they may be related to their marriages. Counseling can become complicated and prolonged, but you can direct the course of the sessions and be upfront about our desired results. Therapists work for you, so you can instruct them to conduct brief therapy that is targeted to your particular relationship needs rather than past issues.

How do you know if marriage counseling will help? Well, it has to be a combination of motivation on the part of you and your partner and skill by the therapist. Each therapist has his or her own style based on the principles they feel most comfortable with. Some styles will work for you, while others won't. My style is behavioral psychoanalytic with a focus on couples homework, and mutual compromise as the key for conflict resolution. I give out homework, so you'll feel like a student if you're in a session with me. It's okay to have a session with different therapists and pick the one with the style you like; just be sure the therapist has at least ten years experience and is the same gender as you. The 10 years of practice means you will get an experienced therapist and the same gender therapist tends to be more beneficial for that gender.

Where to find a good therapist can be a daunting task. There is an Angie's List for doctors and therapists that is fairly new. Going to licensing boards like the American Medical Association (AMA) for psychiatrists, American Psychological Association (APA) for psychologists, American Association for Marriage and Family Therapy(AAMFT), or the National Association of Social Workers (NASW) can help. These boards usually keep updated licensing information, disciplinary records, and referral services in your area.

DATING IN RETIREMENT

The number of women over 65 years old who are single is surpassing 40%. If you are single at this stage, it's inevitable that you think about relationships and love; they are natural and healthy emotional involvements that satisfy a deep need to bond. Our need to emotionally bond does not change with aging, as some have suggested. So, many of us will start dating again with a new agenda. That's right, dating at our age is different in a few ways.

First, we evaluate for different character traits in a date than we did when we were younger. Then, our focus was most likely on a partner who had an interest in child-rearing and a career that offered financial stability. Now most often the children are grown and our careers are almost or completely over. Now we look for someone who can commit long term and is accepting of the uneven road getting there.

"Getting there" means your partner will "be there" for you when you need help, and is okay with whatever happens to either of you, until the end. Ideally, your partner should want to hold your hand on your deathbed while telling you it's all okay. If your partner dies first, your face will be the last thing they want to see. So, your new partner needs to have some adult caretaker skills and intent. He needs to show the skills of generativity, commitment, tolerance, and, if possible, humor.

How do we recognize these skills? For *generativity*, one measure is how involved he is with his adult children. If he doesn't have kids, look for prior experience in an extended caretaker role. For *commitment*, look for the length of prior romantic relationships to be at least ten continuous years. For *tolerance*, one measure would be that he's been willing to do some things that pleased someone else, but didn't really interest him. Another measure would be that he's been accepting of contrasting ideas or opinions. Hoping you partner enjoys *humor* is nothing to laugh about, as it's important too!

Second, our socioeconomic status matters less and less as we age. It may be a part of our identity, but its importance in dating has now diminished. That isn't to say that financial stability isn't important, but the way income is attained matters less. If your partner is cooperative, funny, interesting, and loves you a lot, what his job was in the past doesn't really matter. The good news is that now neither men nor women need the status of a career, or being "well off," to be desirable in dating.

Third, our perceived attractiveness has changed over the years. Of course, it's normal to get grey hair and wrinkles, and to feel fatigued, but with some effort, we don't let it interfere with our lives. This is where fear of rejection and self-confidence can undermine our progress. It might help to know that we all fear rejection, and confidence for both men and women often wavers at this age.

Fourth, I often hear women complain that the old guy doesn't have enough energy. This has to do with his health and how he cares for himself. If he follows all the healthy guidelines in this book, he will have more energy for relationships and life. For a healthy energy boost, I prefer to use a combination of matcha green tea and Spirulina powder, which I'll discuss in four.

I have talked to many women who, for various reasons, have given up on trying to find another mate. Some women don't feel attractive or interested in men anymore, and some say they don't want the trouble of a man. I can understand these reasons very well. We all have a history of relationships, and now reduced libido as we age, but there are many ways to improve this situation, as I'll discuss in the next chapter. If you are finding that dating is too much trouble, remember not to let a prior difficult relationship cloud your judgment about moving forward to a better one.

It's common to be concerned about our self-confidence at this age, but we have all been rejected numerous times in life and we survived it. It's probably the men who are more prone to being rejected since they initiate contact and ask for a date. They take on an attitude of a salesman in that they expect to be turned down many times before they make the right connection. Women can take on the attitude of a shopper, seeking out only the best product to keep and rejecting the rest. This slightly detached attitude removes some emotion from the equation while you are deciding whom to connect with. Of course, dating does take time and effort that requires a positive attitude and some persistence.

My women consultants provided me with the following suggestions regarding confidence. The first is to always look your best. Men are very visual beings, as we all know, and they often go with first impressions. That means they take your entire appearance into consideration. Since looking attractive is important, dying your hair and wearing stylish attire are efforts you can easily make.

The second suggestion is to look available and, if you're comfortable with the idea, even sexy. Think you can't look sexy over 60 years old? Have you seen photos of Connie Stevens, Jane Fonda, Meryl Streep, Tina Turner, Gladys Knight, Glenn Close, Goldie Hawn or Martha Stewart lately? Just being healthy is attractive at any age.

The third suggestion from my consultants is to try online dating, since it narrows the field to men who are really interested in a relationship.

Now that you are ready to move forward, how do you go about dating at this age? You are certainly not going to bars, and dating at work is almost always ill advised or not possible. The best approach is to actively pursue your interests in a group setting, where you will meet others with the same interests.

This may involve taking classes, volunteering, joining a club or team, and participating in other social activities. I've noticed that many libraries have reading and activity programs for the retired. Your local newspaper will list events and entertainment venues you can attend, and where you can apply the social networking skills you've developed throughout life.

If there is still resistance to dating at our age, I sometimes ask the question, "Do you want to grow old and die alone?" It's a blunt somewhat rhetorical question meant to be provocative. But, it gets people thinking more practically about the future of their social health. I would say that having a partner in retirement is more important than in midlife, since this relationship becomes the primary social support for many.

Our final relationship will be more interdependent than previous ones, simply because without work and kids at home, our social circle is smaller. Many of us will have medical procedures that require some help in recovery. Imagine if you became disabled for some reason, what would that be like without a partner who loves you?

Online Dating

I would be remiss to skip online dating since it's and option that's growing quickly for seniors. The concept of online dating is compelling in that you don't waste your time or money with bad dates, and you can narrow down mutual interests of others before you go out, and you can ask anything you want of your date anonymously.

This also reduces the threat of a rejection since you get together only by mutual agreement. This allows you to meet compatible people outside your social circle, people that you would never meet otherwise. It's another form of social networking.

Some of the online sites that cater to those over 50 are Senior Match, Senior Friend Finder, Senior People Meet, Age Match, Mature Free and Single, Dating for Seniors, Dating Agency for Mature Singles, and 50 Plus club. This is not to mention all the other sites that don't cater to seniors, but include seniors as part of the dating population. I'm not endorsing any of these sites, but list them for your review. Some of the sites are free, while others require a membership. The free sites work fairly similar to the pay ones and I could not see much difference. Many websites allow you to browse their selection for a few days before you register.

About 20% to 25% of all relationships start online. My guess is that this figure is higher for the retired because we spend more time at home and have fewer social engagements. It's an enlightening experience to read about a person's interests and traits before you meet them. This information instantly gives both parties something in common to talk about. Many people are online to meet platonically, or for activity partners as well.

One woman complained that she doesn't want her personal information "out there" on the Internet. Well, you are only offering general information about yourself with, just an optional photo. Your phone and address are not listed, of course. You will need a password to access your account. So, I suppose there is some risk if someone hacks the website and copies your ad to You Tube, but its entrainment value is very low, and there is no payoff for the hacker.

If you decide to give online dating a try, you will be asked to summarize yourself. Creating a "profile" gives some people pause, but a well-thought-out summary attracts the right person. Some websites have questionnaires to help match people with similar answers. They attempt to match your interests and your personality traits.

You're encouraged to add photos to your ad if you want to get more responses. This is important because you don't get a second chance to make a first impression. People look at your photo first and must find it acceptable before they read your profile. Women have complained that men often show photos of themselves holding a fish. Men complain that the photos of women are when they were much younger. It's important to put your best foot forward without exaggeration. If your date catches you misrepresenting yourself, it's generally a deal breaker.

Once you have an online ad, expect to receive emails from people tying to find out if you have enough in common. You will progress to a phone conversation, then to a coffee or lunch date, when ready. You'll usually know after the first date if you want to continue. Just like any other dating, you need to meet many people before you meet the right person. You may have 20 dates before you meet someone right, so do not get discouraged; it's a slow process. This may be your last romantic relationship, so taking time to choose correctly is important.

Common Sense Conclusion: More seniors are dating in their retirement years, and are more likely to use Internet platforms for meeting their next partner.

SOCIAL NETWORKING

This may be the most significant area where men and women differ, with women being far ahead. Your social network is the sum of all the people you know and the relationships you have. Some people are high on your network, like family members and best friends. The next tier down often includes extended family, mutual friends, and colleagues. But everyone on your network provides a connection and support on some level.

We all have an established social network that we will see change in retirement. The first thing we notice after we leave work is how important those connections were. Even the casual contacts that didn't seem so important then, suddenly take on importance now. Our employment provided us with personal meaning and great social contacts. So, finding a social support extension or replacement is natural.

It's obvious that women generally have broader and more extensive networks. This networking begins in junior high school for girls and accumulates throughout life. Female networks often have friends from different times and situations in their lives. That is, women wisely keep friends from different jobs or social involvements over time, even as many years go by. Women seem to have a genetic inclination to socialize as a survival instinct.

Women tend to be more skilled at diffusing conflict and maintaining contact, traits that reduce the likelihood of their friendships ending. Women are much more likely to lend a helping hand or to provide some caretaking, which deepens the long-term bond with for their friends. These friends are more likely to return the favor in time of need. The result is an instinctual building of a well- developed support system for life. I believer this is the primary reason for the greater longevity of women.

I am the social networker for my group of college friends and, I have to admit, it's been very frustrating dealing with men. Trying to keep a group of diverse friends together for 41 years teaches you about their poor communication skills and narrow- mindedness. By narrow-mindedness, I mean men often live for the events of that day. You may know the old joke about how a man plans for the future --- he buys two six-packs rather than one. So, I do understand the frustrations of dealing with men and can recommend a few solutions.

Historically, the primary social support for men has been career. Men often rely on their wife or partner as a best friend. They might have many acquaintances or buddies, but the depth (and dependency) of the relationships is reserved for their partner. This balance of work friends, past buddies, and one primary relationship has worked for many years for most men. This will continue to work until the employment landscape changes.

The importance of friends to our health and longevity is beginning to reveal itself. A study(2) with 6,500 subjects tracked for seven years concluded that social isolation or loneliness is correlated with early death in both men and women. But even more disturbing is that, "Americans who said they had no one to talk to about important matters grew from 10% in 1985 to 25% in 2004." This last point shows a very damaging trend toward isolation for elders. The fact that you can die sooner without a partner or close friends should be a wake-up call for those shying away from social contact.

Some studies attempt to measure the benefit of having a large number of friends. But the quality of relationships is certainly more important than the number of friends. I encourage you to evaluate your current network to see if you have any "deadbeat" friends. Keeping in contact with difficult friends, out of habit or obligation, causes stress, and could a health hazard.

As the social networker for my college friends, I'm naturally aware of group cohesiveness and dissension. One friend always showed up late or not at all, failed to return phone calls, and used his wife as the contact person. He socially disengaged to an extreme. It became stressful just trying to get him to commit to a time we could all get together. He appeared to have lost his motivation to keep in contact with us, so I discussed the issue with him. It turned out that he felt apathy toward life outside the house also and just did not care about being social. When I told him that the group would move on without him, he just said, "whatever."

It's never easy to let a long-term friend go, but a minimum standard of reciprocity is needed to continue any relationship. You need to act like a friend to have friends. As a therapist, I could have done more to resolve the situation with my apathetic friend, but the barriers he built were too high, and he showed no motivation. In the process of evaluating my existing network, I wanted to clean out any dead or toxic elements that were more work than they were worth. I wanted a handful of quality friends or confidants that I could really feel connected to and trust.

If you are working, you usually have a built-in social network, but after you quit working, you'll want to consider who in that network may still be a good friend. Most friends at work are situational, but there are a few you can befriend long-term. After you've retired, you may consider calling your old work friends to see who will extend themselves. Expanding your network is something you can do on a daily basis everywhere you go. Since most women are already experts at networking, the suggestions below may help you develop your partner's plan or, if you're single, give you ideas to expand your own network.

EMPLOYMENT: Most work environments offer many social contacts that can be developed into friendships outside of work. If we are changing jobs in retirement, we have an opportunity to make a new set of friends.

VOLUNTEER: Many volunteer jobs provide a work-like social structure, and you'll meet other volunteers who want to extend their social contacts.

JOIN A CLUB: The first organization that comes to mind is the Sierra Club, which combines social activities with exercise like hiking or boating. Choose a club that allows you to express your passion.

JOIN A TEAM: Team sports are great for those of us who really want to stay in shape physically and socially. You would be surprised at how many organized team sports there are for people over 50 years old.

TAKE A CLASS: Classes obviously pair groups of people with a particular interest. You don't have to sit in with the 20-year-olds, since many colleges offer courses designed for seniors -- and at reduced prices, too.

HOME EVENTS: Arranging a jewelry, lingerie, or makeup party in you home not only brings in people, but brings in revenue too.

BUY A DOG: Since you'll walk your dog twice a day, you'll not only get some exercise, but you'll meet others doing the same.

ATTEND RELIGIOUS SERVICES AND FUNCTIONS: Organized religion is one of the oldest and most extensive social networks available. Religion-based groups offer many opportunities to assist fellow citizens in need, and can become a passionate social involvement for us.

HAVE A FRIENDLY DISPOSITION: Make a decision before you go out in public to be friendly or helpful with whoever you meet. As you do this everywhere you go, you'll encounter warmth and friendliness in return.

RECOVER LOST FRIENDS: Getting in contact with old friends can be a welcome surprise. You may find that even formerly difficult friends have mellowed with age.

THE INTERNET: This is a great source for finding people and arranging meetings. Online dating is one form of social networking while meetup.com is a national social website that invites all to join an existing group or to form social groups with diverse interests.

If you use the techniques above, you will develop a larger network. This advice is not just for single women; I know married women whose husbands are so unfriendly that their girlfriends stop visiting them. If this is true for you, make plans to network with your friends outside the home.

Some of us may use the Internet as a platform for digital relationships, which is better than no relationships at all. But the deeper benefits of relationships are from human contact. The best social use for the Internet is a tool that connects us to people, but not to replace them. There are many social involvements available once you start looking.

If you and your husband make a list of all the people you know, you'll become aware of the size of your networks. If he does not include work associates, he may become painfully aware of how small his network is. The frequency of his contact with some of these people may be very low and they may not be supportive. It's always a good idea to network, since our friends and family will become gradually reduced over time.

Maybe your best friend has changed over the years and your number of contacts has decreased, especially after you quit work or relocated. There is nothing wrong with rekindling past relationships. After I let one friend go, I was able to reconnect with another friend I had lost contact with. I had forgotten how much we had in common, and he was excited to have me back in his network.

By letting go of one friend and reconnecting with another, I upgraded my network while keeping my number of contacts the same. We can always be networking anywhere we go, as long as we have an open mind and an attitude of acceptance. The upside is that we are going to have fun meeting a lot of interesting people.

Common Sense Conclusion: Social networking becomes essential for developing and maintaining our social support system, especially as work-related contacts diminish.

The Single Female

Some estimate that about 40% of women are expected to retire alone. Since the divorce rate is closer to 50%, that figure could actually be higher. Toward the very end of life when men die at an earlier age than women, more women are bound to be single. One stroll through a nursing home reveals the vast majority of women residents compared to the men. So, even if you're part of a couple now, there may be a time when you'll be single again.

I believe that interest in people, as shown in their social networking, is the primary reason women live longer than men. I do work with self-isolating women who are trying to figure out retirement, but that is certainly the minority. One of my consultants feels that women intuitively know they will outlive their husbands, and expect to be single in their later years. So, as an anticipated protective measure, it's natural for women to create a supportive network.

Women's superior communication may be a result of higher levels of language proteins in the brain that provide an increased verbal connection to the world around them. Studies (3) show that women speak almost 200% more words than men. Women may be genetically more prone to social contacts. I view a network of good friends as a kind of substitute for a romantic relationship. They may not offer the same level of intimacy, but committed and reliable friends can result in similar psychosocial benefits of well being.

Some women I know accept being single for the rest of their lives. Finding a man they can get along with has proven too difficult and frustrating for them. Their attitude is usually the result of numerous difficult prior relationships. Personal unresolved issues brought forward from childhood could compound their difficulty in finding the right man. We all need to find a social balance that's comfortable and sustainable. Living alone, surrounded by a solid network, with or without a boyfriend, can still be a beneficial and sustainable system.

In essence, you don't necessarily need to be married or cohabitating to benefit from male companionship. Conservative women might find this statement out of line, since it contrasts with the traditional view of being married. I always encourage retirees to find their own individual balance, without regard to what society thinks or what prior generations have done. Your retirement should be designed by you, based on your individual needs and interests.

What is the main obstacle to developing male relationships at this stage? I'm told that menopause is often the culprit. Not every woman is affected in the same way, of course, but enough are affected to make a difference in their relationships. You already know about the hot flashes, night sweats, mood swings, irregular periods, and loss of sexual interest or libido. I will suggest some ways you can cope with these symptoms in the section on sexuality.

It's beyond the scope of this book to go into more detail about menopause, about which much has already been written. The bottom line is that if you feel menopause is interfering with your relationships and your happiness, you need to talk with your doctor to remedy this situation. Don't let something under your control sabotage or undermine your golden years.

If You're Concerned About the Single Male

Many studies confirm that single men die earlier than those with partners. So, if you know a single man without a partner, whether he's your father, brother, ex-husband, or friend, consider him in a high-risk category for mortality. Single women with a solid social network do not seem to be at such high risk for early mortality.

It becomes essential for a single man to mitigate this effect with some type of sustainable social involvement. Many men overlook this need for social involvement, and feel they can adjust adequately to their situation. They deny the healthy and enjoyable involvements that would actually extend their lives.

Men often find designing their own social network awkward, unwanted, or even unnecessary. Many feel they are doing fine with the few friends they have, and that you can't force friendship anyway. But their lack of a network will show itself when they need some help or if it leads to isolation. After my surgery, I needed 24-hour care for a few days until I was able care for myself. If I didn't have any friends step in, I would have ended up in a nursing home during my recovery. If a single man visits a nursing home, the experience will likely motivate him no end to find a social network for himself.

How can he make friends intentionally when friendship is supposed to happen naturally? Well, if he is not working, he doesn't have a built-in social structure. The goal to replace this social structure in some manner may take him out of his comfort zone at first. Few of us have intentionally set goals to go out and make friends, but this is what he has to do at this point.

It's really easier than he thinks, once he starts practicing the networking behaviors outlined here. When I'm out, I try to make casual conversation and be friendly everywhere I go. I talk to store clerks, strangers in stores, workmen, cops, and even with the 82-year-old greeter at the local Walmart. You may have to take your single guy out with you, and role model social skills until he catches on.

PLATONIC COHABITATION

A large percent of retired women live alone. Their retirement comes at a time in life when isolation and loneliness are at their highest, when we see our abilities wane and our need for care increase. Social trends seem disconnected to the needs of older, retired people, and the situation plays itself out in a lonely and dysfunctional scenario for them.

Since we are the first generation to live a long time in retirement, social accommodations that meet our needs tend to lag behind. In the chapter Give Me Shelter, I'll discuss planned retirement facilities like Sun City, Leisure Word, Del Webb, and Four Seasons. If you can afford them, I recommend these wonderfully organized and socially engaging communities.

These facilities are great for upper-middle class people, but the average person in retirement is on a budget. Communities in New York and California usually run in excess of half a million dollars, while similar locations in Florida or Arizona start around $150,000. The improved affordability in these states allows the middle class an opportunity to join in the fun.

Leaving work or relocating to a new area involves some loss of our social network. Any relocation becomes a calculated decision, especially if you're single. It's socially easier for a couple to relocate together than for a single woman to relocate on her own. But if you are a single woman, you may be able to connect with someone in your social network to move and perhaps live with. This arrangement would be economically advantageous too.

If the concept of a roommate is scary at first, I understand completely. Many of us have not had a roommate since our college days or our 20s. We probably have a variety of good memories, and some regrets. We may have the same financial need that once motivated us to find a roommate, but we are now socially and personally more mature and empathetic. It's not that we are set in our ways so much, it's just that at this stage we know what we like. So, over the years our life experiences have vastly improved our social skills.

My consultants tell me there are two main reasons women have a problem with sharing a home: pride and control. They take pride that they don't need help managing their homes, and they want to control what goes on in their homes. If control is an issue for you, you must accept that any roommate situation involves some sharing. Some basic rules can be established so that you and your roommate respect each other's privacy and need for personal space. Whenever people reside together, there are mutual bills and chores that need to be divided up fairly. This sharing is similar to living with a male partner or husband.

In terms of pride, well, we know the poverty rate for elderly single women is high, and that poverty correlates with poor nutrition and depression. Some seniors are stuck in ratty downtown hotels, eating dinner out of a can. There will be a time in most of our lives where, due to advanced age, we will have to accept some assistance. I won't discount the importance of pride, but I question the benefit if it becomes unhealthy or self-defeating.

When I worked my way through college, I needed to have roommates for many years. Besides a form of economizing, it was an educational experience in how to get along with diverse people. I actually met the group of college buddies that became life long friends for over 40 years now. This one experience enriched my life by being able to continually stay in contact with people who care about each other.

The degree of bonding that occurs with roommates can be very profound and long-lasting. When I purchased my first house I offset the expense by having a roommate. This person also turned out to be a lifelong friend. Consequently, the best friendship bonding in my life has occurred as a result of my having roommates.

There are clear benefits -- economically, socially, and psychologically -- to sharing a home. I can't find any research on this topic, but I feel that the increased support of a roommate could actually increase longevity as well. This support can occur not only in the form of psychosocial benefits, but also from just helping each other with medical issues, and being alert for problems.

Until society catches up and organizes these mutually beneficial accommodations for singles, we need to do it ourselves. There is absolutely no reason why you need to experience retirement alone, even if you are disabled.

You might consider buying or renting a home in a planned retirement community and taking on a roommate or two. This way you can enjoy the many activities and benefits of an active community while the roommate pays for some of your mortgage. Remember the TV show "The Golden Girls?" This show conveyed a supportive cohabitation model that can work. Even if you have just a two-bedroom apartment, you would cut the rent in half and enrich your life with a roommate.

In my view, there are two distinct kinds of roommates: friends and strangers. The people you know through your social network should be the first place you look for a roommate. Since you already have an established relationship, you'll have some idea of what to expect. Of course, not all good friends make good roommates, but your chances of this happening are fairly decent.

If you don't have someone on your network that is looking for a roommate, start with strangers. In my own life, all my lifelong friends were strangers before they became roommates. How to go about finding an appropriate roommate is like interviewing someone for a job. You are looking for someone with similar traits to yourself, including your temperament. Of course, you conduct a financial background and reference check, as would any landlord.

I've noticed a few websites that address the issue of finding new roommates. SeniorHousemates.com is a website with ads that include some basic information about yourself with an optional photo. You can sign up for free and search for people by zip code. Roommateclick.com is another free site where you can post or view profiles. Other match-up sites are Homeofseniorinfo.com, Seniorssharing.com, and Ca.easyroommate.com. Some sites even have a list of screening questions to ask the potential roommate. Your local library will also have senior magazines with similar listings.

Getting used to the idea of cohabitation may take some time, but being able to reside with people helps us on many levels, and is a measure of our adaptability. Remember, Darwin never said it was the strongest or smartest who survive; he said that it is the most *adaptable* who survive.

Common Sense Conclusion: More seniors will try platonic cohabitation as the financial, social, psychological, and health benefits become more apparent.

ROLE MODEL BIOGRAPHIES

Many of us are at the beginning of our retirement journey, and naturally look for clues to the road ahead. Reading about how others have successfully accomplished their journey gives us ideas of the vast possibilities available. Learning about the many accomplishments of people in the later half of life can be very inspirational. You may be surprised and encouraged by what can be done with a little determination.

You may have already read some biographies that have caught your interest. Try to identify and learn about at least three people with a remarkable and inspirational second half of life -- positive role models who will inspire your own retirement.

My first role model is Betty Ford. She started out with a passion for choreography and was trained as a dancer. She was a fashion coordinator for a retail store when she started dating Gerald Ford. She was diagnosed with breast cancer at 56 years old, just a year after becoming First Lady. She took advantage of her political position by becoming an outspoken advocate for women's rights.

At 64 years old, after her own recovery from alcoholism, she co-developed the Betty Ford Center for drug addiction. Her effort helped drug treatment centers become more acceptable in society. Despite quadruple bypass surgery in 1987, in her later years she was a tireless leader for the Equal Rights Amendment, the pro-choice position, and drug rehabilitation. Her history of passionate involvements may have helped her live to age 93.

My second role model, due to his exceptionally healthy lifestyle, is Jack LaLanne (who I discuss throughout this book). After making a career out of inspiring others, he wrote a book at age 95. He never planned retirement because he enjoyed being busy with exercise and work all his life.

My third role model is Nobel Peace Prize Winner Mother Teresa. She had an interesting midlife change of heart when she quit teaching theology. She suddenly had a calling to redirect her efforts toward charity for the extremely poor and ill in India. She established centers for the blind, elderly, and disabled. She opened a hospice and a leper colony when she was in her 50s and 60s.

She did not have a retirement separate from the rest of her life. She continued to be very goal-driven and socially involved all the way through her life. Her Missionaries of Charity Foundation has over 600 offices in 123 countries, on all seven continents, and is still very active. She was completely devoted to helping others, and established a legacy for which she may always be remembered. Now that's one inspiring and amazing woman!

A couple of similarities may stand out in these brief biographies. First, beginning early in life, they were all passionately involved with their work or volunteerism. One could say they found their calling and had no need to re-tool upon retirement. This still applies to all of us who have not found our calling yet because we will still work to find it. In fact, this is our prime opportunity to discover it.

Second, as they aged, they apparently continued to show a high energy level and determination. Their midlife intensity of work involvement never waned. So, in addition to passion, motivation appears to be a component of successful retirement. These individuals never planned their retirement because it was the same as their working years. They never needed to retire from a life that was already deeply satisfying.

Third, they never gave into disability or let any limitation interfere with their lives. Determination and persistence helped them adapt, regardless of what curve balls were thrown their way.

These people found their passion in life, pursued it with vigor, and never let anything distract them. They did not retire in the traditional sense, and that is my point precisely. Traditional models have nothing to do with our goal of individualized, passionate, sustainable retirement. Perhaps one answer to a happy and healthy long life is just to find your passion and pursue it.

In choosing role models, it's important to choose someone you can identify with on some level. If you have a family member or friends who have a retirement you admire, be sure to include them in your list of role models. Some people choose those in a similar career or situation, but just be sure you are personally inspired by what they have done in later life.

ANCESTRY

"At the end of your life, you will never regret not having passed one more test, not winning one more verdict, or not closing one more deal. You will regret time not spent with a husband, a friend, a child, or a parent." -- Barbara Bush

I think Barbara Bush had it right about the importance of our personal connections. Consequently, I highly recommend emerging yourself in your family's history as one of your key social connections. If you have already made time and effort to connect the generations, then you are familiar with this process. As you position yourself among your family members, your sense of historical belonging transcends personal belonging in that it includes your historical roots and family characteristics.

I've found that a number of beneficial results occur when doing this research. We revisit what our memory has kept for us. We all have memories of family stories that our ancestors told us. These stories often range from the humorous to the tragic, but they are all unique to our families. They become a foundation for a family identity.

We all know families that follow after each other in careers or lifestyle. I worked with a medical doctor who had two sons and two daughters. He encouraged three of his children to go into law, while the other went into dentistry. This family certainly had its own identity. They were all well-educated, professional, socially driven, but they put personal relationships on the back burner. The children followed the rigid academic direction from their father. Theirs was an achievement-oriented patriarchal family identity.

In your research, look for family themes or characteristics that stand out. If you see that offspring went in man different directions, and your parents think and act outside societies' box, then maybe you belong to a family with a laissez faire independent identity that has emphasized personal awareness and growth.

Each sibling may see his or her family identity differently, since each experienced a different childhood. The importance of family identity is derived from the variation and intensity of the childhood experience. There is usually more than one theme in each family, but there tend to be dominant themes that influenced us most strongly. These themes can be expanded to include generational identities that may have been passed on for many years. Finding patterns in the chaos is what you are looking for here.

The understanding of family tragedies sometimes sheds light on our own path in life. Lets take a look at one example that occurred during the Great Depression. In one family's history, the mother accidentally bleeds to death when attempting a self-abortion at the age of 28. Her three existing children are nine months, four and seven years old. The father cannot afford to care for the children. The orphanages are already full. He places the two younger children in county facilities and the oldest, eventually, in an orphanage. Fortunately, the oldest is adopted after a couple of years and bonds with a supportive family. So, for this child, her family's early identity of tragedy is replaced with bonding and nurturing.

In the above example, a very caring adopted family stayed close to the child even after they raised her. These circumstances completely turned her life around. She graduated from high school, went to business school, maintained employment, got married and raised a family of four. She enjoyed a more or less normal life and died of natural causes. The younger children, who were not adopted, became alcoholics and suffered from depression. So, as you can see, even the timing of early events can determine family identity and influence the trajectory of individual lives.

In the process of your ancestry search, you will probably contact others on your family tree for the first time. This gives you new opportunities to add to your social network and even experience an emotional connection you never had before. Expect to talk about old family stories and learn new ones.

Some contacts will not be the least bit interested in what you're doing, so just give them the opportunity to get back to you later. Others will act as if you are their long-lost friend, even if you never meet. The latter are the most motivated people to help you put the scattered information together. Some of us never become interested in ancestry until we reach the age where our position with other family members matters.

Many colleges offer classes in ancestry, and I recommend them for two reasons. A class helps you organize historical material, since most information is in bits and pieces. That is, a class can be a blueprint or format for writers. It also becomes a forum for feedback from students and faculty, which helps narrow your focus. That is, you will get priceless personal responses as you discuss your ancestry stories, including how well you write about them.. The students in my ancestry class had various writing styles, but our common purpose was to bring the past to life via expository prose for the next generation.

Some classes will publish the better ancestry stories, and that possibility could motivate you as a writer. Since you'll find yourself editing as information comes in out of order, using a scrapbook format seems to work best. To make biographies more interesting, focus on your ancestors' unique or unusual aspects. It could be beneficial for you to learn about the pertinent medical history and longevity of family members as well.

If you have photos, you can pair them with the text, and photos really tend to really bring people to life. If you are wondering how the next generation could understand what life was like in 1880, you can describe life from a historical perspective. For example, you might note that before electricity, people gathered around the fireplace. Then Thomas Edison turned darkness into light forever. Infusing emotion into your narratives adds another level of understanding.

Common Sense Conclusion: Researching your ancestry creates perspective of your family history, connects you to relatives, and expands your social network.

The following narrative of a parent writing to her child is an example from an ancestry class:

The Haight Ashbury

Your Grandma Mary and I relocated to San Francisco in 1956 for her to join her new husband and continue her family expansion. I was always very independent and discovered the city in my childhood by exploring it on foot. I would often take all day for these random explorations. The police had to bring me back home once when I forgot my curfew. But it was this burning curiosity that helped me discover a district called Haight Ashbury.

It was 1968 and I was 14 years old when a school friend and I went to Haight Street. The street was littered with scraggly teenagers who had run away from home without any money. There were 10 to 15 panhandlers or beggars per block wearing tie-dye shirts, bell bottoms, headbands and flower necklaces. My first impression was that something terrible happened for so many youth to be homeless at the same time. I remember being a little confused when I found out they came from all over the country trying to be connected and be included in what they called "The Movement."

All teens go through some rebellion, but this was more organized and extreme. My curiosity led me to attend peace rallies in Golden Gate Park to protest the Vietnam War. I saw local celebrities like Joan Baez and Dick Gregory speak at these very crowded vibrant rallies. These rallies tended to bond the youngsters together in a common cause that only added fuel to the rebellious fire. It wasn't very long until my friends started to look like hippies, and one day I looked into the mirror and found myself with long hair and funky clothes too --oh no!

People were kind enough to open their homes so the kids had a place to sleep – places known as flop houses. I had to stay at one before I really understood what the message was behind this madness. There was frustration with the war, with President Nixon, with conservatism, with music and even with fashion, they complained. Their devoted willingness to sacrifice for peace and social change had a deep impact on me. I had never seen determination to this extent and, I have to admit, it was contagious. You couldn't tell at this point, but this group of shabby kids later became knows as the Baby Boomers and turned out to be one of the most creative and intelligent generations ever.

The Haight Ashbury also influenced you through your parenting style. So, if you find yourself seeking social equality, honesty and clarity, higher education, challenging authority, and thinking outside the box, you'll be able to trace both of our roots to this time of cultural change. If you look into the mirror one day and you notice you're wearing funky clothes, remember it was all meant to be. Peace.

In summary, our social health in retirement begins with our network of friends and family. Making a few adjustments to our primary relationship is key for sustainability of the marriage. Men commonly do not plan their adjustments, so the wife may need to initiate and encourage planning at first. Separation or divorce can have a far-reaching impact going forward, so careful consideration is needed before life-changing events are made. Some of us will try marriage counseling to assist with this adjustment.

Many retired single women will follow the natural tendency to bond and will return to dating. Social networking and dating can be a suitable and sustainable balance for many single people. Since we may find ourselves single and on a budget at this stage,

platonic cohabitation can be an effective solution. Identifying successful retired role models acts as encouragement and a framework for our own retirement. Completing our ancestry helps us find our place in life and connects us with others.

1. Moynihan, C.(8-28-2012) "Marriage may benefit women more than men" mercatornet.com. Retrieved on 2-13-2014 from: mercatornet.com/family_edge/view/11164
2. Vaillant, G. "Aging Well" New York: Little, Brown & Co. 2002. p.113, 123.
3. Mohan, G. (3-26-2013) "Social isolation increases risk of early death, study finds." latimes.com. Retrieved on 2-14-2014 from: articles.latimes.com/2013/mar/26/science/la-sci-social-isolation-health-20130326
4. Macrae, F. (2-20-2013) "Sorry to interrupt, dear, but women really do talk more than men" daily mail.co.uk. Retrieved on 2-24-2014 from: dailymail.co.uk/sciencetech/article-2281891/Women-really-talk-men-13-000-words-day-precise.html

2   HOW TO DESIGN YOUR FUTURE

Older models of retirement, where one plan fits all fail to consider your personality traits, your skills, your interests and your hopes for the future. Customizing your retirement means creating a deeper satisfaction via self-expression of your passions. Designing your future is really about blending self-awareness of your individual traits with socially acceptable outlets. This chapter will focus on developing self-awareness, defining your retirement attitude, and anticipating solutions for future adjustments.

As a result of our unique interests and social needs, we have customized most of our life to fit our personality. However, with the arrival of retirement, our life is in transition. This simply means that we reassess who we really are outside of the working world. Designing this customized plan takes some awareness of individual differences. The first step in designing your future is getting a good understanding of your past involvements and interests. One of the best ways of doing this is life review.

LIFE REVIEW

Life review is the process of writing down in summary form what has occurred in your life. Organizing material in terms of chapters, or life stages, helps categorize these events. This process is not nearly as daunting as you might think, and ends up being very enlightening. This is because you are evaluating the events of your life, how you felt about them at the time, and how you feel about them now in a different light, with wisdom.

Evaluating our past lives is often surprising because we can examine issues we have hidden away for many years. This occurs most frequently when we write about our childhoods. Mid-life is so encompassing, with work and family, that we barely have time to think about how we feel, or how something in the past affected us. Now we can take time to understand ourselves better, to improve our lifestyles, and to design our futures.

Breaking down our lives into broad categories such as childhood, teen years, college, work, family, children, and career or accomplishments, are chapters most people identify as important. The childhood chapter is often crucial because that's where we often find an event that propelled us into a certain direction in life.

I once asked a retired nurse what originally interested her in the field. She described a situation in high school when her grandmother passed away from cancer. The very next year, she lost her favorite aunt to cancer as well. She majored in nursing in college out of instinct, she said. Until she did her life review, she didn't realize that these childhood events developed the curiosity that led her to a nursing career in oncology.

As you write your biography, you will be keenly aware of how each life event unfolded, and how you experienced it. You may notice a pattern or theme developing in your prior lifestyle. Some people have told me that they feel embarrassed because, in their opinion, they haven't done much. The review is not a matter of how much you've done, and it's not about material successes; it's about discovering your interests, your hopes, your disappointments, and your passions for the future.

For those who feel they haven't done much, focus on the more personal items. If you are a housewife who was never employed, but you raised three children, those children are your body of work that becomes your legacy.

For example, Jack LaLanne admitted that he started out life as a junk food junkie. As a child, he was overweight, had a terrible acne problem, and was teased by other kids. He described how weak and physically miserable he felt all the time. Then he had an emotional reaction when he could not get a passing grade on a routine physical exam at school.

The combined negative effect of all these things upset Jack so much that the rest of his life he over-compensated to correct it. Of course, his healthy lifestyle led to a television show that managed to get millions off the couch. Jack became a physical fitness icon and a historical figure as a reaction to his childhood events.

The life review is not an exercise in psychoanalyzing yourself, but simply a way of becoming more aware of your life themes so you can continue what you enjoy into retirement. That is, we are likely to pursue what previously interested us; what we wanted to do, but didn't previously have time for, and also what is dear to us emotionally. In retirement, we can finally pull out those hidden dreams we have always craved.

It's best to start out simple and add details of the past as your memory allows. Some people find it easier to start out with a list of accomplishments that boosts self-esteem. If this is important to you, you might consider some achievement-oriented goals in your retirement plan. Devoted parents often give their children a chapter or two, indicating their future need to plan time with them or with their grandchildren.

One woman wrote the following about her childhood experience in her life review: "One evening our family came to the dinner table as usual. I watched my mother give my sisters a slice of bread with peanut butter on it. She gave me the same, but when she reached into the bag for more bread for herself, there was none left. I noticed a sadness come over her face as she stared down at her empty plate. The kids were hungry, so they ate fast and were on their way. Being a little older, I noticed what had happened. I stayed to watch her clean the table and wash the dishes before I left. She didn't talk about this nor did she talk much the rest of the evening."

She continued to try to understand the meaning behind this and wrote, "To see my mother's sacrifice increased my respect for her as a parent and was a role model for my own parenting. But, more profound and disturbing was the situation that caused this. I was old enough to understand that money was the cause that determined not only our entire lifestyle of poverty, but had determined the lifestyles of many generations before me. I was only 11 years old, but I decided that this was completely unacceptable and I never wanted it to happen again. I began to see money as powerful. It pays the bills, but also provides freedom, security, and stability. I didn't know it at the time, but this was my financial wake-up call that influenced me throughout life."

This lady was motivated to get a masters degree in business, and to become an entrepreneur, an investor, and an investment manager. She retired financially independent at the age of 44, and continues to invest as a hobby. What a great example of turning lemons into lemonade. Her life turned out quite different from her siblings, who still struggle financially. She was influenced at a receptive age in a dramatic manner, but she didn't know what caused this until she did her life review when she was 60 years old.

The life review can be an opportunity to review our early childhood and how the type of care we received affected us. Childhood frustrations and a feeling of parental failures can arise. Raising our own children takes us back to childhood, as we focus on child-rearing techniques we remember from our parents. Retirement takes us back again, as we focus on summarizing our entire lives. Regardless of what shortcomings our past presented, our goal is to gain understanding, put closure on the past, and create an engaging future.

One caveat must be mentioned: if you had an abusive or traumatic past, and bringing up bad memories is disturbing, you can work around this. I don't recommend that you bring up every miserable thing that happened to you in life. You can avoid the traumas in your life and still focus on life direction and interests. Be sure to include the problems you have successfully overcome, because they are triumphs, and they boost self-confidence. You want to focus on those positive life experiences to extrapolate forward.

The conclusion of your life review should produce historical information of your interests and skills, with a priority assigned to each. You should also include significant relationships and their dynamics. This not only provides perspective on what you've done, but on how you feel about it as well. Life review will provide the foundation to build your personalized plan. The goal is simply to find a natural extension of prior interests and involvements applied to retirement.

Common Sense Conclusion: Life review confirms our deepest interests, and what we missed socially and emotionally.

YOUR BUCKET LIST

The 2007 movie *The Bucket List*, with Jack Nicholson and Morgan Freeman, confirmed what many retirement age people do on a more casual level. If this movie encouraged you to put your list into writing, then you've already started your formal retirement plan. This movie shows how the main characters designed their future at the end of their lives. Although the movie received mixed reviews, you can glean a couple of important lessons from it.

The movie conveys the message that the bucket list has deep psychological importance. Imagine the opposite, having nothing special you want to do in life. Goals give us purpose and meaning. Without purpose and meaning, we have no direction and must search for a reason to survive.

As people, it's up to us to determine our purpose in life. Work and family fill most of our lives with a pre-determined purpose. As we transition away from these social obligations, we can design a new meaning based on our individual purpose in life.

We formed new purpose and meaning when we went to school, got married, procured employment, and became parents. We established new purpose and meaning at each major life adjustment point, and retirement is no different.

The other confirmation from the movie is that sharing your bucket list with someone, and participating in the activities of other peoples' bucket lists, increases our enjoyment. Many lists include activities with other people, such as taking a memorable vacation with a spouse, children or friends. I encourage you to involve others as much as possible to make your experience socially and emotionally richer. A typical bucket list has different goals with different people.

Of course, its common that most of us do things with specific people depending on their interests and background. It's appropriate to take this into account when identifying the right friends or family to pair with the right event. If you are not able to pair with people, group events are also a lot of fun; camping at the bottom of the Grand Canyon, or rafting through it, are typical bucket items. Guided tours to other counties offer group discounts as well as social opportunities. So, if you don't have friends or family members with whom to pair with your activity, group events are great.

Working on this list is one of the most enjoyable exercises you can do. The framework is open and fantasizing is encouraged. There really are no limits to your dreams.

Most people end up prioritizing the list in some way. Some like creating two or three lists of different priorities while others assign a numerical value to each item. Some people take photos of their completed adventures and organize them into bucket albums so they can revisit their dream. I can personally attest to the fact that completing any bucket list is exhilarating, will give you a sense of accomplishment, and will make you feel more connected to the world.

Don't let being too busy or the affordability of bucket goals deter you from making your dream list. Remember that many small goals are more attainable than an expensive trip around the world. Maybe there is a restaurant, show, or local event that you'd like to experience. Even if you are completely broke, you still need a bucket list of affordable goals. Goals that include connecting more with people often involve very little money, and tend to be more satisfying anyway.

A couple other concepts the movie covers are the timing of the list and helping others.

It's nice to have your list, or at least be working on it, before you are ill, of course. People usually make their own list, except in the movie, where the two main characters were still searching for goals and needed to help each other create a list.

The concept of going back in time to resolve an unsettled issue sometimes arises during life review. It's not unusual to have some regrets or feel something in your past is unfinished. Perhaps, you turned down a marriage, dismissed a relationship, passed on a job offer, of feel you let our kids down in some way. If you find yourself in a position where you have a desire and opportunity to resolve something in the past, then it may be closure you are seeking.

In the movie, the dying father needs closure on the relationships with his daughter before he dies. Closure will in this example relieve him of guilt, as he seeks forgiveness from past bad behavior. He resolves his emotional distress by revisiting the past. The movie doesn't mention that this daughter achieves closure as well. So, by forgiving each other, they reconnect and gain closure together.

The final point about the movie is that it shows the main characters traveling to many places, yet the focus in each location is their personal conversation. The message here is that the actual locations are less important than how they feel and how they connect, which is true in real life. In the end, it's really these personal connections that are important. So, connecting with people obviously trumps travelling the world alone.

Viewing the movie should encourage you to write your list and help desensitize you to dealing with end-of-life issues. It becomes a positive role model to watch dying people effectively deal with the end of life--a goal for us all.

Talking to others about their list is motivational, and you may find that your friends or family included you in a bucket item. Sharing your ideas with others who are actively pursuing their own goals is exciting and thought expanding. Just listening to their excited voices as they describe their bucket adventures almost makes you jealous and certainly gets you moving on your own list. I'm in the process now of attempting to coordinate the bucket goals of my retired friends. There is nothing more fun than a group of bucket adventurers out to have a great time.

Common Sense Conclusion: Pursuing a list of specific bucket goals provides a keen sense of purpose and meaning, leading to greater life involvement and satisfaction.

DESIGNING A DAILY ROUTINE

You don't want to wake up every morning with uncertainty or confusion about what to do. This eventually leads to boredom, isolation and depression. I've also seen substance abuse increase during the retirement years as a result.

Your daily routine can be a foundation from which you add other activities.

Let's say that you're working 16 to 20 hours a week on Tuesday and Thursday only. That's a welcome change from 40 hours and opens up a great amount of time to fill with enjoyable activities. That's exciting, but how are you going to fill all those open hours week after week? Many people start out with household projects when they first retire. You finally have time to paint the house, re-landscape the yard, redecorate the living room and upgrade the kitchen. These are all worthy projects that will give you a sense of accomplishment.

However, such projects are short term or one time only. There is nothing wrong with that, except that it's not a sustainable routine. They are what I call free time projects. You manage your free time by working it into your daily routine. For example, maybe you are comfortable waking up about 7 a.m., after which you have coffee, read, or watch the news. But now you won't be getting ready for work. Now you have time to manage your financial portfolio, so as part of your new routine, you can add one or two hours of business education to each day.

Another routine item would be housecleaning that must be done, so you add another hour for that. Exercise is key for health, so you set aside another hour for a routine walk that might include talking to neighbors.

The idea is to maintain a similar routine for each day, unless the routine is trumped by a more important issue. This consistency provides a surprising amount of psychological stability and security in your otherwise unstructured life. You might schedule free time in the afternoon to visit friends or family, do volunteer work, play cards, take classes, practice an art or craft, go shopping, stop by a book store, or follow any interest you have. Since this free time will be constantly changing, it will provide variety and spontaneity to your life.

At the end of your free afternoons, you may have dinner and spend time with your partner, watch a movie, browse the Internet, or read a book. Your evenings will likely have a routine already, since we tend to relax before bedtime in ways that come naturally to us, whether we work or not.

So, if you are looking for a daily model of consistency, the one I describe here establishes a routine for the mornings and most evenings, with free time in the afternoons. Give yourself ample time to find your own balance. I guarantee you that the more activities you have planned for yourself, the more interesting retirement will be.

For those of you feeling that the routine I describe may be too much structure in retirement, remember we have all conformed to work and social structures most of our lives, to the point where we unconsciously follow them. Our prior routines have provided direction and purpose, along with consistency, dependability, and security. Maintaining a similar structure now minimizes the pain of adjustment to days no longer filled with work, and keeps self-doubt at bay. As people live further into the retirement years, they often adjust their routines to changing circumstances. I recommend you talk with other experienced retirees about their routine to see what works for them.

Common Sense Conclusion: Designing a comfortable day-to-day routine is the groundwork for needed stability and security in an unstructured world.

ATTITUDES ON A FINITE EXISTENCE

"To live is so startling it leaves little time for anything else." -- Emily Dickinson

Writing or talking openly about the end of our personal lives has always been a difficult and emotional topic. So difficult, in fact, that many retirement books just avoid it. But in retirement, this topic becomes too important and omnipresent to ignore. A great part of this difficulty seems to be the nagging uncertainty of our next phase.

In an attempt to answer questions about the afterlife, many believe that we'll wait in line to enter the pearly gates. But deep down inside, we really don't know exactly what's going to happen. It's natural for this ambiguity to surface during our later years, and for our confusion and anxiety to intensify until we answer them.

We will probably have many questions. What will happen to me when I die? How do I overcome my fear of dying? How do I leave a legacy so that I'm remembered? How do I ever reach a point where I can answer all these questions, and feel relaxed about these answers? Most people, no doubt, asked these same questions in the generations before us. How we answer them determines our attitude for the future.

Questioning life at the end is a natural human process and a necessary right of passage. People in full retirement without answers, or without a retirement plan, exhibit a type of despair and depression associated with greater traumas. This is not a transition that you can take for granted that will solve itself. Addressing the finality of our lives, and arriving at an acceptable understanding of it, is essential for achieving a feeing of calmness and a focus on "going forward."

It's common to experience a little confusion and distress at the beginning of any adjustment. We have been through many successful adjustments before, so adjusting our attitudes now is nothing new. A few of us become so preoccupied, or even obsessive, about death that we live our final years in dread and misery. We must be careful not to fall into the nihilistic or fatalistic thinking that we are going to die at anytime, so why bother to do anything?

To accommodate this view, we have to completely deny our present existence. This maladaptive thinking is both self-defeating and tragic. We don't want agonizing over something we have no control over ruining what's left of our amazing gift of life. So, I highly recommend that all of us come to terms with our existence in an acceptable and positive light.

If we accept and appreciate the wonder of life, we will view our existence on this planet as a one time, amazing gift. The fact that it must end at some point simply has no effect on our current lives, unless we let it. After all, we are used to living most of our lives to the fullest without thinking or planning for death. Just because we are a bit closer to it now doesn't mean we need to become anxiously preoccupied with it. Our goal of making peace with the end allows us to embrace the present without undue focus and worry about the future.

This coming to terms with the end of life often involves spiritual beliefs. Organized religion has always offered a supportive spiritual and social network. People in difficult situations often turn to religion to help them overcome their difficulties and cope with them more effectively.

Christians believe that going to heaven is a reward for spiritual and moral living. They may have less anxiety about death because they see it as part of God's plan. Even if some doubt the reality of heaven, they feel if they put themselves in God's hands, their faith will carry the through whatever lies ahead. If the Christian understanding of the end of life makes sense to you, then you've accomplished the goal of acceptance and you can move forward.

A woman I know, who attended Catholic school, has accepted going to heaven when she passes on because that's what she was told as a child. She confesses any sins and is thereby relieved of any burdens. She does not fear or worry about death and even looks forward to it as a relief from all the duties that are expected of women. She also feels women worry less about death because "We are the creators of life." She has successfully accepted and even embraced the end of life.

Some of us may feel that a religious viewpoint puts control and understanding in the hands of a higher power. If you're not religiously oriented, you will need answers that encompass your particular orientation. If you are scientifically oriented, for example, you might consider the natural order of living organisms. We all have a place and a time to live out our natural existence, and understand that the same natural order pertains to death as well.

Our parents bring us into the world before they die, and so we do the same for our children. The cycle of birth to life to death continues in a more or less predetermined manner as evidenced in our ancestry. So, the goal is to accept our position in the life cycle and accept death as the natural end to that cycle. Once you truly accept the viewpoint that it's natural and okay to die, peace of mind can follow.

The Buddhist view is that the death of your body is a natural part of life. Your spirit, however, lives on, relocates into another life form, and is reborn or reincarnated. The life form may be human or animal or spiritual, as in angels or demons. The form your rebirth takes is dependent upon your karma or how you lived your life. You do not meet your maker as you do in Christianity. The Buddhist goal is to gain positive karma from life, be reborn as a human, and reach nirvana, a state in which all cravings and suffering are extinguished. Consequently, the Buddhist dies not with anxiety or dread, but with an eye to the next life form.

You probably know people who struggle with the idea of coming to terms with death, and who tend to be emotionally unsettled as a result. Some people struggle with denial or other defenses and some become riddled with anxiety. An online article(1), "Accept Your Own Death," starts by suggesting that we not be surprised by death because death comes to all of us. "Life is a temporary passing experience, preceded and followed by nothingness, a moment of wakefulness interrupting a long sleep. Only when we take bodies do we become conscious of time and life; when we leave the bodies, things go back to normal, to silence again." The article suggests that we need to release the idea of immortality, since it exists only conceptually.

Viewing life from different frames of reference provides us with fresh views that we may have not thought of, but that makes sense. I find this last perspective interesting because it points to nothingness as the norm and life as the exception. It certainly seems exceptional to have been given life, and to expect things to return to the norm at some point also seems reasonable. Clearly there are many different perceptions of spirituality and death, one of which may be helpful for you.

Common Sense Conclusion: Coming to terms with the end of life is essential for inner peace and emotional stability going forward.

STAGES OF ACCEPTANCE

Coming to terms with death while we still have many years to live is easy compared to coming to terms when we are at the end of life. This section will address the stages we go through when we are in hospice or are expected to have less than a year to live. These stages are not gender specific.

When you work for a hospice or in a cardiac unit of an acute care hospital, you accept that death will occur. After all, hospice is where people go to die. It's still difficult to witness, but your expectations tend to fall in line with reality. That is, the reality of people departing tends to adjust our expectations of what we expect to happen at the end of our own lives. We become less emotionally distraught and more accepting of the anticipated outcome and more in tune with the life cycle itself.

Most of us haven't worked under hospice conditions and have not been desensitized by such exposure. Some of us haven't had the time or inclination to formulate our own idea of acceptance of death until now. This coming to terms with death is another rite of passage that can be confusing at first. We have usually "practiced" for this event by witnessing the death of our parents or close relatives. We know that whatever emotional task is difficult at first will eventually become easier with time.

Getting older means you probably have had some long-term or significant friends or family pass on by now. This could make you reflect on the briefness and fragility of life. The passing of their loved ones reminds some of the diminishing time remaining for themselves, and motivates them to do more with whatever time they have left. We don't need to dwell on the deceased's death when we can take that which is positive from the situation.

There is a classic book in psychology called *On Death and Dying* by Elizabeth Kubler-Ross(2). You may have heard of the five stages of death and dying that she describes. Doctors, nurses and mental health professionals use this paradigm to understand the patient experience, although the orderly progression of the stages may vary. Still, the final goal is to reach acceptance of death and dying, regardless of whether they're happening to someone else or to you. The five basic stages are:

DENIAL: When we first get a terminal diagnosis, our first reaction is to question its accuracy and ask for a second opinion. Once this diagnosis is confirmed, disbelief and numbness set in for a while. Eventually this denial wears off and anger and rage take over. However, this is not to say that we won't return to the safety of denial in times of high anxiety.

ANGER: We are angry because we don't want to die, and now we have to give everything up. But we tend to get angry with everybody; our doctors are suddenly incompetent, the nurses don't care, our family doesn't understand, and our spouse isn't supportive enough. We may even hate our hospital roommate because she isn't terminally ill.

BARGAINING: Some of us will attempt to delay the inevitable by hoping that being moral and ethical will persuade God to be kind. I believe that in some cases guilt for not attending church may underlie this feeling. Some people give their life savings to the church, unconsciously hoping to buy their way into heaven.

DEPRESSION: When we actually feel and confront our diagnosis, depression sets in. Death is the ultimate loss of everything we know, and it's permanent. There is not a damn thing we can do about it. I feel depression is a tool to prepare for the impending loss. We should be allowed to express this sorrow in a supportive environment that will help us move to the next stage.

ACCEPTANCE: This is the final resting ground emotionally. It's often devoid of much emotion because once we accept our impending death we reach a state of calm and peace. Patients often stop watching TV, want fewer visitors at this point, and prefer to speak less. They have let go of the physical world and are ready to move on. They usually prefer quiet reflection and communicate by holding hands.

In recent years, other researchers have added more stages and, as noted, some question the order of the Kubler-Ross' stages. But the basic framework is still very useful as applied and was my primary tool during my hospice experience.

Of course coming to terms with our existence when we have many years to live, versus adjusting to a terminal diagnosis, are two quite different experiences. You may not experience all these stages in "coming to terms" since your proximity to death is still far away. But, the acceptance process may follow a similar pattern for both situations.

I recommend that you put in the time and effort to come to terms with the end of life prior to a serious diagnosis. You may feel you need to accomplish or finish something before you can let go of life. Publishing this book gave me a sense of closure on life's accomplishments and made me feel more ready to let go.

To reach the final stage of acceptance, we may need to experience some or all of the prior stages. Some agony and confusion is expected when we first started thinking about our own death. I encourage you to persist until you have reached a psychological resting ground of some sort. Some of us can do this alone with some soul searching. Most of us will want to discuss the subject with others, like family or clergy, to see how they reached this stage themselves. You may have difficulty reaching this stage, but once you do, you may experience it as a form of enlightenment.

DISENGAGEMENT AND DETACHMENT

"Involved disengagement" is one social definition of retirement. We become disengaged when we move out of the work force or reduce our outside commitments in some way. For those who continue to work part-time, disengagement will be more limited than with full-time retirement. Some of us are looking forward to and need some separation from a stressful job, excessive responsibilities, or from medical complications. Most retirees embrace and relish this separation at first. Establishing a comfortable balance between how disengaged and how involved we want to be takes experimentation and time.

Disengagement is mostly a transition period where we gain perspective on life. We are rising above the banalities of life to view where our future purpose and meaning exist. Much of our purpose will come to light in our life review, as we focus on the meaning of significant past involvements.

We may or may not continue with our prior interests, but we will understand what involvements are important to us, and which are not. Many of us re-engage with interests that we previously postponed for lack of time. It's not unusual to see retirees begin oil painting, narrative or creative writing, learning music or dance, traveling the world, or even starting a business based on their passions.

Juliette Low did not develop the Girl Scouts of America until she was 52 years old, was partly deaf, and was mourning the death of her husband. Her retirement re-engagement made her famous and cemented her position in history. Being able to work at what you profoundly enjoy can be a life-changing experience.

We all have very personal needs to be engaged at some level with some social balance. Women are usually much better at staying engaged as a result of better social skills. If you are partly or completely retired and new engagement opportunities present themselves, try getting involved and see how it feels. Let yourself experiment a little and take a few chances. Since this is a dynamic process, give yourself space to change and re-balance as your interests and situation change.

I know a couple in which the husband burdened the wife's retirement because he was so extremely stressed out from teaching. He had trouble with the smallest of social contacts and decided to disengage completely when he retired at 65. He announced that he would stop answering his phone and email. He assigned his wife to communicate with the world and take on his social responsibilities. She took his calls and reluctantly started answering his email, and even began signing his name.

His friends felt this was as an invasion of their privacy and a personal rejection of them. The visits and communications that he usually received from family and friends gradually tapered off, as people began to disengage from both of them. During this time, his alcohol consumption started to increase, along with his isolation. His disengagement turned into a regression resembling infantilism.

His wife was unaware at first how his disengagement would affect her. Her husband's withdrawal ended up being a burden for her, to the point where his family and friends became angry with her as well. As her caretaker instincts kicked in, she unknowingly accepted a type of dependency from him. Therefore, we want to be mindful, as we first retire, not to establish -- or let our partner establish -- any unhealthy or self-defeating behavior patterns, out of laziness or for any other reason. It's common for new retirees to disengage too much when they fail to establish sufficient structure in their lives.

Since we cannot let our newfound freedom, with less responsibility, cloud our better judgment. We must refer to our written retirement plan, which we carefully designed with our best interests in mind. In the example above, neither the stressed-out teacher nor his wife had a retirement plan, and as a result, they became confused and disconnected.

But I caution you not to make too drastic of a change, because then you can expect that a stressful adjustment will occur. Keeping a social balance, whether you are working or not, is always key to our happiness and emotional adjustment.

As I mentioned, it's common for the husband to look to you, his wife, for direction and support. The wife in the above example did not understand this phenomenon, and unknowingly followed along with her husband's disengagement. It was only a matter of time before she began to feel suffocated and conflict arose. This situation also shows why it's prudent for you to manage his retirement plan together.

While disengagement is separation from people and work, detachment is separation from objects and places you formerly enjoyed. Detachment is often triggered when a person is coming to terms or making peace with the end of life. "You can't take it with you" is the rationale for letting go, but the situation is more complicated than that.

Our capitalistic culture rewards those with the most wealth, biggest diamonds, upscale fashions, largest house, or the most objects of success. We spent most of our adult lives working hard to collect such things. In our material world, it's not easy detaching from objects that we loved for many years. Learning to give up some objects, or at least view them differently is the beginning of letting go gracefully.

We unconsciously assign values to our material objects. Status objects like a car or house tend to be easier to relinquish as their social value diminishes. Sentimental objects tend to have the most emotional meaning and will remain with us until the end. If you're beginning retirement, then you are just beginning this process of letting go. Some of us won't finish this process until our final days.

The good news is that we have ample time since we have many more years to enjoy. An excellent exercise is to practice giving away your things one at a time. Donate whatever you are finished using. Don't let your work clothes or obsolete items sit idle for years before you get around to donating them.

I'm not suggesting donating items you need or enjoy. We are not transitioning to a completely minimalistic lifestyle, but just cleaning house of obsolete items. You can allow this "downsizing" to occur as a natural process, while being aware of what and why it is happening.

So, it's okay to downgrade the value of objects and to relinquish them when you are finished with them and ready to move on. Once you donate some possessions, you will gain a sense of accomplishment and control. You may suddenly feel more independent and above material needs.

Common Sense Conclusion: Once we establish a comfortable balance between disengagement and involvement, we tend to settle into our long-term goals.

ISOLATION AND LONELINESS

When designing our futures, we naturally include activities we find the most enjoyable. In planning for this happiness, we want to be alert for problems that might develop, and have a solution in place if possible. We can plan to avoid future problems once we have some idea of what to expect.

When we are involved in full time employment, raising a family, and fulfilling many social obligations, we may struggle to find time alone. This situation will change dramatically upon full retirement. The teacher I mentioned, who completely disengaged himself by cutting off phone and email contacts, imposed self-isolation upon himself. Actually, he only semi-isolated himself, since he resides with his wife. It's possible that this disengagement was just an initial reaction to his retirement, and that he will rebalance his life later. Otherwise, he is setting himself up for loneliness and depression.

Our perceptions of isolation may differ. Extroverts naturally crave social contact while introverts are more comfortable alone. Isolation and loneliness occur only when they are undesired. That is, if we choose to be alone and feel no distress, that's not isolation. But, if we are lonely or bored and don't want to feel this way, then our situation becomes one of isolation and stress. In psychology, we use the term ego syntonic to describe behaviors that suit one's self image, and ego dystonic, or behaviors that are in contrast to self image and become distressful.

It will be this first sense of unwanted loneliness or boredom that gives us information about our needs for personal and social balance. The importance of this balance is often first recognized when we do our life review. If you have a history of extensive social involvement, then you want to be sure to continue this involvement in your future plans. In the past, we automatically made friends to counter loneliness and incorporated them into our lives. In the present, we do the same, but consciously and by design.

It's not unusual to feel transitory isolation or loneliness in retirement, whether or not you are married. It's not the end of the world if this happens and is actually a message to you to get moving on your goals. If you are living alone, as many of us unexpectedly find ourselves, then you need to prioritize establishing a larger social network.

PREVENTING RETIREMENT DEPRESSION

The good news is that most of us will not see the severe side of depression, and mood disorders tend to subside as we age anyway. However, depression can begin in subtle ways and slowly progress. Since you will be the first person to become aware of your mood, let's be sure you understand what to look for and what to do.

Women are more likely to internalize feelings of anger or distress rather than act them out. Without an acceptable outlet, anger can turn into depression. Depression in women probably has cultural underpinnings in that they are not allowed to display intense anger or aggression in society— another double standard.

An abundance of studies exist about the etiology, symptoms, course, and treatment of depression. Some authorities even state that retirement depression is normal; however, I strongly disagree. Clinical depression can be a life-threatening disorder and should not be taken lightly.

Most women are usually aware when they are depressed, but are unsure about what to do about it. There are different types of depression, but I am referring here to the reactive type, in which an environmental stressor, such as a trauma or a significant loss, causes us to react negatively. Some examples are severe illness, disability, loss of a loved one, financial problems, divorce, eviction, or any other significant stress. Disappointments can occur at any point in life, of course, and retirement is no different.

Signs of depression to watch for can begin as simply feeling bored or lonely. These feelings tend to be short term and are perfectly normal, unless they start to return more frequently and cause distress. As we begin to feel sad, we sometimes feel anxious, worried or fatigued.

Sometimes depression causes us to become restless or irritable. Appetite extremes often get involved, causing us to overeat or lose our appetite and also lose weight. Sometimes we lose interest in activities we usually enjoy, including sex. We might feel helpless, hopeless, or worthless. As depression progresses, we may have either insomnia or hypersomnia, trouble with memory, concentration and decision- making.

Many of us may have experienced these feelings at some point in our lives. What's important is how many of these feelings occur, how severe they are, and how long they last. How ego dystonic and subjectively distressful they become will be a measure for taking action. We need to be determined not to let these feelings overcome or control us. Most reactive depressions tend to be short term, lasting less than two weeks.

In monitoring ourselves for possible signs of depression, we will need to have some awareness of our feelings. We need to occasionally ask ourselves how we really feel. Are we genuinely happy with our life right now, and if not, what would we improve? Asking this once a month or so and recording the answers can translate into more specific goals. Your partner should also be involved with this process as he may recognize some symptoms before you do. Staying in touch with how you feel can act as a preventive measure against depression.

If you have a history of some depression, then the following discussion about treatment could give you ideas for preventing it from becoming more serious.

When I'm treating a depressed patient in therapy, I request that they make a list of all the positive traits they can think of to describe themselves. Creating this list tends to increase their self-esteem and reminds them of their strengths. I then have them make a list of all the people they know or can contact. This establishes a support network. They are required to make contact with a least two people a day from the list and to make a positive connection with them.

I request they also create a list of goals that provide social direction and purpose. These goals must include a plan for completion. For example, a social goal of joining a walking club is great, as long as the steps for completion are included. This may seem obvious, but the depressed person has extreme difficulty following through on social goals. Many have trouble just getting out of bed, so expectations of social involvement can seem formidable.

I also request they become involved in an exercise or activity program that will release endorphins. This hormone improves mood, reduces stress, mitigates pain, and facilitates sleep, among other physical benefits. For extra social benefits, you can pair up with a buddy or go to a gym for exercise. What I like about this technique is that the positive effects are immediate. All of this is homework that I routinely assign.

The actual therapy session is designed to be very supportive because that's what depressed people need. We need someone to "be there" for us in a non-critical environment. Trust must be established before any significant work can begin.

Then I look for the cause of the depression, which puts the responsibility on the depressed person to sort through the confusion she feels. As part of the therapy plan, I always attempt to get people to be their own problem solver. You know the old saying: give a boy a fish and he eats one meal; teach him to fish and he eats for life. Problem solving is a natural lifelong skill that I always encourage for everyone.

Sometimes the cause of depression is apparent as an identifiable stressor or loss. At other times, it could be hidden in the unconscious or in childhood. The latter clearly involves more exploration and assessment of the patient's prior experience, including their key relationships. In the absence of a clear event, we may feel let down or betrayed in a relationship.

You can be depressed because of an unsatisfactory relationship, including the one with your partner, for years. Once the cause is identified and understood, you can begin to resolve the situation. This involves learning attitudes and behaviors that are effective in changing the relationship. If your partner is part of the problem, he is invited into your therapy sessions and asked to become part of the solution.

Attitudes can determine our frame of reference and ego strength (coping abilities). Maybe you've noticed that after a separation or divorce some people are relieved and even elated. The long problematic relationship that zapped so much of their energy is finally over and they can move on with life.

Others may go through a depression, since divorce and separation are a significant loss emotionally, socially, and financially. A positive attitude, however, has surprising strength. I always encourage my patients to try different frames of reference, using different coping skills.

Since the depressed person's motivation level is usually low, I establish time frames for accomplishing homework goals. A primary behavior that I encourage in my depressed patients is increased social contact, since it's the opposite of depressive withdrawal. It's difficult to be withdrawn if you're in the middle of an interactive group. Social involvements can become self-reinforcing as a result of the contact itself. Consequently, the more socially involved the patient is, the more difficult it is for her (or him) to stay depressed.

Another important assignment I recommend is to read the book *Creative Visualization* (3) by Shakti Gawain. Creative visualization involves constructing your own mind set through directed imagery. One technique is to remain in bed after you awake and visualize what will happen that day. If you have a job interview that day, you imagine yourself in the interview, and what you might say. You visualize the course of the interview and the eventual outcome in a positive light.

If you have a social engagement for that day, you visualize the connection that you want. It can be very interesting how behavior often follows pre-determined thought. I recommend this book to anyone interested in improving his or her outlook, and who want to have some control over their environment. All these techniques are intended to counteract depression on many levels and activate as many coping skills as possible.

Common Sense Conclusion: Maintaining a supportive and active social life, which incorporates physical activities, will help to prevent isolation and depression.

The above framework is for mild to moderate depression. In the event that depression worsens in yourself (or in a loved one), you may need to seek professional assistance. Counseling is indicated if 1) the above techniques don't seem to work; 2) the subjective distress level is too uncomfortable; 3) you can't seem to leave the house: 4) you have any thoughts of hurting yourself or others; 5) your friends or family think counseling might help; and 6) you feel confused and cannot seem to make a decision.

If you are not sure what to do, either check with your doctor or call 800-273-8255, the National Suicide Prevention Lifeline. You don't have to be suicidal to call as they address all mental health issues. They provide free crisis counseling, referrals, and follow up calls. They can set up appointments for you in your city. If it turns out that you can benefit from counseling, you can use your Medicare insurance.

But don't think that you have to pretend to be happy all the time as evidence that you are enjoying retirement. In terms of mood and longevity, happiness or optimism is no longer correlated with longevity as was once thought. Although it may seem that way to the casual observer, this claim cannot be supported.

One of the primary traits correlated to longevity is conscientiousness (4), which is being careful, thorough, or vigilant. These traits contrast with happiness and optimism. The explanation for longevity lies more within the behaviors of following doctors' orders, conforming to a diet and exercise program, and making all the lifestyle changes that are considered prudent. Optimistic people tend to take health risks like smoking and drinking in order to be social with others. Interestingly, those who are more carefree and happy often do not follow health guidelines because they expect everything to turn out positive as a matter of course.

BRAIN HEALTH AND COGNITION

We are all concerned about loosing our mental abilities as we age. The good news is that the expected decline is so gradual that most of us won't notice. Cognition is a broad term that includes comprehension, memory, judgment and reasoning. This includes learning, decision-making, and language skills. These are skills of intelligence that we have used all our lives and taken for granted. Cognitive impairment can occur at any age, but we are referring to Age Related Cognitive Decline or ARCD.

A normal function of aging is that brain neurons shrink and die. One of the primary reasons for this is oxidative stress, or an imbalance between reactive oxygen and the body's ability to detoxify itself. Oxidative stress figures into Alzheimer's disease, atherosclerosis, heart failure, chronic fatigue syndrome, Parkinson's disease, and ARCD. A diet rich in antioxidants foods will help mitigate this effect.

Chronic systemic inflammation caused by cigarette smoking, poor diet, insomnia, and obesity allows irritants to enter the brain. This inflammation causes a delay in reaction time and memory impairment. If you still smoke, preserving your mental functions is yet another important reason why you must stop.

Obesity and diabetes have a surprising effect on brain function. There are a number of studies that conclude that as body weight increases, brain size decreases, which leads to decreased cognitive abilities. There is a relationship between BMI (body mass index) and brain volume deficits in the frontal, temporal, parietal and occipital lobes. Childhood or midlife obesity can be a predictor of later life dementia. The cognitive impairment becomes worse when compounded with high blood pressure. Diabetes studies also show greater brain atrophy and lower test scores on performance and learning for this population. Diet and exercise programs would help counteract this effect.

Hormonal imbalance in women has an impact on cognition and emotions.

Steroid hormones increase neurotransmission, causing an increase in memory in women when treated with estrogen. Alzheimer's patients respond with improved memory and mental functions when given testosterone. Hormone therapy for menopausal women was routine until recently, so consult your doctor to discuss whether it's right for you.

The good news is that keeping a healthy lifestyle is excellent for the cerebral cortex, and results in keeping cognitive functions almost the same until the end of life. Since we are willing to put effort into staying healthy, this cognitive deterioration can be deferred with small declines not noticeable until very old. So, we can enjoy our mental functions virtually the entire time, if we just stay healthy.

We can do many activities to keep our brains healthy. Physical activity, with at least 30 minutes of exercise a day, is extremely beneficial for brain health. Moderate to high intensity aerobic or anaerobic exercise can produce a dramatic increase in memory. Dietary recommendations are similar to those discussed in the chapter. Your Body is Your Vehicle. Exercise paired with proper nutrition is confirmed as the primary activity for the health of the mind and body. So, following the guidelines for exercise and nutrition from this chapter are transferable benefits for improved brain function.

Staying mentally active by doing a variety of challenging tasks also correlates to improved mental abilities. Learning new information encourages the brain to establish new neural networks that can be used to compensate for other age-related impairments in brain function. So, it's important to limit the same old comfortable patterns and try new and interesting activities.

The fun part of improving your abilities is doing crossword puzzles, playing scrabble or Sudoku, or doing any other new or challenging activity that you enjoy. I bought my daughter a Nintendo DS video game years ago and discovered it can be used for games of mental acuity. Such games are designed to exercise different lobes of your brain, based on laboratory research, and involve math and reasoning where you compete with yourself.

Social involvement is also a confirmed trait of brain-healthy people. Having a large network of friends and other personal bonds while engaging in social activities preserves certain cognitive abilities. Since women tend to have larger and more complicated social networks, they are perfectly suited for keeping their cerebral cortex active.

Common Sense Conclusion: Enjoying challenging mental activity with a healthy and socially involved lifestyle helps maintain and prolong our cognitive abilities.

SEXUALITY

"It's not the men in my life that count, it's the life in my men." --Mae West

My female consultants absolutely insisted that I address sex since they strongly feel that it's one of the most overlooked pleasures in retirement. Despite many retirement guides being too uncomfortable to discuss this, I'll still address the expected changes and challenges for both you and your partner. Designing this part of life is especially important because each woman's sexual expression is very personal.

I'm using the term sexuality to include not just sex, but affection, intimacy, and love. How we view sexuality began in childhood with our parents' attitudes. As baby boomers, our formative developmental years were in the '50s and '60s, periods not known for sexual openness. It's true that the summer of love occurred in 1967, but by then we had already formed our sexual attitudes.

But, before I discuss attitudes, here's a reminder about the benefits of sex(5):

MOOD: Sex, along with exercise, can be recommended for depression because the endorphins that are released act as mood elevators.

SELF-ESTEEM: Self-esteem normally increases with a sexual partner and the resultant production of hormones.

STRESS REDUCTION: The immediate feeling of muscular relaxation and anxiety reduction is a great physical and psychological benefit.

LIBIDO: Increased frequency increases desire and counteracts vaginal atrophy. When we have sex, blood flow, elasticity, and vaginal secretion increase, making sex easier and more enjoyable. Vaginal dryness occurring during menopause can interfere with this.

BLOOD PRESSURE: Different studies have confirmed lower blood pressure occurs as a result of coitus. Newer studies point to intercourse as being physically and mentally more beneficial than masturbation.

SLEEP: Feeling sleepy after orgasm is immediate and easily confirmed. Sex can help with insomnia.

IMMUNITY: Studies show that antibodies called immunoglobin A are produced and protect us from colds and flu.

BLADDER: Pelvic muscles that control incontinence are exercised and strengthened, thereby improving bladder control for women.

EXERCISE: Sex helps firm your muscles, increase your circulation, reduce your pain, and offers all the other benefits of exercise.

BURNED CALORIES: The average calories burned during sex is about 200 per hour, but clearly depends on your activity level.

LOOK YOUNGER: Sex increases blood circulation to the skin and causes collagen production. One study had people guess the age of people who had sex and those who didn't. The ones who had sex were perceived as being younger to both male and females by up to seven years(6).

RELATIONSHIPS: Feelings of physical and emotional intimacy are hormonally and personally improved.

If it appears that there is an overlap with exercise and sex, that's because sex is a physical activity. Some studies suggest that longevity can be increased by sex in the same way that exercise increases life. This may be logical, but scientific studies have yet to prove it.

The jury is also still out as to the best way to glean health benefits from sex. Some studies suggest that sex with another person is more beneficial to health than masturbation. Other studies suggest that you must reach a climax to trigger the release of healthy hormones. Some suggest that how often you have sex or climax makes a difference. Others suggest that at least twice a week is the minimum to realize benefits. So, we know that sex is beneficial on a number of different levels, but we're still finding out exactly how beneficial.

Regarding the attitudes about sex that we learned from childhood, our parents most likely reflected society's attitude at that time. Most of us will agree that the attitudes of the '50s and most of the '60s were fairly conservative compared to today. Our parents grew up before contraceptives, so prudence was the primary message that was passed on to women of our generation. Men were raised more carelessly, so women had to be the managers of the bedroom.

Then, in 1960, the Food and Drug Administration (FDA) approved the pill for contraceptive use. But, women's attitudes changed slowly as a result of its controversial launch. Doctors questioned the safety of the pill and in 1988 the original pill was taken off the market and replaced with a newer pill. As its acceptance gained ground, women were relieved not to worry about pregnancy, and the age of recreational sex began. But, AIDS appeared in the homosexual population during the '80s, and affected the heterosexual population by the '90s. An attitude of protecting oneself from disease was introduced out of necessity, and attitudes toward sex became once again more conservative.

Today the issues of pregnancy and sexually transmitted diseases have been put into perspective; women have more control over their bodies, and society has a more relaxed attitude towards sex. This means that religion and morality are issues that each woman must settle individually. You may need to do some soul searching to determine which attitudes about sex are really an expression of your own personality.

Many of us were told to marry before we have sex, but is this still a viable principle to follow? Women were told that living with a man was living in sin. Are these principles psychologically healthy for us, that is, are we following them out of guilt because that's what society told us? Do any of our passed-down principles interfere with us having a better relationship, or with having a relationship at all? These are questions that need to be answered individually.

What I'm suggesting is that you clear your conscience of any inhibitions, so you can be ready for what might be your last chance to enjoy the greatest natural pleasure we know -- romantic love paired with great sex. The unique ménage of sexual expression involves a blending of two people emotionally and physically. Sex satisfies our deepest needs of being loved and accepted on both a psychological and physical level. If you have forgotten what this feeling is like, it's never too late to rekindle it.

Reduced estrogen in women and lower testosterone in men occur around the same age for both men and women. Because this stage is characterized by a loss of interest in sex, both parties can surrender to this urge to forget sex, or both parties can fight to keep it in their lives. The bottom line may be how important this level of closeness is to you personally. Most of us will feel that intimacy and love cannot be discounted and is characteristic of a healthy relationship and life.

SEXUAL ADJUSTMENTS

The larger problem here is not just loss of intercourse, but also the loss of more important feelings of intimacy, affection, and love. The symptoms of menopause that impact the body and mind affect coitus, especially hormonal loss of libido. Some women feel less inhibited since they can't get pregnant at this stage. However, others must deal with symptoms that might interfere with their enjoyment in the bedroom.

Replacing the loss of libido, or sexual interest, is a very individual and delicate matter. My women friends tell me they know menopausal women who are not aware of how much interest they have lost, and not aware of the impact on their lives. They are worried that women may give into their lost desire and lose this pleasurable experience forever. If you lose interest in something, you don't necessarily miss it, so there is nothing distressful to remind you of the loss. But loss of interest in sex may result in a more distant relationship or even complaints from your partner. If you are single, you may simply have no interest in being with a boyfriend.

Rather than possibly lose your relationship or deciding to stay single the rest of you life, what can you do about loss of desire? There are treatment options that you can discuss with your doctor. Hormone therapy may be appropriate for some, while Viagra for women is available. Viagra (and Calais) for women are intended to increase blood flow to the pubic area. Consumer reviews of Viagra from women are still forthcoming, so as a newer medication, time and success of usage will determine its popularity. Hormonal replacement patches that release testosterone have also benefited many women.

Whether you decide to try the above supplements or not, first be sure you are physically healthy. We all need to take care of our medical issues, meaning we don't smoke; we exercise, and are generally healthy. The next focus for restoring interest in sex is the psychology of arousal. Making love may be physical, but we all know arousal begins in the mind. This means we must first re-connect with arousal neuropathways in the brain.

To accomplish this, I assign retro experiences to trigger prior arousal responses. For example, the goal is to have fun recreating that romantic evening with candlelight, soft music, vintage wine, gourmet food, a sexy outfit, and the man of your choice. The thoughts and visualizations that aroused you in the past may arouse you again. Self-awareness of all the little things that go into your experience is key to renewing that arousal.

Employing different modalities -- visual, auditory, tactical, olfactory, and gustatory -- can connect you with your partner. For example, watching a video with him might trigger an arousal response if you are visually oriented, or a nice massage might arouse you if you are tactically oriented. You may need to experiment a bit to find your best source of arousal. Once you know, you can arrange an arousal scenario with you partner.

Fantasy is an ever-present precursor to arousal. Creating new fantasies can always occur as long as you have an open mind. Historically, women have read romance novels, which can be excellent for setting new erotic fantasies into motion. You may have unfulfilled fantasies of being with a certain man, or being with two people, or even being overpowered in some way. These repressed desires can be turned into fantasies that you can pursue and perhaps realize in your life.

An active fantasy life is considered healthy. I hope you are open to playfulness and experimentation in the bedroom as part of your continued pursuit of healthy social involvements.

Your male partner will be going through some physical changes that impact him psychologically, and which might affect your sex life. If you have been in a long-term relationship with him, you may not notice it as much with an infrequent amount of activity. He may experience difficulty maintaining an erection, which is caused by less efficient circulation than he once had. This loss of ability to "perform" may affect his libido. This does not mean he is losing interest in or less attracted to you. Even my healthy athletic friends with active relationships are experiencing this decreased response.

That's because testosterone tends to decrease as men age. Some men are caught off guard when this happens and try to downplay its importance as they try to cover up feelings of inadequacy. Other men take this particularly hard and invent excuses to avoid sex or withdraw from their partner. If your partner is avoiding sex, you know there is something wrong for sure. Since most men will not admit or understand this lessening of libido at first, you can be very instrumental in helping your partner accept and resolve this issue.

This lowered testosterone may be the only sexual issue you'll need to address with him, since it's the main culprit by far. When you speak to him, remember he's a little scared and his ego is fragile because he has lost something dear to him that defines his manhood. If you suspect this is the problem, there is nothing better than an open honest discussion. Try saying something like "Honey, I really miss being more intimate with you and I understand this is normal, so let's talk to our doctor together and figure it out."

In terms of treatment, in the past years testosterone replacement has dramatically increased among older men. However, many men test normal for testosterone levels and do not meet the clinical guidelines for treatment. Additionally, there could be some cardiovascular risk with this therapy. So, you want to get your partner's doctor to evaluate any treatment for its suitability.

The best case scenario I've seen is when your partner agrees to try Viagra. Not only does this increase the circulation leading to an erection, but the erection can be maintained for hours. One woman told me she and her partner have sex for three to four hours now and she has never enjoyed it so much. She stopped telling her friends about it because they wouldn't believe she had intercourse for that long. When I asked how her partner was responding, she said that he thinks he is 25-years-old again because he can go for so long. She is amused that he struts around the bedroom with his new sense of pride. This woman pulled off a big success here and she wants me to tell the world so other women can do the same.

As I mentioned above, some men cannot take Viagra due to a conflict with cardiovascular disease. Sometimes Viagra also conflicts with other medications. If your partner cannot be weaned off these medications, then encourage him to use other methods in the bedroom. You may need to educate him on manual manipulation, cunnilingus, and the use of toys. His male ego may need him to feel like a champion, so tell him how important his involvement is to the success of the relationship. The good news is that you both should have a lot of fun experimenting.

Common Sense Conclusion: As a result of lower libido, both men and women will need to make minor adjustments to continue or re-establish an active and enjoyable sexual relationship.

ADVANCED MEDICAL DIRECTIVES

Even though these instructions direct health care treatment, it takes some soul searching to make the important emotional and personal decisions. Completing these forms tends to give you a sense of control over what doctors can or cannot do to you. These forms are state-specific and can be filed with your state's Advance Directive Registry. Filing with the registry eliminates the need to pass around many copies and ensures that the form is available in any medical situation where you might need it.

Most states allow a Power of Attorney for Health Care so that another person, of your choice, can make these decisions if you are incapacitated. You doctor usually determines when incapacity occurs. The form for Power of Attorney includes a provision about whether you would like someone to begin making decisions for you before you are impaired. The form includes instructions similar to a living will. Here you state your decisions about what you want if you can no longer speak or lose certain functions. You can limit your instructions to take effect only if certain conditions arise. The entire document is revocable when a new directive is executed, so you can change your mind at any time.

In these forms, you will be making decisions on any care, service, or treatment that affects your physical or psychological condition. You can make a provision to hire or fire your health providers and institution. You can approve in advance any tests, medications, or surgical procedures. You can direct the course of your hydration, artificial nutrition tubes, or cardiopulmonary resuscitation. You authorize organ donations and autopsies on the same forms.

Despite the sober nature of this topic, I recommended you complete these forms. It's the type of task you do once and can then forget about. When I assisted others in drafting their forms, I noticed that a fair amount of conversation would occur. So, it's clearly helpful to discuss these issues with family and friends, especially the person you're considering for your power of attorney.

In summation, by completing the exercises in this chapter, you have the foundation you need to design your individual plan for the future.

Your life review provides the primary themes of your life that you want to continue. Your bucket list provides specific goals with a focus on wish fulfillment of enjoyable activities. Your daily routine provides personal stability and reliability, and your free time provides variety and mental challenges.

Coming to terms with the end of life in a positive manner is recommended. You will be aware that some disengagement is typical while you find your social balance. You will also be aware of factors leading to isolation and depression, and will act preventatively. You will prolong and enjoy your cognitive abilities with a healthy lifestyle. Minor adjustments can be made to your sex life so that you maintain intimacy and enjoy sex as you age. Finally, you will register your advanced directives.

1. RHEG(5-25-2013) "Accept Your Own Death" raymondinegypt.tripod.com. Retrieved on 2-13-2014 from: raymondinegypt.tripod.com/articles-01/accept-own-death.htm
2. Kubler-Ross, E. "On Death and Dying" New York: MacMillion Pub. Co. Inc., 1969.
3. Gawain, S., "Creative Visualization" New York: Bantam Books, Inc. 1978.
4. Vaillant, G. "Aging Well" New York: Little, Brown Co. 2002.
5. Robinson, D.M. (10-24-2013) "10 Surprising Health Benefits of Sex" webmd.com. Retrieved on 2-13-2014 from: webmd.com/sex-relationships/guide/sex-and-health
6. Sieczkowski,C.(7-12-2013) Regular sex can make you look 7 years younger, scientist says" huffingtonpost.com. Retrieved on 2-22-2014 from: huffingtonpost.com/2013/07/12/sex-make-you-look-younger_n_3586435.html

3   GETTING ORGANIZED

I've come to believe that each of us has a personal calling that's as unique as a fingerprint--and that the best way to succeed is to discover what you love and then find a way to offer it to others in the form of service, working hard, and also allowing the energy of the universe to lead you."-- Oprah Winfrey

Writing out a dynamic and evolving plan that allows for additions and changes becomes our foundation for our new lifestyle. The last few years prior to retirement bring out a variety of concerns that can be addressed in your plan. When you actually retire full time, you can expect a two to three year adjustment period.

PLANNING FOR A FEMALE RETIREMENT

Most of us wouldn't think of retirement as being male or female, but there are differences in financial, medical, lifestyle, personal, social, and emotional areas. These differences won't necessarily be new to women; of course, it's just a reminder to address these areas for inclusion into your main plan.

LONGER LIFE: The first difference is that, on average, women live longer than men. This is wonderful news for you, but at the same time means you must fund and balance a budget for a longer time. Sustainability of financial and emotional livelihood becomes an essential component for future planning.

The solution is establishing creative income and working longer at what you love. We know that employment prolongs life and keeps us socially connected. So, women who embrace a lifestyle of continual interesting involvements will be giving themselves a longevity gift.

LESS INCOME: Women make less income over a lifetime than men in similar positions. The wage gap is slowly narrowing so that today women make about 75% to 80% of a man's pay. Social security benefits are less since the benefit amount is based on accumulated income. Some women may have worked less in the workplace in order to attend to family needs, and have saved less than women who worked outside the home. This lifetime of dedication to husband and kids can leave women with fewer saving and a lower income history.

Besides employment, you must be smarter in budgeting and skilled at economizing. Learning how to manage money effectively will be essential for you to sustain yourself. When reading the financial chapters in this book, be sure to take your time so you can understand it. Since the intent is to be an overview, you can have fun focusing on the topics that interest you.

MORE MEDICAL CARE: Medical expenses are expected to be higher for women throughout each life stage. The bottom line from many of the studies is that, for various reasons, women just need to see the doctor more often, and end up paying more.

Women tend to be more alert and concerned about resolving medical issues than men. Some of women's medical expense may be for preventative care or for routine exams that men don't need or may skip. So, you pay a little more to enjoy better health care.

You need to make a solid commitment to staying as healthy as possible since your health is mostly under your control. Finding creative ways to reduce medical expenses might involve attending free medical clinics and medical tourism. Medical tourism matches patients with overseas hospitals for procedures at a dramatically reduced cost.

HIGHER LIFESTYLE EXPENSE: Women spend more on hygienic and cosmetic items such as toiletries, makeup, hair, nails, and fashions. In general, appearance is important whether you are retired or not. Women are not about to let their hygiene and appearance deteriorate to any extent like a man might. Men tend to get away with the weekend just-got-out-of-bed look. As women, that would be considered a social faux pas and even embarrassing.

This is where economizing and an attitude of humbleness are key. Changing our shopping habits from high end to discount stores is certainly difficult at first, but adaptability is the key to sustainability. Coloring hair or doing nails at home instead of the salon, for example, would be a manageable improvement to your budget.

LESS HEALTH INSURANCE: It's unfortunate that women are less likely than men to be offered health insurance at work. Part of this difference is due to women more often working at part-time jobs. The combination of a need for more medical care and less insurance coverage can put women in a difficult position. Divorced women are about half as likely to have insurance, since many were often insured through their ex-husband's job.

In retirement, Medicare and related supplemental policies will be the main insurance for most of us. So, taking time to be sure you are covered in all the needed areas is important. An experienced insurance agent can help you carefully weigh the virtues of the various Medigap policies.

CARETAKER DEMANDS: Everyone seems to expect women to be the caretakers for their children and for their elderly parents. Women usually enjoy being a parent and wouldn't have it any other way. Men help some with children, but not as much with elders. When our parents get old and need help, it's women who step forward. Even if you embrace your caretaker situation with joy and purpose, it often keeps you out of the workforce and reduces income.

This is a very personal issue. Many of us want to take care of mom, but may admit to having mixed feelings. Time and energy can really be taxed here, so getting as much support as possible is important. At some point, the demands of care may outstrip your abilities to keep up with everything. This is when you can enlist professional assistance, like home health care or adult day care.

SOCIAL INVOLVEMENT: Excellent social skills, which many women develop naturally, create an amazing foundation for continued involvement and support from others. The strength of this trait appears to mitigate the stress of other life challenges. My women friends tell me that women do most of the volunteering and often take the default role of social planner for the home. Volunteering for women is a natural extension of social skills that involves them in the community, enabling them to connect to new people, including those with similar interests.

Retirement has always been more socially attractive for women; therefore, a situation that affords room for group involvement or social networking is important. Volunteering is wonderful on different levels, but employment can provide a similar social structure with needed income.

INCREASED SELF-SUFFICIENCY: My consultants tell me that many women still expect a man to take care of them. They seek not a knight in shinning armor, but a desirable partner and teammate. That's interesting because men secretly want a woman to take care of them. It appears that deep inside, we all want to be taken care of. It's just human nature to want somebody to "be there" for us.

But, this is less likely to happen to a woman today compared to the past. Prior generations stayed in marriages longer, which increased financial stability for wives. Cultural changes in marriage have increased freedom and a sense of control for women. An extension of this freedom is increased self-sufficiency.

Being independent and self-reliant may build confidence, but you don't want to feel disconnected. Besides being responsible for yourself, you still need a shared existence with others. Relying on a well-established network to connect with others provides the kind of support we all need.

BREAST CANCER: We really cannot overlook this disease, since it occurs 99% of the time in women and often in retirement. The average age at diagnosis is 61 years old. It's just a fact of life that most women accept and plan for by taking precautions. Most are aware of the importance of self-examinations, scheduled mammograms, recent treatment options, and dramatically improved survival rates. Even the media is more accepting and sensitive, as evidenced by the news of Angelina Jolie's decision to have a double mastectomy for preventative reasons.

MENOPAUSE: It may be true that a loss of estrogen in women is parallel to a loss of testosterone in men, but the range and intensity of the experience is quite different. These symptoms of hot flashes, mood swings, hair loss, dizziness and weight gain can interfere with your comfort in social situations. They can become personally distressing unless you feel you have some control over them.

Just as breast cancer is a necessary focus of concern, menopause is in the same category of symptom management. Although, menopause is not life threatening, it can still interfere with your lifestyle and happiness if you let it. Therefore, you will work with your trusted doctor and make all personal adjustments as needed.

EMOTIONAL DIFFERENCE: Although major depression tends to occur less frequently with the elderly overall, some studies show that more elderly women are becoming depressed recently. Women are more susceptible to depression at this stage, and it tends to be more prolonged. Depression can have physical consequences in that you care less about and may abandon your healthy habits. The National Institute of Mental Health views depression in the elderly as a major public health problem.

In the prior chapter, I discussed isolation and depression and suggested preventative measures. Preventative means having a plan in place before an emotionally distressful situation occurs. A physically active and socially involved lifestyle, where you feel connected and needed, is an excellent hedge against depression.

Many studies show that women report happier retirements than men. Self-report may be a subjective measure, but it's this subjective nature of retirement that we are interested in. So, a little anticipatory planning goes a long way in establishing a manageable and comfortable retirement.

TIMING YOUR RETIREMENT

The timing of the woman's retirement is partly dependent on the different factors above. Since women live longer on less money and have extra expenses, creative planning is very important. Timing your retirement to maximize work income, social security, and reduce taxes will be your emphasis.

Many of us will make half the adjustment to retirement while working part time, and the other half will make that adjustment at full retirement. As mentioned, making two smaller adjustments is less stressful and disruptive than one major one. Those people who heavily emphasized their careers above other involvements have the most difficulty adjusting.

Some of the deeply involved workers never make an adjustment to total retirement and end up returning to work. Career-minded women are now part of this category. The combination of poor timing and poor planning can often lead to confusion and distress about what to do.

A number of medical doctors that I know failed to follow this simple suggestion of planning your retirement. This may not be a surprise since the practice of medicine is certainly demanding and all-encompassing. When I asked one of the doctors I worked with why she returned from retirement, she said, "I just couldn't sit on the couch all day." If she had a retirement plan, it would have been obvious that this couch plan would not be adequate to keep a highly educated person interested in life for the next 20 or more years. Since she did not have a plan to move forward, she moved back instead. As a result, she returned to work until she passed away.

Another doctor I worked with returned to work after trying full retirement. He was diagnosed with cancer and had one leg amputated from the hip. He got around work on a motorized wheelchair. He would joke that he became a "half ass doctor." When he wasn't joking, his normal facial expression was forlorn and gloomy. He also stayed at work, despite his disability, until he passed away. No matter how high your IQ or how successful you have been before, if you don't have a plan that includes your timing, you're just not prepared for retirement.

A 68 –year-old social worker I know accepted that her retirement time line is to stay at work as long as possible. She recently decided to get married, and bought a house with her new husband. She admitted that the mortgage was the main reason for her to continue working full-time. She did complete a financial budget that proved to be instrumental in planning her lifestyle direction. This was a measured decision since she clearly understood that renting would change the equation.

The part that I like is that her attitude is completely positive and accepting of the situation. Working full time through retirement just to support a mortgage may not seem worth it to many. But, it's the marital stability and life with her husband that is important to her. You aren't making a sacrifice unless you perceive it that way.

That brings me to the importance of personal attitude or frame of reference. There is no right or wrong way to retire because its up to each of us to redefine this stage individually. Some of us won't want to hear that because it seems easier to follow a predetermined plan. Our parents were more prone to accept direction given to them rather than determine their own. The retirement blueprint used by our ancestors was characteristic of those generations. It doesn't seem applicable to the boomer generation because of the evolution of more independent thought and behavior as well as different economic times.

Beside more independence, we know female baby boomers are expected to live much longer in retirement. Many will live 30 or more years or about as long as they worked full time. This demands a focus on the long-term sustainability of a plan. For women, extended longevity naturally calls for extended employment to keep things in balance. That's why it's essential to position yourself with this in mind, even if your plan must include part time work beyond 70 years old.

Historically, we know that about 70% of retirees are taking social security at age 62. This decision turns out to be one of the worst timed decisions you can make, since you lock in the lowest rate for life. Many people stop working at that time too. A personal friend, Janet, has a bachelor degree and was a long-term rehabilitation counselor for the disabled. She felt she really deserved this early retirement because she put so much into work for so long.

We can all understand her feeling, but less than two years later she was looking for work again. "This social security isn't enough to live on; I'll have to keep moving to a cheaper place and I'm always afraid to spend money," she complained. We know enough now to guess what went wrong; you're correct, she never completed a budget or the rest of her retirement plan, and mistimed it by retiring too early.

Obviously, the timing or age at which you retire requires some thought. Working longer into retirement provides with us with a better financial and social plan. Retiring from our main job and getting rehired in a different field often results in lower wages. So, give yourself some time and flexibility to tinker with your short and long term budget and plans. I'll go into more planning details on this topic in the coming financial chapters.

Common Sense Conclusion: Deciding the best time to retire can reduce your adjustment distress and provide for better financial and social rewards going forward.

THE WRITTEN PLAN

Writing the plan down gives a more objective and organized feel to your ideas. You will also want your partner to plan along with you, so viewing a written plan is a form of role modeling that's more likely to engage and encouraging him. The example of a plan below is from a recently divorced housewife who is working part-time:

PLAN	INTEREST
1. Become a tutor	Love of Children
2. Babysit	
3. Be a clown for kids' birthdays	
4. Advocate for children's rights	
5. Start a reading club	Love of Friends
6. Arrange group activities	
7. Volunteer together	
8. Become a more caring friend	

9. Take a drawing class   Love of Arts & Crafts
10. Travel to art museums
11. Begin new crafts projects
12. Make artistic Christmas gifts

13. Plant a vegetable garden   Love of Gardening
14. Attend garden events
15. Join adopt-a-park program

16. Eat a better diet   Love of Health
17. Walk with others
18. Join a gym and keep going
19. Get more sleep

20. Work part time at same job   Love of Money
21. Shop only when a sale is on
22. Read more about investing
23. Spend less eating out
24. Do my own nails

Since the above plan has many options, she can alter her individual plans and still stay within her area of interest. She has not decided which plans will be routine versus free time activities yet. All these interests were gleaned from her life review, except love of money, which was from her budget. She recently decided that she must love money in order to make saving it a priority.

The second example is a full retirement plan as based on themes from life review and bucket items. This plan is from a single 60-year-old woman retired for five years. The R is for routine activities while the F is for free time activities.

          PLAN   INTERESTS

1. Take classes, F   Lifelong Learning
2. Write and research, R
3. Teach a short-term class, F

4. Conduct group therapy, F   Mental Health
5. Answer questions on Yahoo, R
6. Read ground breaking studies,

7. Enter photo contests, F   Photography
8. Find unique locations to shoot, F
9. Join a photographers group, F

10. Walk 3 x a week, R   Exercise

11. Bike 3 x a week, R
12. Jogging or weights, F

13. Join an investment club, F   Investment
14. Manage retirement portfolio, R
15. 1-2 hrs. of business news or study, R

16. One hour a day of cleaning, R   Home
17. One hour of evening cooking, R
18. Home improvement projects, F

19. Attend a group hike, F   Social
20. Spend more time with partner, R
21. Spend more time with daughter, F
21. Contact at least one friend a day, F
23. Join walking or cycling club, F
24. Be friendly when out, R

25. Arrange a family reunion   Bucket List
26. Reunion with college friends
27. See daughter graduate from college
28. Take Italy tour with my daughter
29. Go to Carnival in Brazil with best friend
30. Go to French Laundry Restaurant
31. Spend a week on Venice Beach, CA

The above plan has an ample number of routine items at 10 and enough free time ideas at 14. The inclusion of some individual plans ensures that she and her partner will look beyond the house for social involvement. As a result of her being retired for five years, her plan is detailed, and has been updated and changed over time. I find that most changes occur at the beginning of the plan, while we search for the right balance. Any changes pour husband makes to the plan you've suggested means that he's getting involved in making it his own.

Since you may begin a plan not only for yourself, but for your husband, let's see how easy it is to get started. Let's take a few bad habits or interests of the average man that a wife might want to regulate. Maybe he likes to drink and watch the game with the boys at your house. He refuses to help out with housework. He compromises his health by continually gaining weight and refuses to diet.

PLAN   INTEREST

1. Buy tickets to the game   Friendships
2. Go to the sports bar to meet
3. Meet at different homes

4. Include the wives occasionally
5. Throw the ball around outside

6. Empty trash weekly   House Cleaning
7. Water and cut lawn
8. Vacuum weekly
9. Wash cars
10. Take out garbage

11. Walk 3 x weekly   Health
12. No snacks after dinner
13. Join a sports team
14. Join a gym
15. No more fast food

The first interest above, friendships, is really a plan to get the boys out of the house and out of your hair. I included five options because he is likely to adapt two or three, and that's still progress. You may need to tell him that the best retirement is based on cooperation with each other. Tell him his involvement and effort is very important and necessary for a successful long-term retirement.

Regarding house maintenance, you need to make him a team player. I find men more receptive if they consider the housework a man's job. Yes, I know this is old-fashion thinking, but you would be surprised how many men feel this way. I don't think this attitude is oppositional, just selectively gender-oriented. So, just select those chores that he is more likely to do.

Health and attractiveness are qualities we should be motivated for, but some people get off track when a major life change occurs. Being healthy and attractive is obviously important to the relationship. Telling your partner that you want him healthy so he'll be around in the future can have a positive impact. Again, among the five options presented here, expect that he will adapt two or three. You may consider a reward for him if he needs more encouragement.

I'm suggesting wives manage their husbands' retirement only if they do not. You may need to encourage him at first, to get him started, but once he gets involved with the plan, and realizes its importance, you can let him direct his own future. You are not over-controlling him; you're just getting him on track and protecting yourself and your future together.

Should you really be this concerned with his adjustment? Well, remember the example of the husband who refused to help around the house at all, and was divorced in his second year of retirement? This situation upset and derailed the wife's retirement plans too.

It's best if you discuss your expectations and plans openly with your partner while keeping his interest in mind too. He'll appreciate this; he won't feel surprised or rejected, and will have a chance to adjust. Besides, if you were a little directionless at some point in life, wouldn't you appreciate your partner stepping in to help?

You are in the same retirement boat, both personally and financially as long as you are together. Remember, adjustment for a man will likely take longer because of his deeper identity with his work. So, a little patience on your part and helpful prompting of him could save you a painful and unnecessary adjustment.

Common Sense Conclusion: A written retirement plan provides an evolving foundation for personal goals with social purpose and direction.

If your partner is helpful and engaged in the relationship, he may take initiative with his plan without prompting from you. This opens the door for a cooperative discussion about coordination of your plans. The areas you may want to coordinate are amount of time together or apart, vacations or other travel plans, meal planning, and daily routines.

If you are single, you won't have to coordinate your plans with anyone. However, singles do tend to want to coordinate with other single friends, and seem to be flexible about contingency planning. When you are single, it's assumed you need to be more socially flexible since you don't have a structured relationship. It's not unusual for a single person to establish routine plans to date or to meet a partner during retirement. Singles may tinker with the plan upon meeting someone to spend more time with them, but you will still have the same basic framework designed for you.

VITAL INVOLVEMENT

As we progress through our lives and confront new tasks, it's vital that we become involved socially, mentally, and emotionally in order to meet the demands of each stage.

EGO INTEGRITY

Most of us are familiar with developmental childhood stages, but extending these into adulthood and old age moved the understanding of human nature forward. The eight stages of psychosocial development are outlined in "Childhood and Society," by Erik Erikson (1). This groundbreaking work was awarded the Pulitzer Prize.

According to Erikson, the eighth stage that occurs during retirement and is identified as "ego integrity vs. despair." The ego is part of the self that integrates pleasure or desire (id) with moral and cultural demands (super-ego). The ego attempts to balance out the id and the super-ego, resulting in behaviors that are satisfying to us and don't clash with society.

As we derive a feeling of wisdom from our past experiences, and as we graduate successfully from each stage of life, we gain a sense of integrity. We also come to terms with the fact that we live only one life, one time in history.

The result is a "consolidation" of life's experiences to take the sting out of death. According to Erikson, if these experiences do not integrate well, we tend to fear death and feel despair. Despair is also the realization that the end is so near that it's too late to relive experiences and gain integrity.

Part of ego integrity is the awareness of the unique time in which we live. As we find our place in the natural progression of one generation after another, we see that such order was meant to be. The ancestral structure that preceded us will continue to precede all the forthcoming generations, and we were instrumental in that process. We must accept that we have only one turn in life to make what we will of it, and that's how nature intended it.

That is something to be proud of, in my opinion, because it's our chance to create a legacy, contribute to the human race, or pursue our passions. It's a chance to add our one verse to the script of life. I'm not sure this takes the sting out of death, but it can bring calmness and resignation to the present. This makes life seem more orderly and, therefore, just a bit more predictable and less frightening.

The other part of gaining ego integrity is the successful accumulation and completion of prior stage experiences. Erikson suggests that the tasks of each stage have either a positive or negative outcome. We progress to the next stage either way, of course. I doubt that many people have had a perfect completion of each stage, but even if we've had prior stage mishaps, we still have some ego integrity.

The "adaptive strength" we are supposed to derive from this eighth stage is wisdom, which we all have to varying degrees. Our ancestry work provides us with a temporal perspective on the uniqueness of our life cycles, while our life review connects us to our prior experiences that led to wisdom. Completing these exercises in this book should help make us become aware of our ego integrity.

Once we are comfortable with our ego integrity, how does that help us, and what do we do with it? Well, the perspective on a finite life cycle brings us a sense of time urgency. If we view our remaining time in terms of life expectancy based on our family's longevity, we can estimate a rough departure time. We can use this time wisely by planning our life within it. The reality of losing time can become a source of motivation to implement and enjoy our retirement goals.

PLANNING VITAL INVOLVEMENT

In terms of what to do, that takes us to another work by Erikson(2), "Vital Involvement in Old Age." In this extensive work, he discusses how the life cycle "weaves back on itself in its entirety." The task of this stage is the process of integration of all prior stages combined with life cycle awareness leading to wisdom. We gain a different time perspective based on where we are in our life cycle. As older adults, we are more aware of our limited time. As this thought becomes inescapable, coming to terms with our existence is helpful prior to understanding ego integrity.

Our accumulated and unique wisdom qualifies us to become mentors to the next generations. Our wisdom allows us to be engaged and take pride in the lives of our grandchildren, according to the author. Perhaps we experienced our grandparents' involvement with us, and have positive memories of them as good role models. Perhaps we see some of ourselves in our grandchildren and have already bonded with them on some level.

Involvement in child rearing, once delegated to women, has come full circle now, and benefits all of us on multiple levels. We can easily transition to attending to grandchildren by drawing on our experience as parents.

What if you don't have children or grandchildren? Of course, that's not the only way to impart wisdom, but that's a good place to start since there is a natural connection. If caretaking is part of the expression of your personality and you have an interest in being a mentor to the next generation, you have many options. A complete commitment would be to adopt a school-age child. At our age, adjusting to a younger child with 24-hour needs is probably a bit much. Adoption is a good idea only if you really have the desire, time, and energy.

Having a babysitting business may meet this need by providing a designated and more limited time for caretaking. Volunteering or employment in a school or children's institution may be less demanding of your time and may offer an opportunity for a deep bond. There are many ways to mentor children, if that is your passion, once you start looking.

Vital involvement can occur in any social situation where you can passionately impart your wisdom in a situation where it is appreciated. One of my passions is working with older adults, helping them reframe and adjust to retirement. This keeps me deeply connected with people, as this is a journey of reflection and emotion. Research shows that any passionate social involvement can produce many benefits and increase longevity. This really starts with our life review and discovering our obvious and hidden interests and personal needs.

Common Sense Conclusion: Our plan for vital involvement is to discover, implement, and reap the rewards of the social application of our passions.

Identity at this stage of ego integrity vs. despair generally takes on two forms. There is the base accumulated identity, carried forward from the past, which includes all our prior life themes. One might call this the core identity. This identity provides most of the material for discovering our ego integrity and passions. The second more situational identity is the result of adjustments and transitions to this stage. It concerns how we present ourselves personally and socially, based on the stage-related changes we've made.

The accountant turned Wal-Mart greeter is an example of a second adaptive identity based on necessary economic adjustments. His prior work identity of accountant is part of his personality, but does not express itself in his current activities.

Following a newly discovered passion allows us to express ourselves in new ways. Living our dreams of being an involved grandmother, artist, writer, or whatever appeals to us becomes our new adaptive and healthy identity. This choice may be the part of the repressed self that has been longing to be discovered and expressed for many years.

PLANNING FOR LONGEVITY

"Don't let anyone rob you of your imagination, your creativity, or your curiosity. It's your place in the world; it's your life. Go on and do all you can with it, and make it the life you want to live." -- Mae Jemison, Astronaut

Various studies show that the strongest correlation for successful aging and longevity is income. In "Aging Well(3)," based on the Harvard Study of Adult Development, Dr. Vaillant discusses this topic in detail. This can be misleading because income is really a result of other traits. What predicts a higher income is a loving mother, good mental health, warm friends, admired fathers and good coping skills—a lot of social support. In other words, what predicts all this is a caregiver who provides reliable love during the first couple of years of life. If this does not occur, mistrust of people and the world develops and generally continues throughout life.

Dr. Vaillant classifies this group without basic trust as the loveless. This group found it difficult to play, trusted no one, and was more likely to be mentally ill and friendless all their lives. The loveless also die sooner, he notes. Not developing basic trust in childhood inhibits any personal or social bonding going forward, an unfortunate set of circumstances not under a child's control. These individuals are not always single, as one may think. Some tend to get involved in unsuccessful relationships instead. Others become convinced that bonding does not work or is too difficult, and end up alone.

How do basic trust and the ability to bond affect your retirement and longevity? Let's take an example from a couple I know, Darlene and Drew. Theirs was a traditional marriage in which she cooked, cleaned, and took care of him for more than 30 years. Darlene started loosing her balance with age and unfortunately took a fall going downstairs one day. After a brief hospital stay, she was released in a wheelchair, without a prognosis for recovery. Her need for the wheelchair and therapy would be indefinite.

Drew, now 72, was fully retired at this point, but did not have many hobbies or friends to occupy his time. It was assumed, by all who knew him, that he would return the favor of caring that his wife had offered him all these years. The stress of this role reversal proved too much for Drew causing him to escape the situation to reduce his anxiety. No formal divorce, he just suddenly moved out and left the country and completely abandon her.

Since both their Social Security checks were necessary to maintain the expense of their current home, Darlene was forced to relocate, to move away from her home of 28 years. Everyone who knew Drew was shocked and angry with him for his irresponsibility. Darlene contacted her only adult son, who claimed he couldn't manage to help her either. She took care of her son for 20 years and her husband for 30 years, yet neither one would care for her at all. Darlene now resides in a budget nursing home with strangers for the rest of her life.

I've known this couple for a long time and it was difficult to watch this abandonment happen. It turned out that Drew was one of the loveless and had trust issues going back to childhood. Most women don't think this can happen to them, and Darlene didn't think it could happen either. My women friends tell me this situation occurs more than we realize, so lets take a closer look.

Darlene unknowingly married a slightly dysfunctional partner who was distrustful in relationships. You probably already know from your conversations with your husband if there is distrust in your relationship. This distrust might be one of the ongoing issues you work on. If he had problems with early caretaking or a dysfunctional mother, that could be a red flag. It turns out that Drew's mother was once diagnosed with schizophrenia. If your husband has no friends in life or is happy being a loner, that could also be a red flag. If he clearly has a problem with trust, bonding or caretaking, it's important to go into couples counseling sooner rather than later.

Regarding longevity, this Harvard study found seven predictive factors for healthy aging. I won't go into great detail here since the next chapter will address this topic in some detail. The most important predictive behavior for longevity was not to smoke or to stop smoking early. Smoking is the single worst thing you can do to your health.

The second factor is having mature defenses for dealing with stress and social issues. In psychology, ego defense mechanisms, or how we cope with the problems of daily living, tend to mature as we age. For example, children may act out their frustrations in tantrums, while adults learn to talk them out. Children are often impulsive, while adults learn to delay their gratification. Children are self-centered, while adults are able to take the feelings of others into account. These are a few examples of mature vs. immature defenses for coping.

The third predictive factor is the absence of alcohol abuse or alcoholism. The fourth is not being overweight, and the fifth is frequent exercise. It seems these last two factors could be combined under physical fitness. The sixth factor is a stable relationship, or marriage, though a stable relationship doesn't always mean residing with a partner. As I mentioned, having a solid network of reliable friends is the primary foundation for stability. Having a stable boyfriend nearby adds to this support. Many people constitute a network, and the deeper the relationships, the better the benefits.

The last predictive factor is higher education. It appears that it's not the years of college that correlate with longevity, but the behaviors that are associated with more education. Educated people become more aware and vigilant in attending to their health and medical issues. They tend to be more compliant with doctor recommendations and medications. They keep routine exams and are more likely to act preventatively. We can all decide to do this without extra education, of course. So, don't feel you must go back to college just because this and other factors are correlated with longevity. It's equally effective to practice specific behaviors that extend our lives.

For planning purposes, we can summarize female-oriented goals as focused mainly on sustainability of income, socialization, and healthy practices. When designing your retirement plan, you will want to include the behavioral goals of longevity, vital involvement and female orientated goals in your retirement plan. This way we can maximize the health benefits from all these areas.

For example, when you include exercise into your plan, you can do it alone or with others. Exercising with another person or in a group, like a gym class, adds an additional social support that is a female oriented goal and correlated with longevity. The one benefit of exercise becomes two benefits of exercise and socialization (with an option for passionate vital involvement as well). Blending these goals together provides us with compounded health benefits to improve our quality of life.

Let's look now at the first plan in this chapter to evaluate it for the inclusion of goals, vital involvement, and longevity planning. This woman has her interests listed as Love of Children with plans of 1. Become a tutor; 2. Babysit; 3. Be a clown for kids' birthdays; 4. Advocate for children's rights. Knowing where our passions lie can direct us to which choices benefit us the most. We can assign a value to each plan based on how many benefits are involved. I will assign a value of .5 if the involvement has less depth or contact time than a full point.

Her first plan, becoming a tutor, has some personal involvement(.5), is academic(.5), with regular contact(1). Babysitting can provide daily social contact(1) that has a financial benefit(1) and affords great emotional involvement(1). Being a clown probably has the least continual contact and depth of involvement(.5), but may have a small financial benefit (.5) and seems fun(.5). Advocating for children's rights may have the least personal contact, but can lead to passionate(1) and intellectual involvement(.5).

The total for each plan is as follows: Tutor = 2; Babysitting = 3; Clown = 1.5; and Advocate = 1.5. So, we see that babysitting has the highest score and would therefore offer the deepest and most comprehensive involvement. Of course, daily babysitting can be stressful as well, so it's crucial that your plan must be derived from your passions. Once you get used to designing your plans in this light, you start including multiple health benefits in all your plans.

Lets take one more example, the second retirement plan of the 60 year old, in which the first goal is lifelong learning. The three plans for this are 1. Take classes. 2. Write and research. 3. Teach a short-term class. The first plan, taking a class, satisfies lifelong learning (1) and has some social benefits (.5). Writing and research may sound interesting, but they have only the one benefit of learning (1) because they are isolating activities. Teaching is educational (1), somewhat social (.5), and may have a small financial benefit (.5). So, in this example, teaching has the highest score and would be the most beneficial on multiple levels.

Common Sense Conclusion: Including specific female oriented goals, vital involvement, and longevity behaviors in our retirement plan results in multiple benefits for healthy aging.

In formulating our retirement plan, we begin with our passions as determined by our life review and bucket items. We then add the female goals of sustainability of income, socialization, and health. Longevity goals of maintaining our weight and diet, improving our relationship, continuing our education, and improving our coping skills are included. We add the vital involvement part of passing our knowledge on socially and we gain an amazing sense of purpose as we combine all these elements together. This allows us to attain self-fulfillment on a deeply satisfying level.

In conclusion, not only are women's plans quite different from men's, but are unique from each other as well. Each woman's interests, experiences, health, passions, and personality are unique and result in a specific design for a customized plan. It's difficult to imagine it any other way.

ESTATE PLANNING

Estate planning is the legal manner in which your wish to distribute your belongings after you die. This may seem like a financial decision, but it's actually more personal. Giving away your personal belongings to those you know can be upsetting, partly because you are going through a rehearsal for what you expect to happen after your death. It's natural to become attached to material objects, each with a special meaning for you, which have become part of your life.

I found that it doesn't matter how much money your have or the value of your objects. Each person has a need to have closure on his or her life as part of getting ready to leave it. Closure not only involves saying goodbye to significant people in our lives, but also making sure the right objects are with the right people.

In working for a hospice, I had been assisting with wills in a nursing home when a frail gentleman approached me for help. I went to his room and sat bedside him so we could talk in privacy. He looked me in the eyes and said, "I don't have much, but I got to take care of it." It turned out that his extended stay in the nursing home rendered him completely broke. We carefully assigned his remaining belongings, even his clothes, in accordance with his wishes. He released a big sigh of relief and appeared noticeably relaxed as we finished, as if an emotional weight had been lifted--he finally had closure.

Many of us do some estate planning when we have children. But, as they grow and have their own lives, our plan needs to be updated to reflect current conditions. I prefer a revocable trust because you can change your mind without altering the whole document. A trust is also designed to avoid probate, which will be your largest expense. Marilyn Monroe's estate was worth 1.1 million, but after probate, its worth fell to .1 million. I won't go into detail about trusts and wills because you will most likely have an advisor to rely on. I went to an attorney for my first trust, but saw a paralegal for my second one, which cost me only a fraction of the first.

Common Sense Conclusion: Preparing a trust and final will provides the psychological closure necessary for moving forward.

PREVENTING FAMILY CONFLICT

It's fairly well known that families often disagree and even file for court when disappointed by an inheritance. It's important to be mindful of the possibility of these feelings because family hostilities may last for many years. That's probably not what you had in mind, but you could accidentally create this result if you're not careful. As you create a pecking order for distribution of your funds, your wishes may get misinterpreted as reflecting the importance to you of each inheritor. Even if their reactions stem out of immature entitlement feelings, their feelings will be intense, and must be defused.

In one family, the mother died and left what she had to her two children. She designated in her trust that the family home be sold in order to raise cash for them. One daughter decided the family home should be kept in the family and should not be sold. Her decision was not in keeping with the wishes of the mother, so the home was sold according to the documents and the money was distributed. However, the daughter never got over this point of conflict and still refuses to contact the rest of the family, more than 12 years later.

As a therapist who has dealt with conflict for many years, I believe clear and open communication is necessary to work out differences. In the above example regarding the family home, if a family meeting had taken place, the issue could have been discussed and probably resolved. If the daughter had disclosed her interest in owning the family home earlier, she may have been given an option to buy the other half. This way one would get the cash they wanted and other would keep the home—both would be accommodated and the family dynamics left intact.

Second, it's a good idea to have your heirs write down their specific "wants." Many people just earmark household items until its time for them to be passed on. Be sure your heirs list even the small things in the house they want. Do not underestimate the importance of this list to them. This way, you can take your time deciding how to distribute items fairly or can negotiate individual items with each person privately. It's important to know what sentimental value your heirs may attach to items so that you don't inadvertently upset them.

My third suggestion to avoid unwanted litigation and family conflict is to begin your distribution before you die. At this point, in 2014, the gift tax exclusion, that you can give without having to pay tax, is $14,000 annually. If you have three children, that's $42,000 a year you can give without them being taxed. This way you can distribute your money in manageable amounts.

I'm a big fan of arranging payments over longer time frames. I find that those who receive large sums of money suddenly tend to spend it just as suddenly. The last thing I want to see is someone carelessly wasting my money, which took many years of hard work and economizing to accumulate.

If the funds are distributed over a longer time or at certain points when the children are more mature, I've noticed less impulsiveness in spending. Giving young people too much money at once stresses their value system and seems to alter their motivation to live a normal life of school and work. Sometimes they withdraw from society, since they no longer need to be employed.

I can't imagine anything more upsetting for parents who have worked hard all their lives to help their children than to see their children spend the money irresponsibly, or even completely waste it. To counteract this possibility, some people arrange one distribution after the child graduates from college, another at age 30, and a final one at age 35 or 40.

My fourth suggestion is to have a reunion of family and friends while you're still around. It's too bad that our culture doesn't have a farewell celebration, so we could see everyone we love and see them enjoy our gifts before we part. I think a reunion of family and friends would be an intimate, caring, and memorable occasion, and would also provide the ultimate in closure for all parties involved. Maybe if we arrange these celebrations for our loved ones or for ourselves, we can push the culture forward to celebrate life instead of mourning death.

If you've had a trust for any length of time you've probably updated it. You may have taken some people out of it or added some people to it. We go through different feelings about people over the years, but as we get ready to depart, we tend to soften and forgive. Rather than exclude those who have fallen out of favor, I like to view my relationships historically. If I'm upset with a long-term friend today, I still take the history of the friendship into account when making trust decisions. I don't want any regrets or ill feelings at the end.

THE ESTATE EXECUTOR

Besides the sensitive issues of writing a trust and considering how your family might respond, you also need to choose an executor or trustee for your estate. Your offspring or friends may react to these choices as well. As parents, we tend to choose the oldest or most stable child as the most reliable. But it's a good idea to ask your chosen person ahead of time if he or she wants this position and will have time for its duties. You don't want a trustee who feels burdened or resentful probating the estate.

It's typical to list at least three trustees, two family or friends and a professional entity as a backup plan. If your family has too many conflicts over who gets the trustee position, you can use the backup plan as your first choice. Taking a diplomatic view with a willingness to negotiate seems to work best.

A couple of examples about why estate planning is so important, and can have wide-ranging effects:

In a recent probate, three children were in line for distribution after the second parent died. But the father was disapproving of one child for not living up to his expectations. He made his feelings clear before he died, but never mentioned he was excluding this one child in the documents. The other children felt the inheritance distribution was grossly unfair and decided to split it in three equal parts, essentially changing the wishes of their departed father.

The above is an example of how your belongings may be re-distributed if you haven't discussed it with family. Most families are not this fair and reasonable as entitlement issues often arise. This is why it's good to have offspring and other beneficiaries list their expectations before you write your trust.

A 66-year-old woman who had worked hard all her life for a hand-to-mouth existence was finally ready to receive her inheritance. When her mother died, she was shocked to learn that the maid who worked for her in her final years inherited the entire estate. Over half a million dollars was at stake here, so the daughter procured legal representation. She was anxious and scared about being involved in a legal case. Her anxiety was so high, in fact, that just to end the stress she decided prematurely to settle the case out of court. She settled for $15,000 and allowed the maid to have the rest. A year later she had spent this money and was homeless for a while. I know this woman personally and it really broke my heart to see this happen.

If we view this situation from the mother's view, her wishes were never met because for most of her life she had her daughter as the sole beneficiary of her will. It was only in the last year of life that she altered her will. I'm sure her wish was not that her daughter receives so little and end up homeless.

As for the daughter, her own anxiety and fear of the legal process defeated her. It caused her to give up her rights to her inheritance, leaving her with frustration instead. If her mother had taken the daughter's personality into consideration by starting the distribution process early, and if the daughter was more involved in her mother's care, this story may have ended up differently.

Common Sense Conclusion: We need to use our best judgment in constructing an estate plan, in considering the feelings and wishes of beneficiaries, and in choosing an executor for our trust.

The bottom line is there is no way to guarantee what's going to happen to the trust or with people after we die. The only way to be sure that your wishes are followed is to do it yourself while you are still alive. We can include a clause that eliminates anyone who files a lawsuit disputing the trust. But such clauses have still been challenged in court. This process is so riddled with conflict that some attorneys specialize as trust dispute lawyers. So, we can take all this into consideration when choosing an executor.

In summary, we will include female-oriented goals as part of our retirement plan. Timing your retirement to maximize financial and social benefits is key for future happiness. Making a written retirement plan allows you to organize and adjust your goals more objectively. The more detailed your plan, with multiple themes and options, the better prepared you will be. You may help your partner or friends start their plan to encourage adjustment. We will include vital involvement and longevity planning in our community activities. Estate planning should be completed with anticipation and thoughtful consideration of family reactions.

1. Erikson, E.H., *Childhood and Society*. New York: W.W. Norton and Co., 1950.
2. Erikson, E.H., *Vital Involvement in Old Age*. New York: W.W. Norton and Co., 1986.
3. Vaillant, G., *Aging Well*. New York: Little, Brown & Co., 2002.

4 YOUR BODY IS YOUR VEHICLE

"You have to stay in shape. My grandmother started walking five miles a day when she was 60. She's 97 today and we don't know where the hell she is."   ---Ellen DeGeneres.

When discussing health, I'm going to present established standards for good health in general. Some areas of health will benefit women more, but good health is obviously important for both men and women. Many of us, including myself, will fall short of some of these standards. Since we could all improve our health, we'll regard this information as fuel for starting a healthy program.

According to 2013 Businessweek.com article(1), *Scary Health-Care Statistics on the Broken Down Boomer Generation,* "Aging baby boomers are fatter and sicker than their predecessors were at the same age." In addition, "Boomers who are in poor health will not only have more expensive health care; they are more likely to retire early, depriving employers of their specialized knowledge." Apparently, we have gotten off track from earlier healthy habits of our youth and some authors are trying to scare us back to better health.

Currently, the boomers are less likely to report excellent health and to do regular exercise, and more likely to suffer from obesity, hypertension, diabetes, and other maladies than earlier generations. The study says that although boomers have a longer life expectancy than previous generations, their health is another matter. Better habits would help prolong their lives, the authors say. The present study demonstrates a clear need for policies that expand efforts at prevention and promote a healthy lifestyle. Here are some statistics from the report:

Pre-Boomer to Boomer
Excellent health status 32% to 13%
Use a walking assist device 3.3 to 6.9
Limited in work   10.1 to 13.8
Functional limitation 8.8 to 13.5
Obese   29 to 39
Regular exercise   50 to 35
Moderate drinking 37 to 67
Hypertension   36 to 43
Diabetes   12 to 16
Cancer   10 to 11

YOUR WEIGHT AND BODY FAT

As younger boomers, we were more health oriented than we are today. Remember when running marathons and being healthy was the thing to do? This positive lifestyle and culture change has reversed only recently. The Center for Disease Control (CDC) reported that during the past 10 years, there has been a dramatic increase in obesity in the United States and rates remain high. More than a third, or 35.7% of adults and 17% of children, are obese.(2) Okay, so maybe we let ourselves go for a while, but we still have time to turn the situation around.

The body mass index (BMI) is most common measure of weight to fat ratio, and is intended as a general health guideline. If you're curious about your BMI, its easy to calculate: BMI = (weight in pounds/(height in inches) squared) x 703. For example, a 5'10" male who weights 180 pounds would calculate that 5'10" = 70 inches and 70 squared is 4900 Then, 4900/180 = 27.2,so his BMI is 27.2. A 5'2" woman who weighs 120 pounds would have a BMI of 21.9. Healthy weight is between 18.5 and 25. If you are over 25, you are overweight. If your BMI is over 30, you are considered obese, and have a 44% increased chance of death.

The BMI is not designed for individual diagnosis, so if your BMI is higher than you expect, remember it's just a general estimate, and don't overreact. Try to take it in stride, and work it into your health program plan. (I was able to lower my BMI by changing my diet.)

The health effects of overweight and obesity, according to the National Institute of Health, (3) are:

1. Coronary heart disease
2. Type II diabetes
3. Cancer (breast, colon, endometrial)
4. Stroke
5. Dyslipidemia (high cholesterol or triglycerides)
6. Liver and gallbladder disease
7. Sleep apnea and respiratory problems
8. Osteoarthritis
9. Gynecological problems (abnormal menses, infertility)
10. Being 40% overweight doubles your chance of death

Some researchers add chronic joint pain, inflammation, social isolation, and even depression to the list. Either way, this is not a list you want to be associated with. So, if your BMI is high, it can be your wake up call to get healthy and live a long life.

THE COST OF POOR HEALTH

In these next few sections, I want to provide you with factual information for your evaluation and consideration. I figure that if I'm asking you to improve something, like your health, having the real facts should be more convincing than opinion. My intent is to dispel any myths about health and aging and to encourage you to design and take charge of your healthy habits.

We'll begin with a condition that we have the most control over: our weight.

The CDC(2) reports that in 2009-10, 35.7% of adults were obese. But, for women who are over 60 years old, the rate increased to 42%, the highest of any category. Rising health care costs are showing no sign of slowing. One study(4)noted that, "Across all payers, obese people had medical spending that was $1,429(42%) greater than spending for normal weight people in 2006." As weight increases there is a corresponding increase in medical expense.

According to a *Motley Fool* (5) article, America's obesity epidemic is increasing. The author lists the following statistics:

1. The amount of medical costs stemming from obesity is $190 billion a year.

2. The obese pay 105% more for prescription drugs.

3. Gasoline costs an extra 3.4 billion dollars to move the extra weight when compared to 1960.

4. Employers lose $164 billion a year in lost productivity.

5. $6.4 billion is lost annually due to employee absenteeism.

6. Airlines claim they loose about $1 billion a year in fuel.

7. The cost of childhood obesity is $14.3 billion.

8. Medicare and Medicaid spend $62 billion a year on obesity-related costs.

9. $580 billion will be lost by 2030 if the trend continues.

These are certainly staggering numbers by any measure. But, what is your cost individually? *Disabled World* (6) in 2010 reported that the individual cost of being obese is $4,879 for women and $2,646 for men. Adding the value of lost life to the costs results in $8,365 for women and $6,518 for men annually. The analysis demonstrates that costs are nine times higher for women and six times higher for men who are obese (as defined by their BMI level). The findings also reveal a significant difference between the impact of obesity on women when it comes to job-related costs of lost wages, absenteeism and disability.

In a study entitled, "Longevity, Mortality and Body Weight,"(8) the authors focus on the causal relationship of body weight to longevity and mortality. The findings show body size is negatively related to longevity and life expectancy, and positively to mortality. They also found gender differences in longevity due to differences in body size. They conclude that overeating and increased body mass have promoted an epidemic of chronic disease and reduced our life span.

It appears that our attitude towards health has changed over time. I understand that we are all busy and tired at the end of the day. In our youth, we were more determined to use our available time in healthy ways. Somehow, life has distracted us and changed our priorities. We cannot continue on this path, but since weight is under our control, it simply becomes another area to manage.

What if I told you that "half the population spends little or nothing on health care, while 5 percent of the population spends almost half the total amount (7)." Lets hope we are not that 5 percent, at least not for a long time.

But, on closer examination, we find a concentration of treatments in specific areas. "The five most expensive health conditions are heart disease, cancer, trauma, mental disorders, and pulmonary disorders," according to the study. One explanation for this concentration is that these disorders often become chronic.

Even the cost of falling down for those over 65 years old is significantly expensive and frequent. "In 2010, falls among older adults cost the U. S. health care system $30 billion in direct medical costs when adjusted for inflation. In 2000, medical costs for women, who composed 58% of older adults, were two to three times higher than the cost for men."(9)

Hospitalizations accounted for nearly two-thirds of nonfatal fall injuries. Fractures were both the most common and most costly nonfatal injuries." Hip fractures not only interfere with our current health, but also tend to change our quality of life going forward, even leading to disability and depression.

According to one study (10): "A hip fracture is a terrible injury. It typically requires major surgery for repair. Operations involve either metal pinning with screws and/or plates or replacement of the hip joint with artificial parts. Infections, blood clotting, bleeding, and failure of the repair work can complicate these operations. After surgery, long and aggressive rehabilitation programs are necessary for optimal success. For the very frail, elderly person, ultimate recovery can be extremely difficult and lead to long term loss of independence, nursing home placement, and even death can result."

Since being female is considered one of the risk factors for hip fractures, lets talk a little about prevention. As muscles naturally weaken and balance may become a problem over time, exercise is key for maintaining both in optimum condition. Our homes must be evaluated for adequate lighting and cleared of any obstacles we can trip on, especially throw rugs. Since a common place to slip and fall is the shower, a seat or rail can be added. I recently replaced my glass shower door with curtains.

If you are having trouble with your eyesight, you must make it a medical priority. Osteoporosis and dietary intake need to be addressed since they have an impact on the fragility of your bones. I personally try to increase my grip strength with exercise, so I can catch my fall if needed. If you know someone who is frail and prone to falling, he or she can wear a preventative hip protector that in the form of padded underwear. As parents, we childproofed our homes; now, as we retire, we will elder-proof our homes.

Common Sense Conclusion: Improving and maintaining your health results in increased savings, improved quality of life, and longevity.

PSYCHOLOGY OF EATING

When working as a therapist in the Optifast weight reduction program, I taught a class on the psychology of eating. Many of you may remember when Oprah Winfrey rolled a wagon onto her TV set with 70 pounds of animal fat, and touted her weight loss in that amount. Well, it was the Optifast diet program that got her started. The system used a very low calorie protein drink four or five times a day instead of food. I saw women over 400 pounds and men over 500 pounds lose significant weight in a matter of weeks.

It's important to make a list of all the causes, or triggers, that make you eat. Watching a TV food commercial is a trigger causing you to feel hungry even when you are not. Neurological conditioning, involving biochemical changes in your brain, results in increased ghrekin, a hormone that causes hunger when you see food. The supermarket understands this phenomenon, and strategically places junk food near the check out area.

But you can control your response by controlling such environmental triggers: mute and look away from TV commercials; stick to your shopping list in the store; don't grocery shop when you're hungry; eat out less; skip food ads in magazines and newspapers; invite food buddies on a walk; and sit away from concession stands.

Another key focus in weight control is on stress, or emotional eating. Some think the obese are 25% more likely to have a mood disorder like depression. In my professional experience in working with the obese and the depressed, I would say the overlap is higher. There is some evidence that depression in children leads to obesity later in life. If depression is related to obesity, then many diet programs are misguided in not addressing this issue.

In my experience, depression is the most common disorder in mental health treatment clinics. I've noticed that if worry or anxiety accompanies depression, food can be used as a tranquilizer because of its calming effect. Oxygen leaves the brain and goes to the stomach and intestines for the digestion process. In this way, the individual uses food as a form of stress reduction or anxiety management.

Besides external triggers and internal stress or moods, a third psychological key for success is the social element. That is, when participating in a program designed to change behavior, group reinforcement or support is essential for broad success. Dieting and exercising are always easier and more sustainable when done in groups. Groups add an essential social and even competitive component, as demonstrated in the TV show *The Biggest Loser*. Consequently, partners or friends who diet and exercise together have the most success long term.

Common Sense Conclusion: Making a lifestyle commitment to maintain normal weight and body fat levels is essential to healthy aging and quality of life.

My experience in the mental health field confirms that, with a little practice, we can successfully reprogram our habits. If we know stress is the primary trigger for our overeating, then we can go for a walk or call a friend. After a month, our unhealthy habit has been replaced with a beneficial one. Such behavior substitution can be effective in many areas of our lives.

DIET AND NUTRITION

The fact that so many fad diets exist is a function of lack of knowledge and opportunism: lack of knowledge on the consumer's part as to the essential ingredients of nutrition, and opportunism on the part of diet businesses trying to capitalize on that lack of knowledge. As boomers augment their education, and begin altering their nutritional patterns, the farmers, food packagers, supermarkets, restaurants and diet businesses will cater to those needs or become obsolete. Emerging boomer dietary demands will drive the direction of future nutritional offerings.

Since a healthy diet correlates to reducing conditions such as heart disease and cancer, *Healthy at 100* (11) examines the diet of societies with the greatest longevity. The Abkhazians in Russia eat mostly vegetarian with some nuts, milk, and a little meat. There is no added fat, sugar or butter in their diet, and they eat under 2000 calories a day. They also get a great amount of regular exercise, have no urgency about time, continue to work into old age, and use music and dance in their social gatherings..

In the Andes Mountains of Ecuador is the Vilcabamba society. Their diet is primarily vegetables with nuts, beans, grains, and a little meat, but no processed foods. They are always walking and climbing, live in a social commune, respect their elders, and don't need glasses or hearing aids as is so common in western society. Dr. Leaf from Harvard (14) confirmed that the Vilcabambans were free from diseases and had longer lives than their western counterparts. He noted the Vilcabamba population of 819 had nine people over 100 years old, while the U. S. rate is three per 100,000 people. "...they took in about 1200 calories a day, low in fat and cholesterol, which would minimize heart disease. In addition, physical activity required by living in a high altitude improved their cardiopulmonary function."

The book, *Healthy at 100*(11) also discusses the Okinawa diet. In Okinawa, Japan, the news reported that the oldest man on record, Jiroemon Kimura, passed away at the age of 116. He broke the record of 115 years by Misao Okawa of Osaka. The Japanese are known to have the greatest number of centenarians on earth. What do they eat? You guessed it, mostly fresh vegetables (seven servings a day), plenty of whole grains, soy products, fish, squid, octopus, seaweed, and lots of green tea. There is no meat or dairy in their diet, but they do consume a low amount of alcohol that is beneficial. They also exercise daily and have a supportive society.

The Okinawa Program, a bestseller in 2001 by Wilcox & Wilcox, is based on the Okinawa Centenarian Study of 25 years. The book is filled with suggestions of how to adapt the diet of Okinawans to western culture. The authors also recommend other lifestyle changes based on this study. In their follow-up book, *The Okinawa Diet Plan*, they expand on the diet with more than 150 recipes, and emphasis on the 10 principles of the diet.

The Mediterranean Diet

A study by the *New England Journal of Medicine* (12), "compared head to head against a low fat diet and ended early, after almost five years, because the results were so clear it was considered unethical to continue. Participants who adhered to the modified Mediterranean diet dramatically reduced their risk of heart attack, strokes and deaths from heart disease." However, this diet does not turn you into a vegan or request you do anything extreme, just eat more unrefined and fewer processed foods.

This diet is characterized by fruits and vegetables (six servings a day), whole grains, legumes and nuts. Fish, olive oil, and red wine in moderate amounts are included. Some variations include occasional red meat, but never processed meat. Moderate exercise and social involvement complement the diet. Since the diet was developed in 1993, much research has been done to confirm the following principles as beneficial (13):

1. Eating the least processed forms of plants is best. Fresh, raw or lightly cooked vegetables, and fruits and whole grains retain fiber and most of their nutrients.

2. Dining with poultry and fish more often than red meat. Lean red meat should be limited to a couple of times a month or less.

3. Using olive oil for cooking, baking and over salads and vegetables. Extra virgin olive oil is highest in monounsaturated fat and phytonutrients.

4. Low fat cheese and yogurt in moderation are acceptable.

5. Physical activity is encouraged as is eating with others. This bit of physical and social involvement complements the actual diet.

6. Herbs and spices are now part of the program. The added flavor and aroma reduce the need for fat and salt when cooking.

7. Fish and shellfish are now recommended more often -- at least twice a week -- for their unique health benefits.

8. Wine is acceptable -- one daily glass for women and two for men.

A study with 57% women included over seven thousand subjects between 55 and 80 years old. These subjects were considered to have high cardiovascular risk with type II diabetes, or at least three risk factors of overweight or obesity, hypertension, smoking, family history of coronary heart disease, and high LDL cholesterol or low HDL cholesterol levels. Subjects were randomly placed in three groups: Mediterranean diet with extra-virgin olive oil, Mediterranean diet with nuts, or a low fat diet. The results, published in the *England Journal of Medicine*, (15) showed that the risk of a cardiovascular event was 29% lower with either of the Mediterranean plans than with the low fat diet.

The common elements of all these diets are fresh fruits and vegetables as their foundation. They combine whole grains with nuts and legumes. Seafood is usually the meat of choice. The calorie restriction averages around 2000 for men and 1800 for women. There is an avoidance of fats, most meats, processed foods, salt, and sugar. The Mediterranean societies also included a fair amount of exercise on a daily basis and social cohesiveness in their culture.

If you are not convinced that extra servings of fruits and vegetables are important, "the latest dietary guidelines call for five to 13 servings of fruits and vegetables a day(2.5 to 6.5 cups per day), depending on one's caloric intake. For a person who needs 2000 calories a day to maintain weight and health, this translates into nine servings, or 4.5 cups a day (2 cups of fruit and 2.5 cups of vegetables)." (16)

Most people feel they eat a fairly healthy diet until they look at their diet in detail. Trying to include five or more vegetables and fruits in a daily diet takes some planning, until it becomes routine. You also have to include enough variety to get proper nutrition. Many complain that vegetables are poor tasting and not appealing to eat raw. It works best if you cook them half way, use spray butter (one calorie), and sprinkle ground garlic and/or fresh ground pepper on top—non-sodium spicing seems to make the difference.

In the American diet, the three big ugly things that are killing us are fat, sugar, and salt. Therefore, substitutions become key. I find that fruit satisfies my desire for sugar; potassium chloride works as a salt substitute for my sodium cravings, and non-fat Greek yogurt is good as a fat/dairy replacement.

The adjustment to a healthy diet doesn't have to be stressful because we can replace virtually everything we eat with something better. We can still eat hot dogs and hamburgers since they may be now made out of organic soybeans. Even French fries can be made healthier when baked without oils or condiments added.

Even if you already have cardiovascular disease, the proper diet can reverse it. A study by Dr. Dale Ornish (17) decided to test this hypothesis by following the American Heart Association diet. His experimental group had a vegetarian diet with 10% fat, moderate aerobic exercise, stress management training, smoking cessation and group support. None of the experimental group received lipid- lowering drugs, while 60% of the control group did. Angiograms for both groups were done after one and five years. The results of the study for the experimental group showed a 91% reduction in frequency of angina after one year, and 72% after five. The control group had a 186% increase in frequency of angina after one year, but a 36% decrease after five years.

The Ornish study control group recorded 45 cardiac events (2.25 events per patient) while the experimental group had only 25 events (.09 events per patient) during this time. Events included heart attacks, angioplasty, bypass surgery, hospitalizations, and cardiac deaths. This is one of the rare studies that measures reversal of disease due to nutrition. This study confirms that's it's never too late to get healthy and prolong your life.

Jack LaLanne was an excellent role model for healthy eating. He wrote *Live Young Forever* (18) when he was 95 years old, just a year before he died. We have all heard of the famous juicer machine that he developed because he had a problem consuming the needed amount of raw vegetables. He swore by his juicer rather than bottled juice because it had no sugar or preservatives.

LaLanne always emphasized clean organic foods, usually bought at a farmers market. He and his wife enjoyed dining out, but not because of the food. His favorite restaurants knew that he would send back food unless it was prepared to his standards. Even more interesting is that the restaurants were happy to accommodate his demands in order to keep him as a customer.

Since the American diet is one of the worst in the world, it is absolutely essential that we all make changes to it. This is our lives we are talking about. We can all improve our diets with a little effort and direction. The above longevity diets can be guidelines for our changes. It helps to have a health partner, like a spouse or friend, who is improving their diet as well.

If all your friends are food buddies, then you need to be careful. You have to determine which of your food buddies can transition into another activity. Can the food friends take a bike ride or a walk together instead? If you find that few friends are able to make this transition, then you will need to join a gym, or maybe a biking or walking club, and make a new set of health-minded friends.

A spouse can take on a pivotal role in weight loss and dietary change. When both partners are overweight, the situation can be either ideal or just the opposite. If both are motivated to improve their health, then it becomes self-reinforcing to work together. If only one is motivated, the other sometimes becomes insecure as the dieting one starts to lose weight and look better and more attractive. I know one husband who started putting out cake and other desserts when the wife returned home from diet class. As she became thin and attractive, she triggered too much insecurity for the husband to tolerate. That's why both partners should be involved with the plan or, at the very least, not opposed to it.

Evaluating restaurant food is often difficult because you have little control over how it's cooked. Even the upscale restaurants are at fault as they cater to the over indulgence of the wealthy. Altering where you dine is an important step in controlling your diet.

On a recent trip to New Orleans, I was careful to avoid the traditional Cajun and Creole deep fried cuisine offered almost everywhere. The Internet reviews provided critical information in helping me find healthy restaurants. I just followed the list of reviewed places and was amazed at how excellent and healthy the choices were. I managed to spend a week in the deep fried South and actually lose three pounds..

Any diet plan should include portion size. Some of us are not aware of the importance of this information. The oversized portions at restaurants are bad enough, but some are offering extra large plates as a way of encouraging business. These are the type of restaurants to avoid as we transition from quantity to quality of nutrition. Over time, we become accustomed to making a visual estimate of calories based on portion size.

Common Sense Conclusion: A predominately plant-based diet with small amounts of seafood, within a low calorie framework, is proven to be the most beneficial diet for improving health and increasing longevity.

TOBACCO CESSATION

The Gallup poll (19) reports that about 9% of us over 65 years old still smoke tobacco. Also, older smokers are less likely to believe that smoking harms their health. New studies show that women lose about 11 years of life expectancy and men lose about 12 years from smoking. Rather than make a long list of all the damaging health problems from smoking that you already know, lets take a look at benefits if you quit at a later age.

People I know claim that giving up cigarettes at our age will not help because all the damage has already been done. Others don't care if it helps because they want to enjoy themselves before they go. You have probably heard of a dozen other reasons as well. According to the American Lung Association (20), "Quitting smoking has proven health benefits even at a later age. When an older person quits smoking, circulation improves immediately and the lungs begin to repair damage. In only one year, the added risk of heart disease is cut almost in half, and risk of stroke, lung disease and cancer diminish. After one year, the women who quit smoking had two times more improvement in lung function compared with the men who quit." Women not only benefit more than men by quitting smoking, but also live longer.

Reuters released an interesting article based on a study that concluded "Smokers who quit may cut heart risk faster than previously thought." (21) This study found that a smoker's body recovered to nonsmoker health levels after about 8 years, rather than the previously estimated 15. This shorter recovery time holds true if a person smokes less than 3.2 packs a day for 10 years or two packs a day for 16 years. This and other studies show everybody enjoys health benefits from quitting smoking, regardless of how long or how much the person smoked.

I already noted that we can successfully reprogram our habits with a little effort. A colleague I know proudly brags to anyone who will listen about how he stopped smoking all on his own. He says that lollipops were his key to success. He simply replaced a cigarette with a sugar-free lollipop every time he felt the urge to smoke. He claims this method has kept him smoke-free for over six yrs.; he has saved money and maintained a slender body type. Not to mention that he's given up one of the worst health habits with a simple replacement behavior. He was exceptionally motivated and probably would have found success with any technique.

In terms of the best way to quit, you may want to go cold turkey, but the long-term success rate for this method is 5 percent to 10 percent. If you use a smoking reduction program, the success rate double. If you try to reduce your smoking, but not quit completely, there are no health benefits. The primary factor involved in quitting is motivation; you must be dead serious and determined.

Some people do very well with a nicotine replacement like the patch, gums, nasal sprays, inhalers or lozenges. Replacement allows you to reduce the amount of nicotine intake gradually. The most successful blueprint for quitting appears to be a combination of 1) using a program or proven method, 2) use of a nicotine replacement, and 3) counseling. Medicare will pay for smoking cessation counseling of 8 sessions each year. The cost will be zero if you don't have any illnesses from tobacco use.

Common Sense Conclusion: Since tobacco usage is the single most preventable health hazard that shortens our lives, we must be determined to find a method to quit.

ALCOHOL, COFFEE AND TEA

Information on these substances has finally evolved to the point where we can recommend a therapeutic amount for healthy consumption. Studies show those who maintain moderate consumption of alcohol score better on cognitive test than non-drinkers. Since alcohol increases hormones that improve insulin sensitivity, it also helps prevent diabetes.

According to *5 Hidden Health Benefits of Alcohol,* (22) alcohol benefits your heart by cutting the risk of heart disease by up to 40%, due to its ability to increase you good cholesterol and lower the bad. Also women who drink one or two glasses a day gain less weight than those who don't. This is partly because alcohol has calories and because it relaxes us so we don't eat to reduce stress. The risk of diabetes is also reduced since alcohol increases hormonal levels that improve sensitivity to insulin which make it easier to process glucose.

Moderate wine drinkers are also less likely to have Alzheimer's disease or cognitive impairments like dementia. This appears to occur because alcohol increases blood flow to the brain. Consistent consumption of alcohol also reduces cholesterol in the gallbladder, which then reduces the incidence of gallstones.

Women and Alcohol (23) mentions that the effects of alcohol in women differ from those in men because women process it slower and need less for beneficial results. The authors studied different intake amounts and noted the positive effects of one drink per day. They concluded, however, that more than one drink can lead to detrimental effects, including increased risk for breast cancer. Since women metabolize alcohol differently than men, their findings point to a recommended one-a-day drink for optimum benefit.

If women drink in excess of this, there is no advantage and results can be detrimental to good health. Red wine appears to be the best alcoholic choice due to its antioxidant effect and the impact on HDL or good cholesterol levels. In conclusion, the current recommendation for women is to drink one 5 ounce glass of red wine, or one 12 ounce bottle of beer, or one 1.5 ounce glass of 80 proof liquor per day.

Coffee drinkers may be confused by conflicting research as well. At one point, I thought I'd have to give up caffeine altogether because it could increase blood pressure. Now we know coffee is a potent source of antioxidants and neurologically protective substances. Caffeine appears to compound the beneficial effects of regular coffee compared to decaffeinated coffee. Using cream or sugar seems to decrease the antioxidant effect, so drinking black coffee is healthier.

The Harvard School of Public Health (24), "...conducted detailed analysis of 28 studies, representing 1.1 million (both genders) total participants and 45,335 cases of type II diabetes. Patients were followed for duration of 10 months to 20 years. One cup of coffee a day translated to about 8% lower risk on average. Two cups cut the risk by 15%. Three cups dropped the risk by 21%. Four cups equaled a 25% risk cut, five cups reduced the risk by 29% and six cups lowered the risk by a third."

The Iowa Women's Health study (25) involved 27,312 postmenopausal women. The women were 55 to 69 years old at the beginning of the study and they were followed for 15 years. "Women who reported drinking one to three daily cups of coffee at the study's start were 24% less likely to die of heart disease during the study. ...they were also 28% less likely to die of other non-cancerous inflammatory diseases," the study concluded.

Coffee's protective effect against cancer is still under investigation, but there might be some evidence that it slows endometrial cancer in women. Recent studies associate reduced risk for basal cell carcinoma, or skin cancer, with coffee intake. Some results show a decrease in cirrhosis and cancer of the liver, but more research is needed in this area.

Certain teas appear to stand above other teas for their powerful antioxidant and cognitive benefits. The green, white, black and oolong teas are all derived from the Camellia sinensis plant. Each of these teas is harvested and processed or oxygenated slightly differently. Amazing-green-tea.com(26) has identified 16 tea benefits:

1. *Antioxidant effect:* The catechins in tea can prevent heart disease, strokes and cancers, and can help slow down aging.

2. *Exercise longer and burn fat*: Exercise endurance increases as catechins burn fat and enable athletes to exercise longer.

3. *Cancer prevention:* Catechins blocks production of destructive enzymes that promote cancer growth.

4. *Slows aging*: Studies apparently show that the more tea consumed, the least likely premature death occurs.

5. *Reduces stress while increasing concentration:* Theanine in tea calms the body by producing alpha brain waves and results in better attention spans.

6. *Cardiovascular protection:* The epigallocatechin gallate (EGCG) in tea apparently speeds the recovery process from heart attacks and strokes while reducing heart disease risk.

7. *Blood Pressure:* Tea drinkers are 65% less likely to develop hypertension.

8. *Diabetes:* Tea tends to regulate blood sugar levels by increasing insulin activity.

9. *Inflammation reduction:* This is especially beneficial for women, who are three times more likely to be affected by rheumatoid arthritis caused by inflammation.

10. *Lungs*: Cell damage caused by cigarettes leading to lung cancer is reduced.

11. *Arteries:* Benefits involve inhibition of arteriosclerosis or hardening of the arteries.

12. *Oral health:* Green tea fights mouth viruses, tooth decay, and bad breath.

13. *Liver protection:* Green tea apparently reduces liver injuries from alcohol and possible other substances.

14. *Osteoporosis:* This risk is reduced because tea preserves bone density.

15. *Immune response:* Antigens found in tea seems to increase our

immunity level.

16. *Hydration:* There is apparently a myth held by some doctors that any caffeine dehydrates you. It turns out that not only does tea hydrate you, but also adds all the above benefits in the process.

While the benefits of green tea appear good, white tea appears to have more antioxidants. Oolong appears to be next, and black tea is last. But the most concentrated and powerful tea is Matcha green tea. This is made from the grounded up leaves of the plant. You dissolve the tea into hot water, creating an antioxidant drink over 100 times more potent than just soaking the leaves in water.

Everyone benefits from tea consumption, but women benefit more since it preserves bone density and therefore reduces osteoporosis risk. Why am I making such a big deal by delving into tea so extensively? Because for women it's one of the most potent antioxidants on the planet.

Maybe some of you have visited tea-tasting rooms that are popping up in most metro areas. In contrast to the English High Tea, these Asian tasting rooms remind you of tasting fine wine in Napa Valley. The teas are brewed and served in specific ways to maximize the flavor and reduce the acidity. The finer teas available in the tasting rooms or online are greatly improved over the cheaper bag tea that causes gastric acid and stomach upset, especially in the case of green tea. It's customized in that the tasting rooms can recommended a tea to you based on your specific taste and how your stomach reacts.

To summarize this section, alcohol consumption of one drink a day has many beneficial effects. The effect of alcohol does not balance out; five drinks in one day are not equivalent to one drink for each of five consecutive days. Coffee can cause insomnia and irritability especially as our metabolism slows with age, so caffeine intake should be balanced with decaf coffee. Certain teas provide strong antioxidant effects, but may be a problem if you are pregnant, have anemia or are allergic.

The current daily recommendation for maximum benefit for women is two to three cups of coffee, three to four cups of white or green tea, and one alcoholic beverage.

Common Sense Conclusion: Consumed in moderate amounts, alcohol, coffee and tea provide substantial benefits for the long-term improvement of both health and quality of life.

In terms of mentioning the most powerful foods for women, I would be remiss to not mention spirulina (Anthrospira Platensis). Spirulina is a bluish-green one-celled algae that grows in the form of a spiral. It is about

60% plant-based protein with a huge number of nutrients and vitamins. It's a great substitute for red meat, since it has more protein without the fat and cholesterol.

Spirulina nutritionally provides eight essential amino acids, ten non-essential amino acids, eight essential minerals and ten different vitamins. It also provides an energy boost, so it can be used as a substitute for sugary cereals. The benefits of spirulina include improved vision, digestion, immunity, and even an anti-cancer effect. I personally mix spirulina with match green tea powder in my orange juice in the morning to sustain my energy all day. I have so much energy now that I don't need to drink coffee because of the caffeine in match tea.

CALORIE COUNTING

It's impossible to discuss diet and weight loss without some reference to calories. Most people are not calorie counters or food label readers, but this is where a little change can offer a big reward. It helps to know that it takes 3500 calories to loose one pound of fat because we may base our exercise routine on the big calorie burners. The following calories are metabolized or gained for each gram eaten from the categories below:

Carbohydrate--4 calories
Protein--4 calories
Alcohol--7 calories
Fat--9 calories

It is correct that one gram of fat is more than double the calories of a gram of protein or carbohydrates. This is what we look for when reading food labels. A working rule is not to eat anything that has 25% or more fat. People often overlook calories from alcohol or other beverages, but these can derail a health plan quickly. Many juice drinks are something other that actual juice. Scientists now warn of negative effects occurring from natural fructose in so-called healthy drinks like juice and smoothies.

Label reading and calorie counting is essential in moderating our nutritional intake. We often look for lower fat and sugar contents, but killers like high fructose corn syrup, partial hydrogenated oils and genetically modified products (mostly in processed foods) are hidden in the small print. In time, we'll base most of our nutritional decisions on these labels. Thin people often habitually make label reading an ongoing part of a healthy lifestyle.

Here are the average calories you'll burn if you weigh about 165 pounds and work out for an hour:

Cross country skiing = 1240 calories

Running, eight minute mile pace = 940
Cycling, moderate pace = 920
Jumping rope =   920
Rowing =   910
Handball =   900
Swimming =   550
Sand volleyball = 540
Walking 3 mph = 200
Walking 4 mph = 330
Walking 5 mph = 540

EXERCISE AND QUALITY OF LIFE

This section is a reminder of how essential exercise is, especially as we age. The American Heart Association article (27) *Physical Activity Improves Quality of Life*, outlines why exercise is proven to improve both mental and physical health. Mentally, exercise increases oxygen flow to the brain that produces endorphins that tend to act as painkillers and mood elevators. Endorphins are hormonal compounds that are similar to opiates in their effect and can act as a great stress-reducer. This is where the term "runner's high" came from.

This article confirms that with exercise the immune system is enhanced, while the risk of developing cancer and heart disease is reduced. Also, blood pressure can be reduced 4 to 9 mm with exercise, which is roughly equivalent to the same effect of some antihypertensive medications.

Without regular physical activity, the body slowly loses its strength, stamina and ability to function well. According to the American Heart Association, moderate exercise, such as brisk walking for just 30 minutes a day:

Reduces the risk of heart disease.
Burns calories to control weight.
Improves blood cholesterol levels.
Manages high blood pressure.
Helps to quit smoking.
Prevents bone loss.
Boosts energy levels.
Acts as a stress reducer.
Relieves muscular tension.
Counters anxiety and depression.
Promotes better sleep.
Improves self-image.
Increases muscular strength and balance.
Reduces risk of stroke by 20% to 27%.
Helps delay or prevent chronic illnesses.

Increases energy and mood.

EXERCISE AND LONGEVITY

For each hour you exercise, you will generally gain about two hours of additional life expectancy, regardless of your age when you start. Let's take a closer look at the details to see how this works. I'll present only the key results from research.

One study (28) had over 400,000 subjects who exercised 92 minutes a week or only 15 minutes a day. Despite this minimal amount of time, the results were positive. "The exercise group was about 14 percent less likely to die for any reason over the next eight years. They were about 10 percent less likely to die from cancer and lived about three years longer on average than the couch potato group." In addition, each 15 minutes of exercise per day reduced dying from any cause another four percent and from cancer by 1 percent. So, even a small amount of exercise has positive results.

The article, *Exercise for 9 More Years* (29), reported on a study of 1200 pairs of twins. Telomeres, which are the protective ends of our chromosomes that shorten as we age, were measured. Since the telomere length is correlated to longevity, twins provide a perfect DNA control group. The first group involved three hours a week (for a half hour a day) of vigorous exercise while the control group did no exercise. The results showed an extra nine years of telomere length for the exercise group. These results hold up even if you smoke, are overweight, or are have been sedentary. One of the keys is to be sure to break a sweat when exercising.

A study (30) of 713 women between the ages of 70 and 79 was conducted in senior citizen communities. This study measured the relationship between fitness and longevity, comparing women who exercised and ate well to women who were sedentary. The results were that, "...women with both the highest level of physical fitness, as measured by survey responses, and the highest consumption of fruits and vegetables, were eight times less likely to die than the women who performed the worst in both of these categories." No surprise that fitness level and longevity increased, but it's encouraging to see such an improvement in this older age group.

One article (31) mentions, "One way exercise increases longevity is by reducing the risk of common killers as heat disease, type II diabetes and cancer." The article discusses how lifespan is correlated with different activity levels. That is, the more frequent and vigorous your exercise program, the more you can extend your life. It concludes with, "Exercise cannot only add years to your life, it may reduce the risk of spending your later years in a nursing home." I concur in the opinion that the quality of life throughout retirement is equally as important as longevity.

The Journal of Aging Research (32) reviewed, "13 other studies describing eight different cohorts suggesting that regular physical activity is associated with an increase of life expectancy by .4 to 6.9 years." The increase seems to depend on the type and length of workouts. "Eleven case control studies on life expectancy in former athletes revealed consistently greater life expectancy in aerobic endurance athletes, but inconsistent results for other athletes." The results here confirm that aerobic exercise is the best for longevity and it's actually the easiest to work into an exercise program.

In a study (33) done in England with over 20,000 women and men ages 45 to 79, found that a combination of lifestyle changes added up to 14 extra years of life compared to a control group. The key ingredients for this increase were: 1. Don't smoke. 2. Eat five servings of fruits and vegetables. 3. Exercise. 4. Use alcohol in moderation (one or two drinks a day). The authors gave one point for each "bad behavior" and found that if a subject scored a 0, she or he was four times more likely to die over an 11-year period than those who made lifestyle changes. Those who practiced two of the bad behaviors had only double the risk of death over 11 years.

The lifestyle changes prevent lung cancer and respiratory illnesses (smoking); they help the heart and cardiovascular system (exercise and alcohol); provide proper nutrients for bodily repair (fruits and veggies). About 80% of the improved longevity is from not smoking, if you practice all four good behaviors, you maximize your benefits.

So, whoever told us that we should rest and take it easy in retirement was simply wrong. Our bodies quickly deteriorate with inactivity, allowing illness and weakness to occur. We really cannot afford to be ill informed at this stage, and we certainly don't want to be unconsciously hurting our health.

Common Sense Conclusion: The health and longevity benefits of exercise are so abundant and well established that we must embrace exercise as part of our healthy lifestyle.

WALKING FOR LIFE

Exercise and Longevity: A Little Goes a Long Way, published in the *New York Times* (34), concerned an eight-year study, of over 13,000 men and women, that looked directly at fitness, and not just verbal reports of participants. Subjects walked on a treadmill to determine their fitness levels. The least fit was the sedentary group, next the inconsistent walkers, then consistent walkers (half an hour to a full hour). The results were measured in deaths per 10,000 people. Among the women in the sedentary group, 40 died; in the inconsistent walkers' group, 20 died; and in the consistent walkers' group, only 9 died.

The above study showed the most dramatic improvement in women who went from being sedentary to the first level of fitness. This activity level requires only a half hour of brisk walking five days a week. This is good news for the average person; you don't have to be a marathoner or an athlete to benefit from exercise if you're willing just to walk.

Thus, brisk walking for 30 minutes a day, something most people can manage, is really a baseline for exercise. Since exercise and its benefits are on a continuum, more exercise will generally result in greater benefits.

Not enough is mentioned these days about the cardiovascular effect of aerobic exercise. The goal is to get your heart rate up to about 80% above its normal resting rate three times a week, for at least 30 minutes. Of course, it involves intense exercise to get your heart rate up that high. If you ever tried to get your rate up or break a sweat walking, you know how difficult it can be. To facilitate this, you can time your walks to remind you to always keep a decent pace, walk with hand weights, and look for hills or stairs.

If you have ever been an athlete on a sports team, the half hour a day walk seems barely enough. You may need a customized workout program that addresses your individual needs and goals. There are many free examples of exercise plans on the Internet and many gyms offer exercise planning and coaching services. Having a workout buddy is equally as important for exercise as dieting. When you're low on motivation, your partner can encourage you to go for a workout together.

Exercise doesn't have to be expensive, as evidenced by Jack LaLanne, who looked like he never spent a dime on equipment. Remember his TV show where he used common household products for his workout? He once hooked two gallons of milk on both ends of a broomstick to make a barbell, and he used a dining room chair for stretches and pushups. His daily goal was to exercise two hours in the morning no matter what his age. If that seems like a lot of time, remember he did live to 96.

Walking appears to be the most sustainable activity for those who have not followed an exercise routine previously. Since walking is already embedded into our daily lives, we don't have to change any behaviors, only extend them. You will need good shoes to reduce impact on hard surface walking, but walking on the grass or another soft surface is also fine. Always consider a walking buddy, group, or club in your neighborhood to keep your motivation high. If one does not exist, you can start your own and add a newsletter to go with it.

Treadmill walking is excellent for those who are alone or easily bored, because you can watch TV. If your treadmill is in a gym, you also get the social component. Walking on a treadmill that has a 5% incline almost doubles the number of calories burned. This is especially helpful if there are no hills in your neighborhood.

Maybe some of you have used a pedometer to gauge your distance. When you use a pedometer, you are likely to increase the distance and time you walk. This happens as a combination of your increased awareness and beneficial guilt -- we all feel a little motivational guilt when we feel we are behind on something.

It's common for walkers to lose weight once a pedometer is introduced to their walking routine. The amount of weight loss varies, of course, but almost everyone loses weight to some extent. If you are considering a pedometer, you'll find they're very inexpensive, but the cheapest pedometers tend to be less sensitive to soft steppers or soft surfaces, and may not record your steps. So, spending just a few dollars more to get a good one is worth it.

Some people claim they don't have 30 minutes a day to exercise. First, you don't have to do all 30 minutes at once; all you need is three 10-minute sessions. Second, your walking should already be incorporated into your life even if you are working. So, just extend your walking efforts by taking stairs, parking away for the entrance, taking the long route in the office, and so on.

Remember, one hour of exercise results in about two hours of extra life. So exercise actually gives you more time by extending your life. The truth is that we don't have time to not exercise.

Some people invent excuses why they cannot exercise. I don't understand this point. I don't have the energy, and I can't exercise because I smoke, are popular excuses. Another excuse I've heard is that women shouldn't sweat. I can understand that sweating in certain social situations may be considered a faux pas, but exercise is designed so that not sweating is the faux pas. Breaking a sweat is considered essential to gaining the benefits of exercise.

If your energy level is low, exercise increases your endurance. If you pair exercise with proper nutrition, expect to have more energy and improved endurance. As for not being able to exercise because you smoke, well, we know cigarette smoking is the single worst thing you can do to your body and must be stopped. It's never too late to improve our health on any level.

Besides walking, cycling for seniors has gotten a tremendous boost in recent years. Not only are more seniors biking, but they are doing it in organized groups and events. The low impact nature of the exercise helps relieve pain in the joints, and is key for sustaining seniors' quality of life. Many former runners and basketball players find cycling suitable for an aging body.

Cycling is effective for all levels of conditioning, since your workout can be mild, moderate, or intense. The most common complaint is the design of the seat. Since women need wider seats, just replace the one that comes with the bike. If weather extremes occur where you live, try an indoor bike or the gym as a good substitute.

As we age and balance becomes an issue, some bike riders switch over to a tricycle, usually with a large basket attached for cargo. This increased stability is well suited for the older rider. I can envision many retirees, including myself, cycling this way until it's time to pass the torch.

I cannot say enough about incorporating a social aspect into your exercise regimen, in the same way you apply it to your diet plan (see Psychology of Eating). Unless you are one of the few people who are highly self-motivated, having an exercise buddy or joining a gym goes a long way towards the enjoyment and sustainability of your life.

Common Sense Conclusion: Establishing a daily exercise routine that is both physically engaging and socially reinforcing is essential for long-term sustainability.

SLEEP

Few of us think about sleep as being as being a health issue--until we go without it. The prevalence of insomnia in America is about 25% to 50%, depending on the study and its parameters. These statistics do not include other sleep disorders such as apnea. The studies often examine a certain type of insomnia, such as transient insomnia that may last only days or weeks. Other studies examine chronic insomnia and its etiological variations. Regardless of the type or the cause of insomnia, it significantly impacts our health and longevity.

Many studies report the more common effects of sleep deprivation such as poor concentration, judgment and memory. Chronic insomnia is reported to facilitate more serious symptoms such as heart disease, diabetes, and cancer. Because attention span and concentration are impaired, some studies have tied auto accidents to sleepiness. Since sleep is when cell repair occurs, the body naturally rejuvenates and detoxifies itself. When the body is not allowed to sleep, it cannot repair itself, resulting in faster aging.

The groups more at risk for sleep problems are women with a history of insomnia, those with psychiatric or medical problems, and those using medications. It has long been known that prevalence of insomnia increases with age, so we all become the primary risk group.

According to *Women, Sleep, and Age* (35), women experience more difficulty falling and staying asleep, which results in less alertness, not just in retirement, but also throughout life. The difficulty starts with loosing sleep because of childcare and that nightly feeding schedule. Then the menstrual cycle brings about hormonal changes leading to sleep problems. Later, menopause symptoms interfere with sleep. Our sleep naturally becomes more restless as we age because our circadian cycle is less effective.

The article recommends exercise early in the day to jump-start your circadian rhythm. Being outdoors exposes you to sunlight, which stimulates wakefulness. Keeping the same daily routine, especially in the evening as you prepare for sleep, helps. I personally like the idea and beauty of watching the sunset every night to help set my inner clock.

Another women's study (36) confirms that women spend more time in bed, but get less sleep. They site various reasons, like women's tolerance for a snoring partner because he is the breadwinner. I know many couples that sleep in separate rooms for this reason and I really don't think your partner cares what room you're in while he is asleep. But, the primary reason they site is that women have trouble unwinding due to the stress of work and family care. The last reason is certainly the case when we're working and have children in mid-life. But, most of us have seen our children move on and we are probably better at managing the hustle and bustle at work. If not, then we might consider some stress reduction techniques.

A week-long sleep study (37) had one group sleep 5.7 hours on average and another group sleep 8.5 hours while controlling for physical activity, food, and light exposure. Whole blood RNA samples were taken after each sleep period. Results showed insufficient sleep is correlated with obesity, cognitive impairment, and cardiovascular disease. In addition, the full week of poor sleep intensified these symptoms and appeared to alter gene expression as well. Gene expression, in general, is how the gene is formed and acts. Many inheritable genetic traits, such as IQ, would be impaired with too little sleep. The study concludes that insufficient sleep of less than six hours impacts the development of over 700 genes.

Despite the old theory that we all have a genetically determined sleep requirement, the consensus is that we need at least six hours of sleep nevertheless. We all need a certain amount of rapid eye movement or REM sleep. More REM is produced in infants and lessens as we age. We produce less of the slower Delta waves known for occurring during sleep, and often feel sleepy in the day. Consequently, we tend to wake up earlier than we want and get tired earlier in the day.

Treatment often involves progressive relaxation for stress, cognitive therapy, pre-sleep preparation, and sleep restriction to certain times of the day. My personal favorites of the natural remedies are meditation and biofeedback. There are many over-the-counter medications from antihistamine to melatonin that you may have tried. People tend to have different responses to them, from no effect to daytime sleepiness.

When nothing else works, some of us have tried prescription drugs, but often received only small amounts due to their addictive properties. Kripke (38) reported more than a three times increased risk of death for those who use hypnotic sleep aids such as Ambien, Lunesta and Restoril. Worse yet is the self-medication route where alcohol or other recreational drugs are used.

In the *No More Sleepless Nights Workbook* (39), the authors have put together a program that can help up to 90% of poor sleepers get considerable relief. Their belief is that insomnia is a symptom caused by something we are currently unaware of and not a separate disease. The authors encourage you to track you sleeping habits and reduce substances known to interfere with sleep. Caffeine is first on the chopping block. We tolerate it less because it has a prolonged effect on us as we age. It also has the effect of increasing our metabolism. The authors point out that the insomniac's metabolic rate is already about 9% higher than the average person, so reducing afternoon caffeine drinks could be very helpful.

Nicotine is another stimulant that interferes with restorative sleep. It increases blood pressure, raises the heart rate, and augments brain wave activity. The average smoker wakes often during the night from the temporary withdrawal of nicotine.

Controlling alcohol consumption also helps sleep. Many of us have used alcohol to help us relax in order to fall asleep. This is actually counterproductive because the sedative effect of alcohol wears off in the middle of the night and you awake. The authors point out that studies show that alcohol fragments sleep, increases nighttime awakenings, and is less restorative than regular deep sleep. They recommend avoiding all alcoholic beverages two hours before bedtime.

Common Sense Conclusion: Making adjustments to get a minimum of six hours of sleep remains essential to restoring the body and prolonging health and life.

Many of us are dealing with health or disability issues around the time we retire. This does not change the equation for health, it only suggests we adjust our lives accordingly. For example: A retiree who has a metal rod placed in her lumbar area was avoiding activities because her doctor told her that she must be careful not to fall down. She is on disability and retired early as a result of her serious injury. But, she started gaining weight due to her fearfulness of venturing out and lack of exercise.

When she was walking the dog one day, she tripped and fell, but was uninjured. Suddenly, she realized she could re-embrace activity with a few minor adjustments. She began walking more, but too long a distance produced lumbar pain, so she bought a bicycle. This low impact exercise turned out to be just what she needed to take pressure off her back. Now she enjoys biking for local errands on a daily basis, and doesn't realize how much exercise she is getting. Survival has always been about adaptation, and old age motivates us to perfect these skills.

TRANSCENDENTAL MEDITATION

Many of us will remember the teachings of Maharishi Mahesh Yogi, who introduced the technique to the West in 1959. Transcendental Meditation (TM) is a simple relaxation technique practiced for 15 to 20 minutes once or twice daily while sitting comfortably with eyes closed. Some of us even practiced the technique back in the 60s and 70s. Why do I recommend this practice to seniors? Because it's going to significantly improve your health and well-being, and reduce your medical bills.

There are mountains of studies regarding the many health benefits of meditation, so I'll summarize the most beneficial. One study (40) that summarizes others breaks down the benefits into five categories. The first is stress reduction, which affects almost every system in our bodies. The sympathetic nervous system is calmed, which reduces the cortisol and adrenaline that are correlated with stress. Meditating to relax for sleep, or before a stressful event, is often helpful.

Meditation also lowers the risk of heart disease and has been known to lower the incidence of strokes, heart attack, and death compared to non-meditators. The author reports that through TM heart disease can be lowered by nearly 50% and high blood pressure can be managed also. I know too many middle-aged people who are on hypertension medications, and fail to follow other healthful behaviors like exercise, sodium reduction, and meditation. TM is apparently the only meditation practice that has been proven to lower blood pressure and to get approval from the American Heart Association. Its benefits also help manage depression, in that mood becomes more stable, and also has a positive effect on anxiety and stress management as well.

The final benefit of reduced medical expenses seems a little confusing at first. But "Inpatient days decreased by more than 50% in every age category, children, young and older adults and out-patient visits were reduced by 47% to 69%. Surprisingly, admissions for benign and malignant tumors dropped 55%, heart disease by 87% and more than 30% for infectious diseases. (40)"

These figures are too meaningful to overlook and can apply especially well in retirement. In order to understand this, both inpatient and outpatient visits dropped because meditation reduces our response to pain. For us to see a doctor outside of our routine visits, we usually need to feel discomfort or distress. Tumors and infections may have dropped as a result of an improved immune response, and lower heart disease from deep relaxation is already documented. The conclusion is that stress and anxiety compound or even create health problems that we normally would not have.

A Harvard study (41) states that deep relaxation actually changes our bodies on a genetic level. Long-term practitioners of relaxation methods exhibit more "disease fighting genes." These genes that are activated by meditation help fight inflammation and cancer. They also help reduce blood pressure, pain and arthritis on a genetic level. Apparently, genes can be "switched on," or triggered by the parasympathetic nervous system during deep relaxation.

This study lists the primary benefit as increased immunity even in cancer patients. They mention another parallel study done at Ohio State where relaxation techniques increase natural killer cells in the elderly, resulting in greater resistance to tumors and to viruses. Inflammation, correlated to heart disease, arthritis, asthma and some skin conditions, was reduced.

The sheer number of studies that show a vast array of physical and mental benefits from meditation provides confirmation of its importance to the aging process. Other studies cite improvement in the areas of cognitive functioning, sleep, energy, self-confidence, social tolerance, sense of well-being, job satisfaction and learning ability, as well as reduced rates of disease, use of alcohol and other drugs, decreased pain levels, lower anxiety, and even fewer feelings of loneliness.

Even if you have a history of being a couch potato, you can still practice while in a sitting position with specific techniques of meditation, yoga, or any form of deep relaxation. Sitting in a yoga position with an erect spine, eyes closed, in a dark room, and allowing your mind to wander is where you start. Some people like to use a mantra, that is, a word(s) that's repeated quietly to help center their thoughts.

I was taught to allow the mind the freedom to transcend to any place it chooses to go. If stressful worries come into focus during this process, you just reset to a starting base with your mantra or let your thoughts take their own course. You can always bring your thoughts back to a relaxing image like sitting on a beach. There are many resources to discover how to meditate on your own if you haven't practiced before. But, until you get the hang of it, starting in a class is useful.

A long-term meditator in her 60s recently discussed her mastery of the technique. She said that ever since her parents taught her meditation as a teen, she has been practicing off and on. She can fall into meditation any place and any time because she can immediately trigger the relaxation response. Her skill at filtering out noise has been well developed with years of practice. But when starting out, most of us will benefit from a quiet place.

After you've found a comfortable and quiet location, try using guided imagery. With your eyes closed, picture your last enjoyable vacation. Try to visualize the details, hear the sounds, feel the weather, smell and taste the cuisine. Re-live the entire experience and you have transcended the present. Try other positive imagery by remembering when you were on a beach, walking in the forest, sailing, in a museum, or just being with the person you love. We all have intensely positive memories that work perfectly as a precursor to deeper relaxation and endorphin production.

Biofeedback is a simple technique of giving your mind feedback about your body, and this technique can help you learn to relax. Many of us have seen a stress card that changes color when our fingers warm up. This is similar to the "mood rings" of the past. It is a measure of the vasodilatation or relaxation of our arteries. As our arteries open and allow more blood to flow, our fingers warm up.

Other common biofeedback measures are EEG (brain waves), EMG (muscles) and palm perspiration(a measure of anxiety). The key benefit of biofeedback is that you get real time messages as to what your body is doing so you can make adjustments. For those of us having trouble relaxing, buying a finger temperature gauge is an easy and inexpensive way to get started with biofeedback.

Common Sense Conclusion: Studies confirm that deep relaxation like meditation result in a wide array of physical and mental benefits, including fewer medical visits and expenses.

OUR FIVE SENSES

As we age, there is very gradual decline in our senses that is considered normal. We know that the body's peak athletic period is between 25 and 35 years old, with a noticeable drop off after 40 years old. Some studies show that the body's athletic ability declines at a rate of about 2% per year after 40. Most of us have reluctantly accepted our athletic abilities change, and we can live with that. But it's the senses we use on a daily basis that are of most concern for us.

Vision

The most significant difference occurs with the eye lens and pupil, which account for most of the age-related vision problems. Adequate vision in dim light becomes more difficult as the diameter of the pupil decreases. You may notice this at different ages, but everyone is affected to some degree. Maybe you already have a little difficulty seeing in the dark and have started making adjustments. As our vision changes we need to be alert to safety precautions. No more walking down the stairs without light, less night driving, and adding light in key places in the home. You may have also noticed that it takes longer to adjust in a dark room and glare seems to bother you more. These changes prompt us to allow more time for eyes to adjust and to cover up shiny objects.

As the lens of the eye starts to loose elasticity, we have more trouble focusing on close objects. This condition, known as presbyopia, begins around age 45 and progresses as we age. Increasing light and adjusting reading distance can help, but this is what usually sends us to the drug store to get reading glasses. It's common to increase the reading glass magnification as we age. Some of us feel that wearing glasses changes our appearance and is unfashionable. There are contact lenses and surgery for those interested. But how fortunate we are to have such an easy and affordable fix as putting on a pair of inexpensive glasses.

Cataracts affect about half of all Americans over 65 years old to some extent. A cataract is a clouding of the lens behind the pupil and iris, and the leading cause of blindness for those over 40. The key sign is blurry vision, however, along with trouble driving, reading, recognizing faces; seeing halos around lights may also occur. A cataract often starts off small, but as it clouds more of the lens, blurriness increases. If you are experiencing any of these symptoms, you should have an eye exam. The most common and recommended way to treat cataracts is with surgery. The good news is that its one of the most perfected outpatient surgeries available.

There is also a natural yellowing process that occurs, and it affects our color perception. This is a slow process that alters how we see blue, how colors are contrasted, and how basic colors appear. The yellow lens apparently absorbs and diffuses blue light. This makes it difficult to distinguish between colors and to distinguish foregrounds from backgrounds. That is, we may have trouble seeing when one step ends and another begins. Recommendations to improve visibility are to use more warm red colors in the home, to put markers or tape on the edge of stairs, and to use halogen or fluorescent lighting instead of incandescent.

Eye health can be maintained and improved by following a few basic guidelines. First, smoking is very damaging. Second, avoid cities known for their smog or any other air pollution problems. The Environmental Protection Agency (EPA) reports the smog levels of different cities throughout the world. Third, eat five servings of vegetables and fruits per day to increase the effect of carotenoid antioxidants. Foods high in carotenoids are spinach, mangoes, tomatoes, kale, and cantaloupe. Fourth, avoid excessive sun exposure and wear hats and sunglasses with UV protection. Fifth, schedule regular eye exams at least every three years even if no symptoms are present. Medicare does not cover eye care unless you added it into your Part C.

Hearing

Age-related loss of hearing is called presbycusis. Small hair cells located in the inner ear help us distinguish sounds. They change sound waves into nervous system signals that the brain recognizes as distinct sounds. As these hair cells die or become damaged, our hearing sensitivity decreases. Since these hair cells cannot regrow, this hearing loss is considered permanent. Factors that predispose or magnify this problem are exposure to loud noises, smoking, diabetes, family history, and some medications.

The progression of presbycusis is slow and barely noticeable at first. Besides asking people to repeat themselves, you may experience problems at higher pitches, as in women's voices. You may have trouble with sounds such as "th" or "s," or with hearing in noisy places. You may get tinnitus or ringing in the ears.

Hearing loss often causes us to avoid people and withdraw socially, which can led to isolation and depression. Since presbycusis cannot be reversed and can lead to deafness, its important that you see an audiologist if you experience any symptoms.

Studies show that about a third of us between 65 and 75 years old have some type of hearing loss. About half of us between 75 to 85 years old have hearing loss. Once over 85 years old, our chance of going deaf in at least one ear is 30%. Controlling the loud noises in our environment and wearing earplugs can help prolong our hearing. Current treatment mostly involves addressing the symptoms. This includes hearing aids, telephone amplifiers, sign language, and, for deafness, cochlear implant surgery.

Many of us will use a digital hearing aid at some point. With this new software, amplification can be programmed for each individual type of hearing loss or listening preferences. An amazing range of options exist, including customization across all pitches, hearing sounds from the front of the wearer, reducing digital background noise, connecting with FM systems, detecting telephone signals, and having Bluetooth compatibility. Even the most basic of digital hearing aids far surpasses the most sophisticated of analog hearing aids of the past. Our generation is lucky to be the first to benefit from digital technology. Medicare does not cover hearing aids, so you may consider an additional policy that does cover them.

Taste and Smell

Gustation, or taste, is the result of a chemical reaction between a substance in the mouth and the receptors, or taste buds, on the tongue. There are three to five thousand taste buds and each has up to 100 cell receptors. Apparently, taste does fade with time and can become noticeable after 60 years of age. This loss can be compounded with tobacco smoking, tooth decay, nasal or sinus problems, beta-blockers, ACE inhibitors, and Alzheimer's disease.

Our olfactory sense, or sense of smell, diminishes with age, a condition that doctors refer to as hyposmia. This loss of smell is from normal degeneration of the nerves and cells, which reduce the number of sensory cells in the nose. Apparently, about half of us between 60 and 80 years of age will be affected to some extent. It can affect up to 75% of us when we are over 80 years old. It's thought that the neurological transmission of olfactory signals is impeded as our skulls harden with age. Regardless of the reasons, it's a naturally occurring loss that we will all experience to some extent.

A diminished sense of smell also affects taste, and explains why the elderly complain about lack of flavor in food. The problem that develops here is that loss of taste and smell lead to loss of appetite and malnutrition--a common and serious problem in the retirement years. The loss of smell also presents other safety problems in that we cannot smell a gas leak or smoke from a fire. Fortunately, home smoke detectors are required in most states.

Since we tend to gradually lose our taste and smell concurrently, we are often unaware that it's happening. But now that we know it's going to occur, we need to be alert for small changes in our eating habits. We usually have appetite patterns and favorite food; if either of these seems to change, it's a sign for us to reevaluate our diet with an emphasis on proper nutritional balance.

Touch

Tactile sensation, or touch, is part of the peripheral nervous system. We know that various studies confirm that tactile and thermal pain thresholds in the elderly are significantly increased. That is, it takes greater stimulation for us to feel touch and pain. Our sensitivity or acuity of our fingertips also declines with age. More specifically, the velocity of our sensory nerve conduction declines. The rate of decline is not consistent across studies, but usually appears noticeable between 70 and 80 years old.

The implications of reduced sensitivity can affect us in various ways. Touching gives us needed information about the physical nature of life. For our safety, we need to feel what is wet or day, sharp or dull, smooth or rough, and hot or cold. As this ability diminishes, we will naturally compensate, based on our prior experience. That is, at this age, we don't need to touch a stove or iron to know it hot. It's this range of remembered life experiences that will help us compensate for our loss. When we type, for example, if we cannot feel the keys, we still can view the letters being typed and receive feedback that way. It's really a matter of using other senses as compensation.

A reduction in sensory information perception can affect our intimacy in the bedroom and the relationship we have with our partner. If one partner refrains from sex due to lack of sensitivity, the other can easily feel rejected. This can create stress and discord in a marriage despite no fault on the part of either partner. I will discuss intimacy further in the chapter on social health.

So, a great deal of successful aging has to do with being aware of what's to come, adjusting our expectations, planning how to deal with it, and down-playing the emotional reaction. As with all issues in aging, it's not about dread of loss of abilities, it's about the satisfaction of adapting to our ever-changing situation.

Common Sense Conclusion: We will enjoy the use of all our senses well into retirement as long as we maintain our healthy lifestyle and act in a preventive manner.

From my hospice experience, I've noticed that most elderly people will enjoy good to modest health until the final few weeks or months before they depart. There are exceptions, of course, with more severe chronic conditions. But the loss of sensory abilities mentioned here tends to follow a mild course until these final days -- providing you put some effort into maintaining a healthy lifestyle.

MEDICARE AND HEALTH INSURANCE

If you've had no health insurance previously and have saved lots of money because you've been healthy, congratulations. However, that's not a good idea going into older age. The risks of medical issues increase and you should plan on being disabled for short-term periods. If you have surgery and are disabled during your recovery, you'll need a plan. If you have a secure partner, have good friends that extend themselves, or have relatives nearby, you're in a good position. Otherwise, you could conceivably end up in a nursing home for recovery.

If you've had health insurance through your employer and you want to keep it, you have a couple of choices. Some employers allow part-time employees to continue their health benefits if they're employed a certain number of hours. We all know retirees who continue to work just for the health insurance. If you don't like your job, but need to stay, this becomes counter to our philosophy of working part-time at what you enjoy. So, recognizing all the psychological and social benefits of employment becomes relevant to quality of lifestyle.

Despite the fact that Medicare has been around for seniors since 1965, its complexity only seems to increase. At the time of this writing, enrollment in the Affordable Care Act ("Obamacare") is taking place. Millions of people on Medicare that are in the process of being moved to Obamacare are expected to be mostly immigrants, person living illegally in the United States, and the poor. Some people are concerned that Affordable Care insurance will weaken Medicare, resulting in increased costs for those over 65 years old.

Medicare Part A, which covers inpatient hospital care, skilled nursing care, hospice, and some home health services, is expected to stay intact. If you or your spouse paid Medicare taxes for 10 years, you won't pay for Part A. You are entitled to start this coverage on the first day of the month you turn 65 years old.

Part B still covers office visits, laboratory costs, ambulance, mental health care, physical therapy, and medical equipment. This part is optional and carries a premium usually deducted from your Social Security check. Remember to sign up for Part B during the open enrollment period or you may have a penalty if late.

Part C Medicare Advantage includes plans offered with private insurance firms. This changes coverage for visual care, dental care, and prescription medications. Because the program changes are so new, the impact of the cuts is not fully known. It's not clear how this will affect our Part D prescription medication coverage at this point. So, it's not possible to go into details and make recommendations until the dust settles.

Despite various program changes, be sure to enroll in a timely manner anyway. The enrollment period is three months prior and after your 65th birthday month. For example, if you were born in June, your enrollment period is March through the end of September. This is a very time sensitive matter because penalties may be assessed for missing open enrollment periods. Once you decide on your coverage, you are allowed to make annual alterations during open enrollment from October 15 to December 7. There are special enrollment periods if you relocate or leave your employment insurance behind. Check with your plan administrator if you are keeping your current insurance, so you can figure out how both insurances can work together.

Medicare has had a huge funding deficit for many years and talks of an overhaul are common. Congress views this as an expensive program and likes to tinker with it almost every year. We should not be surprised to witness more cutbacks because the cost burden is slowly being shifted back on to the retiree. Supplemental care plans (Medigap) offered by private insurance are designed to complement Medicare and can help manage these changes. These expected cost increases adds more motivation for us to stay as healthy as possible.

Common Sense Conclusion: Maintaining adequate health insurance is essential to quality of life and a hedge against financial catastrophe.

The primary reason retirees file for bankruptcy is due to medical bills and prescription medications costs spiraling out of control. Filing for bankruptcy can eliminate your medical bills, but if you own a home you'll need to check the homestead exemption laws in your state. Your credit rating will need a few years to recover, but your Social Security is usually exempt from liens. If you're in a bad situation, bankruptcy does offer protections; it's just that you don't ever want to be in a bad situation. We will all certainly have more medical procedures going forward, and having adequate insurance can benefit us on a couple of levels.

In summary, we will all reassess our physical health and recommit ourselves to being as healthy as possible. Smoking is such a detrimental health problem that it must be stopped. Transitioning to a plant-based diet is correlated with longevity in many different cultures around the world. Consuming moderate amounts of alcohol, coffee, and green tea provides many health benefits.

Establishing a challenging and fun exercise routine with others prolongs life. Maintaining at least six hours of sleep is essential for cell repair and general health. The practice of meditation is proven to be beneficial physically, mentally, and economically. Accepting some loss of sensory modalities is just part of aging that motivates us to be even healthier.

Figure 1: website staff(2014 copyright) "The Okinawa Diet program" okinawa-diet.com. Retrieved on 2-7-2014 from: .okinawa-diet.com/okinawa_diet/food_pyramid.html

1. Coy, P. (2-7-13) "Scary health care statistic on the broken down boomer generation"; Businessweek.com.; Retrieved on 2-6-2014 from: businessweek.com/articles/2013-02-07/scary-health-care-statistics-on-the-broken-down-boomer-generation
2. Ogden, C.L., Carroll, M.D., Kit, B.K., Flegal, K.M,(1-2012); "Prevalence of Obesity in the United States, 2009-2010" cdc.gov; retrieved on 2-6-2014 from: .cdc.gov/nchs/data/databriefs/db82.pdf
3. NIH Publication staff(10-1998) "Clinical Guidelines on the Identification, Evaluation, and Treatment of Overweight and Obesity in Adults" nhlbi.nih.gov; Retrieved on 2-6-2014 from: nhlbi.nih.gov/guidelines/obesity/ob_gdlns.pdf
4. Finkelstein, E.A., Trogdon,,J.G., Cohen,,J.W., Dietz,W.; "Annual Medical Spending Attributable to Obesity:Payer and service specific estimates"; content.healthaffaairs.org;

Retrieved on 2-7-2014 from:
http://content.healthaffairs.org/content/28/5/w822.full.pdf+html
5. Speights, K.(4-4-2013) "10 Flabbergasting costs of america's obesity epidemic" fool.com;
Retrieved on 2-7-2014 from: www.fool.com/investing/general/2013/04/04/10-flabbergasting-costs-americas-obesity-epidemic.aspx?source=isesitlink0000001&mrr=1.00
6. George Washing Uni. Medical Center(9-21-2010) "Individual cost of obesity report"
disabled-world.com. Retrieved on 2-7-2014 from: .disabled-world.com/medical/obesity-cost.php
7. Stanton, M.W.(6-2006) "High concentration of U.S. health care expenditures"; ahrq.gov;
Retrieved on 2-6-2014 from:
www.ahrq.gov/research/findings/factsheets/costs/expriach/index.html
8. Samaras, TT; Storms, LH, Elrick, H; (9-2002) "Longevity, mortality and body weight";
sciencedirect.com. Retrieved on 2-7-2014 from:
sciencedirect.com/science/article/pii/S1568163702000296
9. Stevens, J A; Corso, PS, finkelstein, EA, Miller TR(2006) "The costs of fatal and nonfatal
falls among older adults." cdc.gov; Retrieved on 2-7-2014 from:
cdc.gov/HomeandRecreationalSafety/Falls/fallcost.html
10. Shiel Jr.,W.C. (3-18-08) "Hip fracture prevention - hip protectors"; medicinenet.com;
Retrieved date 2-7-2014 from: medicinenet.com/script/main/art.asp?articlekey=15600
11. Robbins, J, "Healthy at 100" New York: Ballantine Books, 2007
12.   (2-25-2013) "New England Journal of Medicine Mediterranean diet study mirrors
recommendations in new clean cuisine diet book" sbwire.com. Retrieved on 2-7-2014 from:
sbwire.com/press-releases/mediterranean-diet/clean-cuisine-diet-book/ssbwire-213725.htm
13. Nelson, JK, Zeratsky, K.(5-19-2009) "The new Mediterranean diet pyramid"
mayoclinic.org. Retrieved on 2-7-2014 from: mayoclinic.org/healthy-living/nutrition-and-healthy-eating/expert-blog/mediterranean-diet-pyramid/BGP-20056170
14.   Leaf, A.(1971) "Dr. Alexander Leaf, M.D." zoominfo.com. Retrieved on 2-8-0214 from:
zoominfo.com/p/Alex-Leif/66923497
15.   Predimed study investigators(4-4-2013) "Primary Prevention of Cardiovascular disease
with a Mediterranean Diet" N. Engl J Med 2013; 368:1279-1290. Retrieved on 2-8-2014 from:
nejm.org/doi/full/10.1056/NEJMoa1200303#t=article
16. Harvard staff(2014 copywriter) "Vegetables and Fruits: Get plenty every day";
hsph.harvard.edu. Retrieved on 2-8-2014 from: hsph.harvard.edu/nutritionsource/vegetables-full-story/
17. Ornish, D. et al. "Intensive Lifestyle changes for reversal of coronary heart disease," JAMA,
12-16-1998; yogasite.com. Retrieved on 2-8-2014 from: yogasite.com/ornish.htm
18. LaLanne, J. "Live Young Forever" New York: Robert Kennedy, 2009.
19. Saad, L.(7-24-2008) "U.S. Smoking rate still coming down" Gallup.com; Retrieved on 2-8-2014 from: gallup.com/poll/109048/US-Smoking-Rate-Still-Coming-Down.aspx
20. Lung Ass. Staff(2-2010) "Smoking and Older Adults" lung.org. Retrieved on 2-8-2014
from: lung.org/stop-smoking/about-smoking/facts-figures/smoking-and-older-adults.html
21. Berkrot, B, Pierson, R. (11-20-2013) "Smokers who quit may cut heart risk faster than had
been thought." reuters.com. Retrieved on 2-9-2014 from: reuters.com/article/2013/11/20/us-heart-smoking-idUSBRE9AJ0U120131120
22. Fetters, K.A.(6-25-2012) "5 Hidden health benefits of alcohol" livestrong.com. Retrieved on
2-9-2014 from: livestrong.com/article/557658-5-hidden-health-benefits-of-alcohol/
23. Roehm, E.(2011) "Women & Alcohol, special considerations" nutritionheart.com. Retrieved
on 2-9-2014 from: nutritionheart.com/women-alcohol/
24. Ding, M; Bhupathiraju, SN; Chen, M.; van Dam, RM; Hu, FB;(9-27-2013) "Coffee--evenedcaf--could help cut diabetes risk" Retrieved on 2-9-2014 from:
huffingtonpost.com/2014/02/03/coffee-diabetes-risk-decaf_n_4718996.html
25. Andersen, L. The American Journal of Clinical Nutrition, May 2006; Vol. 83: pp. 1039-1046. Retrieved on 2-9-2014 from: cbsnews.com/news/coffee-health-drink-for-older-women/
26. Amazing green tea staff.(2014 copywrite) "Green tea benefits 16 things that make
miracles possible." amazing-green-tea.com. Retrieved on 2-9-2014) from: amazing-green-tea.com/green-tea-benefits.html
27. AHA staff. (7-24-2013) "Physical activity improves quality of life." heart.org. Retrieved on
2-9-2014 from:
heart.org/HEARTORG/GettingHealthy/PhysicalActivity/StartWalking/Physical-activity-

improves-quality-of-life_UCM_307977_Article.jsp
28. Stein, R.(8-17-2011) "Exercise extends life, study says" washingtonpost.com. Retrieved on 2-9-2014 from: washingtonpost.com/blogs/the-checkup/post/exercise-extends-life-study-says/2011/08/16/gIQAN6lOJJ_blog.html
29. Stibich, M.(2-27-2008) "Exercise for 9 more years." longevity.about.com. Retriveed on 2-9-2014 from: longevity.about.com/od/lifelongfitness/a/exercise_DNA.htm
30. Huffing staff.(6-5-2012) "Exercise, diet improve longevity for older women" huffingtonpost.com. Retrieved on 2-9-2014 from: huffingtonpost.com/2012/06/05/exercise-diet-improve-lon_n_1568599.html
31. CatheDotCom staff.(1-4-2012) "Exercise and Longevity: can you add years to your life by working out?"cathe.com. Retrived on 2-10-2014 from: cathe.com/exercise-and-longevity-can-you-add-years-to-your-life-by-working-out
32. Reimers,CD, Knapp,G., Reimers, AK;(2012) "Does Physical Activity Increase Life Expectancy? A review of the literature" ncbi.nim.nih.gov. Retrived on 2-10-2014 from: www.ncbi.nlm.nih.gov/pmc/articles/PMC3395188/(J Aging Res. 2012; 2012: 243958)
33. Karthika(1-8-2008) "The 4 do's of everyday that helps you to live extra 14 years" medindia.net. Retrieved on 2-10-2014 from: medindia.net/news/The-4-Dos-of-Everyday-That-Helps-You-to-Live-Extra-14-Years-31593-1.htm
34. Hilts, P.J.(11-3-1989) "Exercise and Longevity: A little goes a long way" nytimes.com. Retrieved on 2-10-2014 from: nytimes.com/1989/11/03/us/exercise-and-longevity-a-little-goes-a-long-way.html
35. Breus, M. (9-1-2011) "Women, Sleep and Age" blogs.webmd.com. Retrieved on 2-10-2014 from: blogs.webmd.com/sleep-disorders/2011/09/women-sleep-and-age.html
36. Macrae, F., (2-10-2014) "Why women can't sleep peacefully" www.iol.co.za. Retreied on 2-11-2014 from: www.iol.co.za/scitech/science/news/why-women-can-t-sleep-peacefully-1.1644458
37. Moller-Levet,CS, Archer, SN, Bucca, G, Laing, EE, Slak,A, Kabijo,R, Lo, JCY, Santhi, N, vonSchantz,M, Smith, CP, Kijk,D-J. (1-23-2013) "Effects of insufficient sleep on circadian rhythmicity and expression amplitude of the human bold transcriptome" pans.org. Retrieved on 2-2-2014 from: pnas.org/content/early/2013/02/20/1217154110
38. Kripke, D.F. et al. "Is Insomnia Associated with Mortality?" Sleep, 2012, Vol. 34, Issue 05
39. Hauri, P et al. "No More Sleepless Nights Workbook" New York: Wiley & Sons, 2001.
40. Garcia, M.(6-10-0213) "Five reasons transcendental meditation is good for your health" voxxi.com. Retrieved on 2-11-2014 from: voxxi.com/2013/06/10/transcendental-meditation-tm-good-for-health/
41. Sydney Morning Herald staff(8-20-2009) "Relax-it's good for you" smh.com.au. Retrieved on 2-10-2014 from: smh.com.au/lifestyle/relax--its-good-for-you-20090819-eqlo.html

5   MONEY MAKES THE WORLD GO AROUND

Copyright 2006 by Randy Glasbergen.
www.glasbergen.com

**"We can afford to retire in 20 years, but only
if our credit cards retire in 10 years."**

Financing our lifestyle in retirement is actually the primary concern of both men and women. Although our financial needs are similar, we tend to have a different relationship with money. There are many ways to adjust our retirement budget and invest our savings. We'll discuss the best ways to safely manage money for long-term income. First, we need to dismiss the doubters.

The media is busy with dire predictions about retirement for boomers because of our supposedly apparent financial ignorance, poor saving habits, stock market and real estate losses, poor health, debt, and the end of pensions and Social Security. These critics often conclude that a comfortable retirement is financially out of reach for this generation. Most of these critics are not retired themselves, yet take very dogmatic and exaggerated positions. Some may have even managed to shake up your future outlook on life.

THE PERCEIVED DOOM AND GLOOM

Lets take a look at what the media would have us believe. According to Emily Brandon on money.com(1), the boomers face a variety of problems. "Many older adults have found themselves forced into retirement earlier than planned," she states. This trend began to accelerate during the recent recession, causing less participation in the work force for these seniors.

She mentions falling income and declining retirement benefits as problematic. "Some 44% of full time workers in their 50s have neither a traditional pension nor 401k," and there are "Few options to recoup losses," she states. Some of us were not offered a retirement plan at work, and few of us saved on our own. This means we will have a greater reliance on Social Security and a need to manage money and investments better. We may not be able to recoup all our losses, but we can certainly establish another income stream.

According to Bankrate.com (2), "Previous generations could rely on defined benefit plans or pensions. Pensions that provide a fixed monthly income for life, regardless of what's happening on Wall Street, have been vanishing as employers shift the investment risk of retirement to their employees." Of course, we are aware of the loss of pensions, often replaced with 401k or other alternatives. Many retirees have also counted on the equity in our homes as part of our retirement savings, but have now been compromised. From 2006 to 2012, the average value of homes declined about a third.

Since our home is often our largest investment, the loss of a third of its value has in many cases made it less valuable than what we paid for it. This is certainly a setback to our accumulated or net worth. The good news is that the economic cycle in real estate has now reversed course, meaning that our home may once again be gaining in value.

However, we don't read as much encouraging news about this recovery; the focus still seems to be on the doom and gloom.

According to LifeGoesStrong.com (3), "41% of boomers said they are expecting to have to scale back their lifestyle in some way in retirement and 31% believe they will struggle financially." This study reports that 73% of us are planning to work into retirement. As a survey, this measures intention and not actual behavior, but this figure indicates a large increase over prior generations, and a notable change for boomers.

So, 73% of us say we plan to work into the retirement years, but only 31% of us are going to scale down our lifestyle. These figures indicate confusion about financial planning. Typically, most retirees downsize as income tapers off, so I find it surprising that only 31% plan to do this. Obviously, a good budget would indicate if we really need to work.

According to a Pew study (4), "Early boomers (1946-1955) were approaching retirement in better financial shape than the age group before them." Those born after 1955 face a more uncertain retirement because of reduced savings, high levels of debt, and losses during the recession from 2007 to 2009. They report, "Over the last two decades, Depression and war babies have been shedding debt, while boomers and Gen-Xers have been accumulating it."

Since debt is often related to having taken out a mortgage, older retirees are probably selling and downsizing to reduce their debt. So, this could just be replacing and old debt for a new one. But what worries me the most is: "Replacement rate analysis shows that the youngest cohorts will not have enough assets for a secure retirement." This is the group born after 1955 that is expected to struggle the most and may have to plan the most creatively.

Based on the theory that people should have enough savings and wealth to replace at least 70 to 80 percent of their income in retirement, late baby boomers appear to be falling short: most will replace only about 60percent of their income in retirement, according to the report.

I could go on, but you have probably read about the demise of the boomers' retirement for a long time. There are no shortages of retirement experts who are not themselves retired, but who offer dire predictions. I've read many of these pessimistic books and articles and find most based on the theory that the economy is stuck in a recession and people cannot recover or adjust from setbacks.

Sure, there was a stock market crash, an economic recession, unemployment, and real estate depreciation. But, all this has happened before, and most of us have recovered.

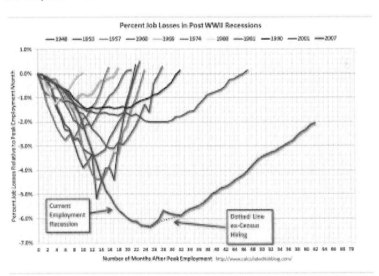

Figure 1: The above graph illustrates the severity of job losses during each post-WWII recession. It also illustrates that every recession has had a complete employment recovery. Our current recovery is distinguished by its depth and breath of the bottom line.

There is no question that the last recession of 2008-09 was the worst the United States has experienced since the Great Depression of the 1930s. The reason it didn't turn into another depression is due to the active involvement of the Federal Reserve Board (The Fed).

The Federal Reserve Act of 1913 divided the country into 12 regions with a federal bank overseeing each area. These banks act as any other bank by providing loans, but are non-profit government entities. The Fed Reserve also sets monetary policy, or manages the flow and supply of money by setting national interest rates. If it decides to increase interest rates, borrowing will slow, resulting in slower growth and less inflation. It usually reduces interest rates to create the opposite effect, that of encouraging borrowing to facilitate growth. The interest rates were reduced during the recession for this very reason.

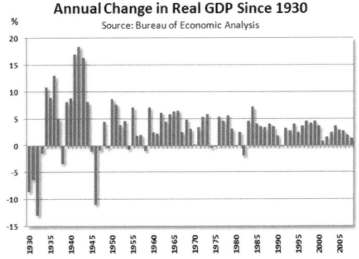

Figure 2: Real U. S. Gross Domestic Product or GDP is nominal GDP adjusted for inflation. This is considered a more accurate figure of growth.

Recession is defined as negative growth for at least two consecutive quarters. After the depression of the 1930s, growth did bounce back significantly in the decade to follow. In hindsight, the Great Depression looks like just a blip historically. The figure above confirms that economic growth not only recovers, but also tends to accelerate after negative growth.

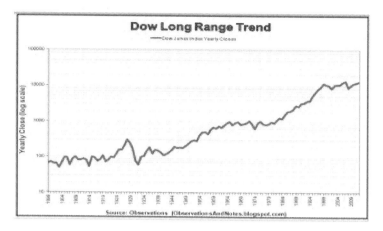

Figure 3: The above graph is the Dow Jones stock index. The market has been down many times before, but appears the most resilient of all the indexes. Even the terrible recession-related market crash of 2008-2009 has recovered.

If you had some investments in the stock market at this point, you'll probably never forget how scary it was. This kind of experience can be a wake-up call, especially as we age. If safety was a small concern before, it certainly became a major issue as we looked to our futures. No matter how much money we lost during this time, the market not only recovered, but now, in 2014, has reached all time highs.

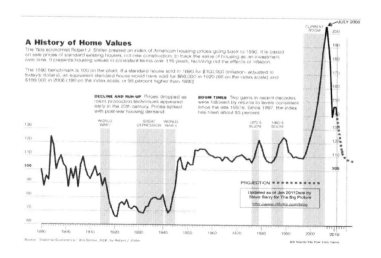

Figure 4: The History of Home Values from 1890. The real estate cycle moves very slow, but given time has always surpassed past values.

In reviewing the prior four charts -- unemployment, the economic cycle as measured by GDP, the stock market as measured by the S & P 500 index, and the real estate market – we see that all show a history of recovery from their slumps. The real estate market is still in the process of its current recovery and will take a few more years to fully recover. But we can clearly see that all prior slumps have recovered. The media and many so-called experts have predicted the bust of boomers based on a permanent slump, which is not historically accurate.

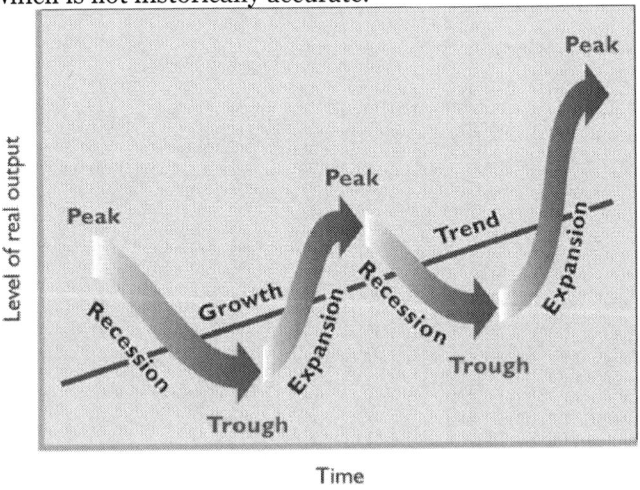

Figure 5: The economic cycle repeats itself and is constantly changing.

The economic or business cycle is just a measure of gross domestic product or GDP. It's an overall measure of economic growth or lack thereof. The above example is only a display of its cycles, and is less symmetrical in reality. But the point here is that the cycle is not stuck in one phase, as some will have you believe. In 2014 we are in a slow expansion or recovery with positive GDP results. GDP is sometimes considered a measure of the economic health of a country. Expansion often equates to more employment and consumption, which should continue for a while, until we reach the next peak.

Why is this important for us? So we understand that the economy goes through different phases or cycles. It is certainly important if you are seeking employment or planning to start a small business. Our economy is based on consumption derived from employment dollars. So, beginning your business during an economic expansion is obviously beneficial for your growth.

Common sense conclusion: The doom and gloom writers have based their predictions on flawed data, as if they never reviewed economic history. We are not in a permanent recession even though it may feel that way sometimes. Different areas of the economy recover at different rates and some areas of employment may evolve, but what history tells us is that economic recoveries have always taken place.

AFFORDABLE RETIREMENT

A common question I get from retirees is "How much money do I need to retire?" I then explain that it's not necessarily a set amount, but really a matter of your income streams from multiple sources. That's right, you don't need a million or more dollars to retire as you may have been told. If you have no savings, but your retirement income is adequate enough to pay all your bills with a little to spare, then you're secure. It's this sustainable security that's our long-term retirement goal, especially for women.

The single most worrisome issue in retirement, for both men and women, is being able to afford it. This worrying is partly based on self-proclaimed experts creating misperceptions of the economy. As noted, the economy's recovery improves the expected outcome for retirement. From an investor's point of view, this recovery is a time of opportunity and not despair. For the average person, it's a time of increasing prosperity, if taken advantage of, and not of helplessness. Either way, you must have a plan and be determined to make the most of our retirement.

Even if the doom and gloom writers were correct about a permanent recession, everyone adapts to their current situation in one form or another. We baby boomers have been changing society with our vast size from day one, and this trend is expected to continue. We can expect female baby boomers to be the harbingers of a new type of creative retirement, where part-time employment or self-employment becomes the cornerstone of future retirements.

I expect boomers to adapt successfully to any adverse economic situation with the same gusto they've displayed in prior life adjustments. Darwin was inadvertently talking about the boomers when he said that it's the most adaptable that survive. We boomers will not only make surprising adjustments, we will create the retirement blueprints for the future generations.

In time, retirees adjust expectations to suit their particular financial situations. This process is helped along once we perceive the need for downsizing. The status symbols of our earlier working years, when we were in the thick of social competition, take on less importance as we age. Those expensive fashions and the big car or house just don't carry the same prestige they once did.

As we age, we become more reflective, and the ways we build our self-esteem changes. In my experience, this transition evolves into "who we are" and "how we contributed to life" with our children or ourselves, not how much money we make or the size of our house.

You are probably already in or near the process of material detachment and downsizing to a smaller budget. If your children have moved out, you may have already downsized to a smaller home. You just didn't need the five bedrooms, suburban, high maintenance house anymore. Maybe you had a garage sale or donated your work clothes or furniture to charity. You are most likely spending less on household items since you are past the acquisitive phase of life. It's not a surprise that affordable retirement and downsizing go hand and hand.

Common sense conclusion: Downsizing our lifestyle is a practical and essential ingredient for managing our retirement finances.

LIVING ON A BUDGET

Many experts attempt to gauge the percent of our past salary we need to live comfortably during our retirement. Most claim that somewhere around 70% to 90% of one's prior salary is necessary. However, there is not one formula that fits everyone, and the results can be misleading. I live on about 50% of my prior salary after downsizing. Obviously, the percent you need is a function of your salary, the cost of living in your area, and your lifestyle, some of which are under your control.

If you reside in the expensive areas of New York or coastal California, and you relocated to Florida or Arizona to retire, you are also probably living on about half of your salary. Since you downsized and relocated, you altered your cost of living significantly. We all need to completely assess our cost of living in our current location and in a couple others we might be considering. The first step in this process is to write out a flexible budget using your actual receipts and expenditures.

Of course, everyone's' budget will be different, but similar in the to need balance it. Your budget will be the foundation for future decisions, so its accuracy is critical. I strongly encourage you to develop a written budget even if you never have. That's because it takes more care to fund our activities when we are not working. There are many sample budgets on the Internet, so you can find one that suits your needs.

It can be difficult to figure in one-time-only or unexpected medical and emergency expenses; however, this is the area we most underestimate. Some studies suggest that about two thirds of us underestimate our medical expenses in retirement. The best way to deal with this uncertainty is to have a reserve or emergency fund. Utilities tend to be a seasonal expense, higher in summer and winter, so I always use a monthly average. No matter how you decide to budget, just be sure to leave yourself a little extra.

MULTIPLE INCOME SOURCES

Traditionally, retirement was known as having three legs: Social Security, pensions, and private savings. In this day and age, we need a forth leg, which I call creative income. Social Security will be there as an entitlement program. This means the government will find a way to extend the benefits as a result of the massive need. It's highly improbable that Social Security will run out, and that the government will let millions of people starve, since they can simply print more money. It was these printing presses that provided lower interest rates with their bond buying.

Social Security

You will qualify for Social Security as part of your retirement income if you have worked work for a minimum of 10 full years. However, if you did not work, you are still entitled to spousal and survivor benefits. Unfortunately, many people fail to apply for these additional compensations. Survivor benefits for family members has a different and relaxed calculation that you can review at the Social Security Administration (SSA) website (5).

As a spouse, you are entitled to social security when you are 62 years old, even if you never worked. Spousal benefits are up to half of the higher worker's benefit. One spouse receiving benefits does not reduce the amount of the other spouse's benefits. If you have a history of employment as a spouse and qualify for your own benefits, you can choose to lock in the larger amount. According to the SSA, if you are full retirement age (65 to 67), you can apply now and have payments suspended. By doing this, you allow your spouse to apply for benefits while your benefits still accumulate until you are 70 years old. If you are married, you want to make sure your husband understands this.

If you are divorced, you can still qualify if your marriage lasted 10 years or more, if your ex-spouse is unmarried, and if he is at least 62 years old. If you remarry, you cannot collect benefits unless the marriage ends in divorce, death, or annulment. If you stay remarried, you cannot collect benefits. Most of us know retirees who don't get married for this very reason. But, being a woman and single, you want to anticipate a longer retirement on average and don't want to accidentally sabotage higher payments.

So, the big decision is when to begin payments. If you were born in 1937 or before, your were eligible for full benefits at age 65. Now the age of eligibility is 66 or 67, depending on the year you were born. If you decide to start benefits at 62 years old, you lock in a payment rate 25% lower than your full retirement amount.

Your benefits will be reduced when your income is over $25,000 if you are single, head of household, or filing separately. For couples filing jointly, the baseline is $32,000 where you are required to pay up to 50% of your benefits if you receive them at 62 years old. This figure can increases up to 85% taxation of you benefits when the combine income exceeds $34,000 if single and $44,000 if married.

According to SSA (5), your "combined income" calculation is: a) adjusted gross income plus b) non-taxable interest plus c) half of your social security benefits. Sorry if this is confusing, but this is how the social security explains it.

It may be surprising that in the past almost 70% of retirees began payments at 62 years old. There are certain circumstances where this may be appropriate, like illness or extreme poverty, but for the average woman, you want to get locked into the highest rate possible. If you are in reasonably good health and have a history of longevity in you family, waiting for the higher rate you can receive at age 70 makes sense. You should calculate not just the total amount of your check, but factor in inflation as well. A smaller check means a smaller cost of living increase.

If you continue to work past 62, your benefits are more likely to be reduced in the years before you fully retire. Since your working years will increase your possible "combined income" and your taxes, waiting to receive benefits until after you are fully retired makes sense. That is, there is no reason to take social security if you are single, making significantly over $25,000, or part of a couple making over $32,000, because your benefits will be reduced by up to 85%. Waiting longer to collect payments results in less taxation and less benefit reduction, since you are not working and collecting at the same time. So, waiting until full retirement at 65 to 67 years old eliminates the benefit reduction, but you will still pay taxes at your regular rate.

A too common scenario would be a 62 year old who works part-time to augment income, while receiving social security. A better scenario to maximize benefits is to work full-time and put off social security until 65-67 years old in order to maximize work income and avoid benefit reduction that ends upon full retirement.

An even better scenario is to work full time until 70 years old and then follow your passions part-time while receiving the highest social security benefit possible for life. This last scenario is key for women, who usually make less over a lifetime and have greater longevity than men. You win with this last scenario with increased work income, which results in increased social security benefits and lower average taxation.

Women's greater longevity sometimes leaves them without a partner and without a second income. Poverty rates for elderly women are higher than for their male counterparts. Most longevity charts reveal that women live about four to five years longer than men. That may not sound like much, but many relationships involve a man who is older by five to ten years. That means that at the end of life a woman could live ten years or more without a partner, a time when people tend to need assistance the most.

If you are a single woman, you most likely have considered this. But if you've been in a long-term marriage, it's more difficult to imagine suddenly being single. It's this complacency and failure to plan for the unexpected that causes panic. So, if possible, locking in your maximum benefits at 70 years old is the best plan.

If your savings produce substantial income, you would need to figure them into the calculation over time. One retiree I spoke with said her investments produce about $25,000 to $34,000 annually. This investment income is expected to continue about the same throughout her life. If she started benefits at 62, she would receive reduced benefits. If you expect investment income to push you, waiting until full retirement age or longer would obviously be another advantage for you.

The SSA website (5) has a section for women under the tab "information for...". This section addresses the various marital and working situations for women and how they can receive the best benefits. But, if you have questions about the information, you won't get much help by calling them. This subject has become so complicated that a new career has developed to address it: benefit or social security counselors. Some of these people are attorneys or financial pros, and some are self-taught entrepreneurs try to wing it. If you decide to get one-time counseling, just be sure your consultant has an appropriate background and reasonable fees.

If you are thinking that working until you are 70 is too long, consider your longevity. According to the SSA, a woman reaching 65 today will on average live until 87. Over 25% of us will live into our 90s. So, working until 70 still leaves us with 15 to 20+ years of retirement --that's a long time, more than past generations.

You should know the amount of your expected benefit at different ages of retirement. You cannot complete a budget without this information, and it helps with decision-making if you can see the different benefit amounts you will receive at different ages. Take some time to explore the SSA website and their procedures, as your benefits may become your primary income.

Only the top 10% to 20% of seniors are considered affluent. The rest of us have formed some reliance on Social Security. According to the Center on Budget and Policy Priorities (6), Social Security provides 90% of total income for 36% of recipients. For 65% of the elderly, it is still the majority of total income. So, Social Security is more than just an entitlement program; for millions of people, it's become a lifesaver. This study concluded that Social Security is particularly helpful for women.

"Women represent 56% of all Social Security beneficiaries age 62 and older and about 68% of beneficiaries age 85 and older. The Social Security system is progressive in that lower wage earners receive a higher percent than higher wage earners do. Women who are low wage workers receive back more benefits in relation to past earnings than do high wage earners."(7) This is due to a combination of benefits for a non-working spouse, survivor benefits, and longer life spans.

In terms of the chance that the program won't be around, the article calls those people alarmists. They correctly mention that since the mid-1980s the government has collected more in taxes each year than it has paid out. The shortfall between income and benefits paid for the next 75 years is only about 1% of gross domestic product. This shortfall is already being addressed by increases in the full retirement age and by tax changes. The article concludes that the fund would last until 2035 if nothing were done. But the age and tax adjustments already made would solidify the program for the next 75 years and beyond.

Common Sense Conclusion: Social Security cannot end due to the large-scale human dependence on the program for basic needs, congress's mandate to continue this program, and the government's ability to print money to bail it out. So, do not live in fear by expecting the worst; this entitlement program is not going away anytime soon.

Some financial firms offer free Social Security workshops to assist us in the decision-making process about benefits and other issues. These workshops can be interesting to attend, but the sponsors might try to sign you up as a client. Some of them offer a computer application that shows the best combination of benefits at the best time. For example, you can take half of your spouse's social security at 62 and then switch to your full benefits at 70. That way, you take advantage of both types of benefits.

Pensions

In terms of your pension, consider yourself lucky if you have one. Many pensions take the place of Social Security, especially for those employed by government programs. I've had clients who have worked for the state government and privately. These individuals can collect both a pension and Social Security, since they paid into both of them.
However, as I already noted, fewer than 15% of people have a pension because they are being phased out and replaced by the 401k and other plans.

During the economic boom of the 90s and early 2000s, generous pensions were promised until the economic cycle changed. The last recession has seen more companies and state and local governments attempt to reduce their obligations to retirees. It's possible that this income stream is in jeopardy, depending on the financial stability of the company. If you are set to receive a pension, you might consider an option to take a lump sum up front, if offered, which would alleviate any anxieties over a future changes.

Private Savings and the Markets

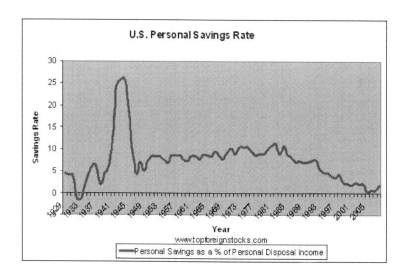

Figure 6: Personal Savings Rate in the United States.

This chart shows a big spike in savings after the Great Depression of the 1930s, and a smaller spike after the recession of 2007-2009. This pattern confirms that we are a nation of spenders until a crisis occurs, or necessity arrives. Retirement is the arrival of that necessity.

Private savings is often the weak spot in most of our portfolios. Even if we have a lot of equity or high net worth, our actual cash savings may be low. I consider the equity in our homes as a form of savings, especially if we expect to sell at some point.

If our savings are still low after we sell our home, then we will be motivated to create more income. Some of us feel that creative investing is the way to increase savings. However, as a stockbroker, I noticed the wide range of investment skills among the public, often characterized by overconfidence.

With a few stock market successes, people easily become overly confident in their abilities. I worked with a medical doctor who was a comfortably retired millionaire. His confidence led to risk-taking in the stock market, and he ended up loosing over one million dollars and had to return to work at age 73. Just because you're an expert in one area doesn't mean you're an expert in other areas. Making sure your principal is safe must be your priority because you don't have time to go back and earn it again.

I am not saying to stay away from the stock market altogether, but to invest knowledgeably and conservatively as part of your overall portfolio. One example of how to do this is to keep a small percent of your savings in an S & P 500 index fund that follows the general market. It's not possible to provide specific investment advice here because it must be appropriate to the individual 's situation. However, I can certainly advise that, because of its complexity and volatility, the stock market is clearly not for everyone.

The problem that many investors run into is over-investing in one area and selling too soon. If you have most of your savings in the market and there is a 50% correction, like in 2009, you're likely to sell at a loss, even if you know that the market will recover.

This is the problem with human nature and the stock market. Wild swings scare people, and they retreat to a loss for self-preservation. This is a variation of the old fight or flight instinct. The investor often loses money by reacting emotionally in a volatile but otherwise positive market.

Market Psychology

In an attempt to take emotion out of the market, various strategies have developed. One strategy is to focus on dividends, which are payments made to you as a fixed amount per share of stock you own. Dividends are similar to the interest rate on you savings account. Just as your interest rate might be 5%, dividends paid to you can be set at 5%. You often receive this payment on a monthly basis that can be cash or reinvest. This payment is often called a dividend yield.

One strategy to earn high dividends involves investing in stable, large, above-average-yielding, conservative equities or stocks. A variation of this strategy is buying the 10 top dividend-yielding stocks in the Dow Jones Industrial Average. This theory is that the higher yielding stocks are at the low point in their business cycle. Consequently, you expose yourself to market appreciation as well as yield. I have been involved with this strategy in the past and seen how it can work in a recovering market.

At the time of this writing, in 2014, the S & P 500 Index is at an all- time high on weak earnings, and the Federal Reserve is beginning to allow interest rates to increase in the near term (not good for stocks). These developments are two red flags, so I would wait for the correction (or whatever adjustment the market makes after the Federal Reserve bond-buying program stops) before entering the market.

You may have heard many times that "you can't time the market." From my experience as a stockbroker, I can tell you that I've always found this statement confusing because "technical analysis" of chart patterns is a whole area of stock market analysis that focuses just on timing. I can also certainly tell you that both growth and value investors use technical analysis when picking equities.

I have used this analysis myself for many years and there are times when it works very well --- or doesn't. I'm not going into detail here about the various ways to analyze the market, but for those of you still interested in stock investing, I highly recommend, *How to Make Money in Stocks* by William J. O'Neil (8). It's a classic in the field, and part of the reason I was able to retire.

The thesis that the economic cycle returns prices to their original or higher level still prevails. But could you imagine how disciplined and emotionless you must be to wait years for the market to recover? Remember that even Wall Street professionals lost a lot of money and had to be bailed out during the recession of 2008-2009. So, even the experts who do this for a living took a big loss. The news reports that Wall Street is increasing leverage and risk-taking again. Unless you have enough personal experience, knowledge, and confidence, then leave the high risk investing to the gamblers.

Some investment advisors rationalize that we must invest in the stock market since we will live 20 plus years into retirement, and will need the better returns the stock market might provide. The S & P 500 track record for the most recent decade of 2000 to 2010 saw a price change of -2.7%, and when dividends are added, -1.0%. Add inflation during that time and the return is -5.1%. You have to go back to 1950 for the returns to average in the 9 to 10% range before subtracting for inflation. Those negative returns are coming at a time when many boomers are expecting to retire.

These types of figures are crushing for the investment industry, which has no explanation as to why the average person should risk her life savings for these unpredictable and unsubstantial returns.
Compare the rate of return for tax-exempt municipal bonds. A 5% tax-exempt(no federal or state taxes) return is equivalent to 7% to 10% of taxable income without the wild market swings.

The stock market is very complicated and anti-intuitive. It has ruined many people and will ruin many more. A few years ago, when I hired a contractor to install sprinklers, an elderly man and his son arrived. His low back pain from an injury was apparent right away as he had his son do all the work. He explained how his back deteriorated after years of physical labor, yet he couldn't retire.

When discussing retirement, he revealed how he tried to get ahead by day trading on the stock market. He sadly disclosed that he lost $450,000, his entire life savings, in the market. I asked why he didn't stop when he was down to $100,000. He claimed that he was always trying to make it back. He and his elderly wife moved to a trailer park after they lost their house.

Common sense conclusion: Don't expect betting on the stock market to provide for your retirement needs. People who are increasing their risk in order to make up lost ground are setting themselves up for failure.

This last example brings up the issue of financial awareness of what your partner is doing with your money. I know men who hide money from their spouse or risk it all, as in the example above. For self-perseveration, women need to be involved with the savings and investment end of retirement. I believe the best way is to invest and manage money together as a team.

If you have never been involved in this area, it's time to get involved. If your spouse is used to doing it all himself, just tell him that you are now studying investments (or money management) and you want to be involved with "our" money. Taking the role of student turns your partner into the teacher, so you get to ask questions while he can explain his strategy.

FIXED INCOME INVESTMENTS

Some of us may find fixed income boring because it's less volatile with better price stability than the stock market. However, this is the type of low risk boring we can depend on. It pays out a predetermined amount rather than a jackpot winning or losing. Not only is it a lot safer, but it takes less maintenance. It's less complicated and more appropriate for long-term sustainability. So, if you are a woman who is new to investing, please take your time and try to understand the basics. Women need to be financially wiser than men since good money management skills are required to extend their budget for longer.

Many retirees hold various fixed income and bond investments. Bonds and bond funds have been the cornerstone of the retired for a long time and I have personally bought and sold many over the years. Historically, they have been the perfect investment vehicles because they are a long-term buy and hold without much maintenance.

As of this writing, the Federal Reserve, which sets interest rates, has begun to allow rates to be determined by market forces – they will reduce their bond buying, which kept interest rates artificially low. They feel the economy is beginning to recover enough to be sustainable on its own. They are letting rates increase, which will lower bond prices. As interest rates increase, bond prices decrease -- it's an inverse relationship.

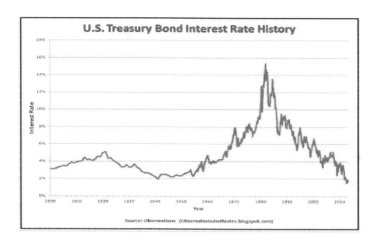

Figure 7: United States bond yields going back 100 years. The above interest rate cycle has reached bottom and is beginning to turn up.

The long rate drop was accompanied by increased bond prices. An investor who held bonds from about 1985 through 2010 enjoyed regular dividend and price appreciation -- the golden years. The 35-year bull cycle in bonds is now over and rates are beginning to cycle back up. The very slow moving curve is expected to last for many years. Yes, timing is involved in bond investing too.

Normally, you do not want to hold bonds *funds* when rates are increasing. However, if you buy individual bonds at par value, when the bond expires, your par value is returned to you regardless of what the bond is selling for in the secondary market. Par value is basically face value of a bond. For example, the par value is $100 while the bond expires in 2020. The price in the secondary market may vary between $95 and $105 over the bond's life, but does not affect your dividend. Regardless of what happens to the bond price during its life, you receive your $100 par value refunded to you upon expiration of that bond in 2020.

If you need to sell the bond before its expiration date, you would take the secondary market price, which could be lower or higher than par. That's why you ladder (use different expiration dates) and put only a portion of your portfolio into a long term investment -- the amount you won't need for awhile.

I'm watching the price of individual municipal bonds in my state to drop to or below par value so I can buy them. Of course, the interest I collect will be tax-free if they are municipal bonds. This would be a conservative tax-effective, long-term hold strategy.

Kathy Jones, Vice President of Charles Schwab Fixed Income, (9) said, "While the prospect of rising interest rates means bond prices will fall, a bear market in bonds does not necessarily mean investors will face steep losses. Limiting duration to high quality, intermediate term bonds and reinvesting principal and interest as rates rise can help mitigate impact of rising rates." When she refers to high quality bonds she means according to the rating agencies like Moody's, Fitch, and S & P. Their job is to rate the quality of bonds. A rating of AAA from S & P is considered the highest rating and gradually decreases to AA, A, BB+ and lower-rated bonds. Only the A or higher rated funds are considered investment grade.

PIMCO (10) has enjoyed an excellent reputation as a bond strategist for many years. Their website discusses a plan for the high yield municipal bond market. "On a tax adjusted basis, municipal bonds may offer greater returns than a taxable debt sectors, such as treasuries and corporate bonds. During credit sensitive time periods, such as a recession, municipal debt defaults frequencies tend to be lower than corporate debt." The tax advantage and the safety of municipal bonds are well established, and I look to PIMCO for advice on bonds.

In a Forbes article about investment themes (11), M. Kahn cites bonds as effective for income and growth. "It has long been my contention that, for income-oriented investors, bonds can provide for a dependable and consistent stream of income, and principal protection when held to maturity." Notice he mentions holding the bonds to maturity. "Rising interests rates should not impact the interest that bond holders receive on their holdings nor should they change the ability of these investors to revive par value on their bond holding at maturity." So, holding individual bonds, not bond funds, to maturity will negate the effect of interest rate increases, since rates have no effect on our dividends or par value at expiration.

Floating Rate Funds

Many dividend-investor retirees are concerned with increasing interest rates, so it's natural that they consider floating rate funds.
In theory, these funds should perform better during an economic recovery with increasing interest rates. These funds are either open or closed end for new investors. The interest rate will adjust periodically as will the return. These funds invest mostly in floating rate bank loans and often use leverage to boost return. Some funds restrict when you can sell your shares to a monthly or quarterly schedule.

The primary risk is the lower credit quality of the borrowers' loans themselves. This risk often places this asset in the moderate risk level. However, it's attractive to income investors when short-term borrowing rates are expected to rise. So, timing and lower values decrease this risk.

A similar example is real estate that supposedly is in the moderate risk level. After real estate prices fell over 50% in many areas, the timing and reduced values decreased the risk of further loss. Valuations are taken very seriously on Wall Street when analysts recommend a stock. Many analysts recommend a buy or sell rating for a stock based on valuations.

There is an old Wall Street adage, "Don't fight the Fed." This means don't fight the direction the Fed is going or you'll end up paying. The Federal Reserve's influence over credit and interest rates the last few years tended to dominate market direction. The Fed has announced its intentions to let rates increase, an action which determines the type of investments that will benefit. Floating rate funds are designed to follow the rates up. The fund paying 4.7% on my portfolio below is Credit Suisse Floating Rate Fund (CHIAX) and is surprisingly stable over time. There is a front-end charge, and the dividend percent changes on a monthly basis since it's variable rate.

Real Estate Investment Trusts

Real Estate Investment Trust, or REITs, have been a favorite of fixed income investors due to their substantial dividend. The dividend is made possible because REITs are required to distribute 90% or more of their taxable income to shareholders as dividends. Investopedia (12) defines them as "a security that sells like a stock on the major exchanges and invests in real estate directly, either through properties or mortgages. REITs receive special tax considerations and typically offer high yields as well as high liquidity." REITs are another way of investing in real estate without buying a property and dealing with tenants.

The two major categories of REITs are equity and mortgage. Equity REITs own property and derive their income from tenant leases or from interest payments if they are financed. Mortgage REITs do not own property, but own the loans that pay interest and fees. The failure or success of a mortgage REITs depends on its skill to buy agency securities (mortgage loans) with higher spreads over borrowing costs.

REIT.com (13) lists the REIT attributes: "1. Diversification: Low correlation with broader market with a higher returns and lower risk. 2. Income: Reliable income creates wealth accumulation. 3. Inflation Protection: Returns consistently outpace the Consumer Price Index. 4. Liquidity: It trades like a stock. 5. Performance: It outperformed the S&P 500 index over most periods and has better returns than corporate bonds. 6. Transparency: Market and tax transparency."

Some advisors feel REITs can be part of a retirement portfolio, and I agree as long as they are a small part and your investment purpose is for income and diversification. Rising interest rates affect mortgage REITs far greater than equity REITs, since their margins (profits) become compressed.

Equity REITs have a better forecast at this point in the cycle, due to a recovering economy that increases rental rates. The limited supply of new multi-family construction should also create greater demand leading to higher rents. At the time of writing, the REIT investment is GOV ticker symbol, an exchange-traded fund (ETF) that pays 7.1%. This is a federally owned company that leases to other government enterprises. Government entities tend not to go out of business or loose funding like private companies often do.

Master Limited Partnerships (MLP)

Master Limited Partnerships also provide high yield returns because they have no corporate income tax. The Tax Reform Act of 1986 and the Revenue Act of 1987 created this offering. Congress granted this exemption from taxes to encourage faster infrastructure development. Distributions or dividends, usually paid quarterly, are taxed at your regular rate, but you can write off depreciation, partnership costs, and other items against this income.

The benefit of this investment lays in double-digit yields, a very stable business model, and the possibility of increased yields. Most of the MLPs are energy pipeline companies -- crude oil and natural gas. Once these pipelines are built, they require little maintenance and expense.

The companies in the pipeline business are paid by the volume being pumped through the pipe, not the actual cost of crude oil itself. It's just a method of transporting the oil. So, even though oil prices may change, it won't affect the price of transporting it. MLPs tend to be correlated to the stock market in times of economic stress like the last recession. The MLP tax structure is better suited for an after-tax retirement portfolio, but not for retirement accounts like IRAs.

Some advisors feel MLPs are considered suitable for retirement portfolios as long as the risks are understood. These risks include volatility, interest rate risk (increases borrowing costs) and management risk. So, we look for increasing company earnings. We also look for lower debt than their competitors. And we always pay attention to analysis ratings.

The MLP investment in my portfolio paying 11% is LRR Energy (LRE), which engages in the acquisition, exploitation, development, and operation of oil and natural gas pipelines. As with any dated suggestion, evaluation at the time of investing is needed. It's always important to do your "due diligence" or your homework on the company before making any investment.

Certificates of Deposit and Money Market

Certificates of Deposits, or CDs, have proven their safety with insurance from default, flexibility of duration, and liquidity (easy access to your money). The risks are low, but there is some interest rate risk in that you get locked into one rate even if interest rates increase. There is also some risk of insolvency of the issuer, but this is what insurance is for.

The problem I have with CDs is that the interest rate paid to you doesn't quite keep up with inflation and you have to pay taxes on it as well. The result could be a net loss. If the five-year rate would increase to 3% or higher, then I would recommend CDs as a safe, conservative part of your portfolio.

Money market funds offer safety, liquidity, and low fees. Taxation of interest can be exempt if the fund invests in municipal products. The rates they pay you are historically low on this product because they are based on short-term maturities. Money market funds are usually a temporary place to park cash when you are deciding on your next investment.

Tax Deferred Retirement Plans

Your individual retirement plan, 401k, 403b, IRA, or SEP IRA, has great benefits and I hope you've been diligent about contributing to it. When you want to withdraw money from it, take it out slowly, before the required withdrawal age 70 ½, to avoid stiff penalties. In general, between the ages of 59 1/2 and 70 1/2, you can take as much as often as you like without the 10% penalty. You will pay taxes on the withdrawn amount at your income level.

There are a few exceptions for withdrawal before 59 1/2 without penalty. A disability, family death, medical expenses or premiums, higher education, or even down payment on a residence may qualify you for early withdrawal without penalty. Contact the IRS if you are interested in these exceptions.

However, I recommend using your retirement plan for its original purpose. The tax deferred nature of these vehicles dictate that certain investments are appropriate. The higher taxable yields, like MLPs and REITs, are appropriate. Municipal bonds are not appropriate because they are already tax-exempt.

There is a debate among advisors over the withdrawal strategy for these funds. Since we are legally obligated to withdraw all the money during an 11-year span, how do we maximize this benefit? We would have our money sooner if we withdrew the amount in one or two years, but less of it after taxes.

If you have $100,000 to withdrawal, for example, you can divide the payouts to span 10 or 11 years so not to trigger much taxation. It would also be prudent to let the amount you withdraw in any one year be dependent your taxable income. That is, if your taxable income increases that year, you can withdraw less from retirement accounts. Increased income means less withdrawal and vice versa.

CNBC ran a surprising online article (14), "Can't figure out your 401k? You're not alone," on August 13, 2014. The author reported that 57% of Americans are confused over how to manage their 401k plans and want a simpler way to know which investments to make. A survey revealed that 52% complained that explanations of their investment plans were more confusing than their health care benefits. 46% complain that they don't feel they know what their best investment options are and 34% suffer from a great deal of stress over appropriate allocation of funds.

The highly independent and self-sufficient boomer generation doesn't like to be dependent on advisors. That's a positive because no one takes better care of your money than you. But your independence means your top priority must be education and safety regarding your financial situation.

Retirement is the perfect time to increase your investment skills because you finally have financial need and the time to develop financial knowledge occurring together. You can narrow down the endless number of investment books by focusing on those that address retirement. The theory that an aging investor should incrementally alter his or her portfolio holdings to bonds and other safer investments holds true for most of us. We don't want to risk loosing our money, but we must be willing to take a minimal calculated risk in order to generate some income.

The concept of individual risk tolerance now comes into play. We often learn our risk tolerance when we take a loss. Professional investors understand that taking some losses is par for the course. They do their best to manage losses by selling quickly before they mount. However, as retirees, our risk tolerance should be fairly low because we know we cannot make up for a large loss. The ranking below is an introduction to investment risk.

HIGHER RISK: Stock or Commodity options or derivatives, Precious metals, Mining, Commodities, Futures, Small cap or penny stocks, Day trading, Hedge funds, undeveloped land, Art and collectibles, Venture capital, Emerging market stocks.

MODERATE RISK: Rental real estate, Junk bonds, Blue Chip Stocks, Stock mutual funds, large quality stocks, International stocks, Variable annuities, MLPs, S & P 500 index fund, mREITs.

LOWER RISK: Federal and State Government bonds, High grade corporate bonds, bank deposits, Bond mutual funds, Floating rate funds, Life insurance cash value, Municipal Bonds, Zero-coupon bonds, Personal real estate, Fixed annuities, pREITs.

SAFEST: C.D.s, Money market funds, Treasury Bills, Saving accounts, Cash, Savings bonds EE and HH.

You may have seen graphs or pyramids of investment risk before and noticed they are all a bit different. Many of them list real estate only once. I placed rental real estate in the moderate risk level and your personal residence in the lower risk area based on my personal experience. Most of my portfolio is concentrated in the lower risk category.

Investment property is more likely to default than the home you reside in. Since, real estate prices are cyclical, your place on the cycle can determine your risk. That is, if you bought at the bottom of the price cycle, you have less risk of price decline.

If you bought real estate at the price peak in 2005 or 2006, your risk increases. That is, if homes appreciate at four to five percent annually and, in the last five to six years, they have appreciated at an average of almost 20% -- then they are overextended way past their average. Conversely, if you purchased a home in 2012 to 2013, after real estate had depreciated close to 50%, you would be buying it at a lower risk time.

I also divided REIT investments into two categories as mentioned in the REIT section. Mortgage REITs appear to have moderate risk at this time while property seem to have a lower risk.

Take a few minutes to review the risk above and familiarize yourself with the different type of investments and the risks they carry. Even if you are managing your IRA or 401k, you still don't want risky investments. I counseled a retiree who became influenced by a radio show touting gold as a retirement haven. She was not aware that many advisors recommend their own book of investments so people will buy what they own and increase the price. After this price increase, they often sell at a profit. Large volume selling brings down the price of gold. She lost over 80% of her retirement savings when this happened. That's why we must be aware of risk.

Maybe you have noticed the many financial ads for retirees offering to solve all your problems. "Just give us all your money and we'll show you how to manage it," they claim. As more boomers retire, I expect these "hurt and rescue" ads to proliferate. Hurt and rescue is an old sales technique where you hurt people with a big problem and offer to rescue them with a solution. So, expect to see a lot more of these ads.

The various investment vehicles described here should help you with the task of deciding how to allocate or balance your 401 portfolios. As the Fed decides to discontinue its bond-buying program, don't be surprised to see a major market correction. I would wait before I allocate a maximum of 10% to stocks because of the risk the market will fall during the Fed's unwinding.

If you are just starting to invest, the learning curve accelerates when your education involves other investors, such as you would find in an investment class or club. A class is beneficial, but you'll get actual investment experience in a club. The interesting and unsettling characteristic about investing is that everyone seems to have a different opinion. Evaluating all these different viewpoints will sharpen your critical skills. If you can't find an open investment club with a retirement orientation in your area, consider starting one of your own.

Annuities

Annuities are insurance products designed to address two retirement fears: loosing money in the market and outliving your money. Annuities are often considered fixed income, although some have variable rates as well. As a stockbroker, I also arranged for teachers' 403b tax-deferred plans that are the non-profit version of the 401k. This company's tax-deferred retirement program put them all into annuities.

There are many different versions, some fixed, some variable, some combined, some immediate, some delayed, some pre-taxed, some after-tax, and some that provide upside potential without downside risk. In the latter example, the insurance company guarantees that you never have a losing year. To pay for that protection, for example, you agree to receive to 75% of the S & P 500 gain. If the market loses ground that year you accept no gain and no loss. If the market increases 20%, your return will be 15%. This system is designed to mitigate the fear and pain of market uncertainties and loss.

The way an annuity addresses "outliving your money" is to guarantee life-long payments similar to Social Security. To pay for that benefit, you agree to forfeit the remaining funds to the annuity company upon your death. If you die the next day, all the money goes to the company.

Let's say you are 65 years old and think you might live 30 more years, but your life expectancy is 20 more years according to the actuaries. You decide to have the annuity begin payments when you are 75 years old, and you receive the amount based on the 10 years you still have to live. The annuity company pays you for ten years. Your account balance will be zero after 10 years, but you get the same payments until you die. The company loses money if you live longer than expected and makes money when you die early. The company is sure to charge fees for various services, like taking a loan on your money, along the way.

Other risks of annuities are inflation and company failure. Social Security benefits have annual cost of living increases, but annuities don't, unless you buy an extra package for this protection. There is always a minor chance the insurance company can go under. You have a contract with the insurance company that is not insured by the government (like bank deposits, for example). Your state may offer some protection through the state insurance commissioner, which usually stops at $100,000. So, you will want to put no more than that amount into any one company.

It's always wise to check the credit ratings of the annuity company as well. Normally, if you die a month after receiving payments, you may forfeit the remaining amount to the company. The way to counteract this is by having a joint life annuity that is shared with a spouse. I won't go into greater detail here since each company has many variations and you usually sit down with an agent who outlines all the possible choices.

Annuities are designed as retirement products, but whether it's appropriate for your retirement depends on a number of factors. First, does your expected longevity exceed the average? Second, is your financial situation such that you feel you could outlive your money? Third, are you young enough to be around long enough to collect the payments? Fourth, do you have enough savings now to afford a significant initial deposit?

I like the concept of not outliving your savings, so an annuity may be helpful for women with greater expected longevity, but the primary task is to find an annuity with low fees. If it appears that an annuity might be appropriate for you, contact at least two independent agents who work with different companies so you have choices. After asking which annuity is the most cost-effective, ask each agent which annuity they would buy for themselves and why.

Some annuity holders complain that they can't gain early access to their money without taking a high interest loan on the principle. So, just be sure you do your due diligence to understand the cost structure and redeeming policies before you buy an annuity.

Long Term Withdrawal Rates

Wall street likes concepts that are designed to take the chaos and confusion out of investing. Many of us have been told by advisors that we should withdraw 4% per year out of our deferred retirement plans and savings. Once we do the math, we find this general principle to be too general to apply. If our total savings is under $100,000, then less than $4000 a year won't leave us very much to live on. That amount of savings would send us back to the job market, and postpone withdrawals altogether.

It's understood that this withdraw rate is meant to extend throughout the retirement years, but it doesn't address variable economic scenarios like recessions or individual needs. Once these advisors become retired themselves, they will find that each year they will have different expenditures.

If you have surgery one year for example, you'll withdraw more than you planned for that year. If you sell your house, you'll probably add to your savings with the equity. But, regardless of the percent or how well worked out the formula is, it's important to plan for unexpected expenses.

After being retired for years, most people spend just what they need to get by and save or reinvest the extra. We all seem more frugal in old age because our incomes are lower, but we still want to do the same things as before. We just remember to check our budgets before we splurge. But outside of being more careful with money, our financial habits change slowly. So, don't feel constrained by general theories that fail to address your individual situation.

INVESTMENT PORTFOLIO

Many of us do not trust the markets or advisors, feel that investing is gambling with a tie on, feel unprepared to invest, or distain Wall Street for a variety of reasons. As a prior stockbroker, I more than understand how you can distrust the markets or advisors because I feel the same way.

The generation that lived through the Depression of the 1930s had market aversions. After the big collapse, many were not comfortable re-entering the market for the rest of their lives. If that is your position, then I respect it. But remember, if you don't get some type of return on your savings, it loses 2% to 3% annually, or whatever the rate of inflation happens to be. Therefore, this section is for those who are not willing to accept this loss and must have safety before investing in anything.

The expected response to presenting a working portfolio is that I know every advisor will disagree with it. That's because there are so many choices; each investor has their own style, and there are multiple strategies. As economic conditions change, the investments may change as well. But, this is what's worked for me. The purpose of giving you a sample portfolio is to get you thinking and planning your own. Since this is a retirement portfolio, it's going to be mostly a dividend/interest-producing plan that may look different from riskier investments you made earlier in your life.

Safety is the first consideration, with 60% of funds in municipal bonds and money market funds. I'm not recommending bond funds, but only the bonds themselves. You can withdraw non re-invested dividends from the money market for living expenses. The 10-15% in the floating rate fund, designed for increasing rates, is very stable and lower on risk as well. The clear risk here is in the MLP, REIT, and S & P 500 funds, which are needed to kick up the return to 6-7% annually. We all need to find our own balance between investment safety and returns. Below is just one example.

% portfolio	Investment Type	Expected Return
50%	Individual State Municipal Bonds	5.0%
10-15%	Floating Rate Fund(CHIAX)	4.7%
10%	MLP(LRE)	12.8%
10%	REIT(GOV)	7.1%
10%	S & P 500 Index Fund	9.0%
5-10%	Money Market Fund	.8%

Since safety comes first, your state municipal bonds should be General Obligation (GO) or high quality revenue bonds, and rated high by the rating agencies. The default rates on municipal bonds are low anyway, but having them insured or pre-funded reduces risk even further. Even though city and county bonds are considered on the safer side of the scale, a couple of high profile defaults like Stockton, CA, in 2012, and Detroit, MI, in 2014, have occurred. The media may hype each story to get maximum effect, but the truth lies in the actual numbers.

Moody's (15) calculated default numbers of bonds from 1970 to 2010 and found that during this period no defaults on municipal bonds occurred when rated AAA. Even bonds rated A defaulted less than one in 2000. City and county municipals with A rating have less than one-tenth the defaults of corporate bonds rated AAA. So, not all bonds are created equal, as the ratings become our guide.

Keep in mind that the local municipalities are authorized to declare Chapter 9 bankruptcy under 11 U.S.C. 109, and default on their bonds. States, on the other hand, are not authorized by the United States Code to declare bankruptcy and cannot default on their bonds. Since the states cannot default, this extra protection makes it safer to stay with the state G.O. bonds.

Individual State General Obligation Municipal Bonds, bought at par value or below, will return 100% of your principle at maturity while you receive a tax-exempt yield. This tax-effective, long-term hold strategy is appropriate for taxable retirement portfolios.

Investing in municipal bonds in your own state can exempt state and federal taxes. Many people think that these types of bonds are only for the wealthy in a high tax bracket. Since the Bush era tax cuts have expired, the threshold for taxes is $9,750 after subtracting the standard deduction and personal exemption. Since the tax structure has changed, tax-exempt returns take on greater importance for all levels of investors.

Common Sense Conclusion: Individual State General Obligation Municipal Bonds, bought at par value or below, can be the foundation for a safe retirement account.

The 10% allocation in the S&P 500 index fund is for growth and dividends. As mentioned, it's prudent to wait for the Federal Reserve to discontinue its bond-buying program and see how the market reacts prior to investing. This may take a number of years to completely unwind, so patience is required.

Since I like competing opinions, let's take a look at other respected advisors' recommendations for retirement. Morningstar.com is a company that's well respected and used by many. C. Benz (16) wrote an online article, posted August 30, 2012, entitled "A Sample Retirement Portfolio Using the Bucket Approach." The three buckets, or groups of investments, are for short, intermediate, and long-term holding periods.

			Yield
Short term:	4%	Cash(CDs, money market)	
	4%	PIMCO Enhances short maturity(MINT)	.88%
Mid-term:	9%	T. Rowe Price short-term bond(PRWBX)	1.74%

10%	Harbor Bond(HABDX)	2.36
7%	Harbor Real Return(HARRX)	1.67
7%	Vanguard Wellesley Income(VWINX)	3.02

Long-term:	27%	Vanguard Dividend Growth(VDIGX)	1.97%
	13%	Harbor International(HAINX)	2.02
	7%	Vanguard Total Stock market(VTSMX)	1.80%
	8%	Loomis Sayles Bond(LSBDX)	5.72
	5%	Harbor Commodity Real Return(HACMX)	1.58%

This allocation is about 59% stocks, rendering it way too risky; the bond fund yields don't keep up with inflation; the funds don't have a par value to redeem at maturity, , and the bond fund prices are expected to fall.

Okay, lets take a look at another professional recommendation. *Kiplinger* is very well respected, and posted an online article in May 2007 that is still online. K. Marquardt (17) recommends different risk portfolios based on individual tolerance. I won't compare the higher risks plans because that's outside the scope of safety. The safer long-term fund portfolio is:

60%	Fidelity Spartan Total Market Index
20%	Fidelity Spartan International Index
15%	Fidelity Spartan Extended Market Index
5%	Vanguard Emerging Market Stock Index

This relevancy of this recommendation is easy to assess because it's 100% in the stock market with expensive funds. Some advisors are only stock-oriented and do not provide a balanced approach. This recommendation was made just months before the market began its major correction of 59%. The subsequent losses would hurt any investor, and have no business in a retirement plan.

Let's take one more example from *The Motley Fool* (18) website, "A Retirement Portfolio You Can Set and Forget." Of course, that's what we all want to do, but is it realistic?

	Conservative	Moderate	Aggressive
Large-cap stocks	20%	35%	50%
Small-cap stocks	5%	10%	15%
Foreign stocks	5%	5%	10%
Bonds	60%	40%	20%
REITs	10%	10%	5%

The above portfolio is divided by risk tolerance. REITs are in the same risk category as equities according to figure 7. The conservative approach is 60% bonds and 40% stocks. The bonds recommended are one fund: Fremont Bond (MBDFX), with a yield of 2.89%. This website recommends rebalancing the portfolio annually only if assets are 10% or more away from the target percent. It's interesting that these recommendations were made when the great recession and stock market correction had already started four months earlier.

This last conservative plan above is the closest to my working portfolio in that the safe part is 60% bonds versus my 55% to 60% bonds and money market funds. The risk here is the stocks and REITs at 40%, while my risk is 30% of stocks, MLPs, and REITs. The big difference is that this plan has all bonds in a fund. There is no par value to redeem at the end of the bond holding period in a fund.

The other challenge is that this plan turns you into a stock picker for 30% of your portfolio, if you don't like the fund choice. You will need education, experience, ample time, and risk tolerance to address this need adequately. My plan puts a maximum of 10% into a stock index fund, so you don't have to embark upon the long journey of becoming proficient at stock or equity analysis.

Whatever approach you decide to implement, just be sure you take the time to understand it. Once you're invested, maintenance of your portfolio can demand be very little effort, unless you arrange a more complicated account. Expectations of returns beyond 6% or 7% are unrealistic for a conservative portfolio. You will have a buy and hold portfolio with adjustments that are dictated by changing economic conditions. In this case, it's the change in interest rate direction that's the condition for change away from bond funds into individual bonds, and from stocks into floating rate funds. You may go years before another economic condition dictates a needed adjustment.

OUR RELATIONSHIP WITH MONEY

Would it surprise you if I told you women are better money managers than men? If you went through the public school system, you probably didn't receive much business or financial education. Even in college, it's not a requirement, so you have to sign up specifically to get it. Consequently, many women have not had a chance to understand investments and to develop a relationship with money. If that's the case with you, now is the time to establish that relationship so you can better sustain yourself in the future.

How do we improve our relationship with money? Well, we have to spend time working with it. When trying out any investment program, I like starting small in order to get a feel for how it works. Rather than put 10% of your money in a floating rate fund or MLP, start with a much smaller amount, like $500. Then watch the movements of your funds to assess their stability over time. You can also use charts to view the historical stability of the fund. This approach will really help you understand price movements. As you feel more comfortable with this investment, you can slowly add more to it. In this way, you will be improving your understanding and relationship with money.

Why not construct a pretend or "mock" investment portfolio, so you can learn the process while not risking any money? That's a good question and I'm glad you asked!

When you have actual money at stake, you view it more seriously and tend to remember the experience. When you have your personal money on the line, even in small amounts, you tend to have a heightened awareness of possible loss. So, your motivation to learn and succeed increases. Having money at stake makes you emotionally involved with the market and accelerates your learning curve. Joining an investment club or taking investment classes also accelerates your learning curve. All of these experiences add to your education and confidence for investing.

Very few studies of the differences between how men and women deal with money exist. But we know there are gender differences anyway. Our society is based on capitalism, so profit is our orientation. Money gets intertwined with socioeconomic status and becomes a symbol of pride and accomplishment, especially for men. For them, whoever has the most money is considered the most successful.

Women usually do not view money as the ultimate goal, tend not to flaunt it with objects symbolic of success, and don't involve it in their identity to the same extent as men do. Becoming a millionaire is usually not considered the final accomplishment and stopping point for women. For women, money is more a tool that enables them to enjoy the benefits and freedoms of life.

Historically, women have been considered less skilled at mathematics than men. I'm not sure if this idea is factual or relevant. Even if true, day-to-day business and investing skills don't require math skills above a basic level. People with superior math skills are not especially successful at investing, or else all the math professors in the world would be billionaires. If women are less confident due to feelings of poor math abilities, they could just be listening to society talking to them.

My experience as a stockbroker confirms that women are more risk averse, that is, less inclined towards risk-taking and aggressive investing. I find this attitude beneficial and practical. The risk in aggressive investing can yield a significant gain or loss, but has no place in a retirement portfolio designed for safety. Women are more likely to invest conservatively and follow proven advice. They are less likely to be seduced by get-rich-quick schemes or other investment fads.

Women are also less likely to discuss investing and business in their daily conversations with friends, but as a matter of choice rather than as an intellectual defect. Women generally prefer to discuss more personal issues. But when in retirement money becomes a cause for concern, it's likely to gain greater prominence in discussions.

If you are thinking that all this investing stuff is just too complicated, it turns out that women are better investors than men. According to the latest study (19), women hedge fund managers out-performed men by 6% over a nine-month period in 2012. The four ways women make better investors:

WOMEN ARE LESS COMPETITIVE: Men become preoccupied with beating an index or rivals and less focused on actual return. Men tend to invest for the short term and for bragging rights.

WOMEN TAKE FEWER RISKS: Women on average make lower risk investments and seem more protective of their money in general. (Women take fewer risks in other areas of life too, like wearing seat belts and not smoking.)

WOMEN DO MORE HOMEWORK: Women are motivated to be in control by doing more research, and less likely to fall for the hot tip of the day.

Women stay in investments longer, thereby incurring fewer transaction costs.

WOMEN REALIZE THEY ARE NOT IN CONTROL: Realizing that many factors are involved in the markets that they cannot control gives women the necessary perspective to avoid panic. Consequently, women are better at anticipating the next market divergence.

Once you decide to learn the process of investing, you can feel confident that you are likely to be a better investor than many men. This is your opportunity to expand your horizons and activate your inner investor!

FINANCIAL ADVICE

On the other hand, women are more likely than men to seek financial advice. You'll need to devote some attention to detail in choosing the right advisor, but it's important that you combine professional advice with the knowledge you get in an investment club, classes, and self-study. Having personal knowledge and using multiple sources of information is the best hedge against poor investment advice.

The goal here is to get you involved in your own planning that is safe, sustainable and not complex. It's natural that some of us are just more comfortable with professional financial advice, and that's fine. There are different levels of advice, which can be distinguished by title. A certified financial planner (CFP), a personal financial specialist (PFS), and a chartered financial consultant (ChFC) are the best-trained advisors. These individuals usually charge a set management fee of about 1% of your portfolio per year. You probably used a Registered Representative (RR) or stockbroker when buying and selling stocks. The RR will recommend investments and charge a commission on most trades.

Some generic titles like financial planner, investment planner or consultant are not registered or certified and should be avoided. So, if you are looking for an advisor, be sure they are certified. Your advisor should have at least 10 years experience since it takes that long to really understand market complexity. Now that we know how good female advisors are, we are more likely to consider this option.

Personalities and motivations of advisors vary, and some will be oriented toward their own profits. This is your main concern in hiring a stranger. Be sure to check backgrounds at the National Association of Security Dealers (NASD) and your state's security regulators. There are many online resources available regarding how to interview your advisor, and I highly recommend you review them.

Some of the discount brokers offer a tiered system where you can receive full advice, occasional advice, or no advice. If you are in a mostly fixed income portfolio, you may need only advice at the beginning of your investment cycle, since this kind of portfolio is a long-term hold. Then you should re-evaluate your portfolio every three months; you won't need to pay a full time manager. Many of the larger discount brokers have departments that specialize in fixed income. Getting and paying for advice only when you need it seems most efficient.

Barrons Review (20) has published a list of the top 100 women financial advisors, and this year the winner is a 65-year-old woman. Her diverse background affords involvement on different levels as she becomes personally involved with each family. She ends up counseling her clients on many issues besides financial, since they call her to solve a variety of problems. This list might be a good place to start looking for your own advisor.

In summary, your objective is to have a realistic view of economic retirement based on facts, and not opinions of doom and gloom. You can afford life after work if you make a few adjustments, in most cases downsizing your lifestyle. You don't have to worry about Social Security being discontinued, due to its broad-based public dependency and its entitlement mandate. Establishing a working budget becomes your foundation for future decisions.

Safety becomes your priority for any investment. Over investing in the stock market to make up lost ground only creates risk. Individual municipal bonds bought at par value can be the cornerstone of a retirement portfolio. Understanding your relationship with money and becoming educated about the world of finance is crucial. Many of us will pay for advice only when you need it and will consider hiring a woman for that advice.

1. Brandon, E. (10-31-11) "The Recession's Impact on Baby Boomer Retirement" www/money.usnews.com, Retrieved 2-2014 from money.usnews.com/money/retirement/articles/2011/10/31/the-recessions-impact-on-baby-boomer-retirement
2. Kahn, C., (no pub. date)"Retirement of baby boomers at risk." Bankrate.com, Retrieved 2-3-14 from: www.bankrate.com/finance/retirement/retirement-baby-boomers-1.aspx
3. Kerr, J.C., (11-10-11)"Poll finds more boomers working past retirement." News.yahoo.com; Retrieved 2-3-14 from news.yahoo.com/poll-finds-more-boomers-working-past-retirement-080836311.html; _ylt=AoSO8x2qGvBSyF8A8tJXNyoA; _ylu= X3oDMTBydmltOXBoBHNlYwNzcgRwb3MDNgRjb2xvA2dxMQR2dGlkAw--
4. Risotto, A. (5-16-13) "Retirement Security Across Generations" The Pew charitable Trusts, Retrieved from: /www.pewstates.org/research/reports/retirement-security-across-generations-85899476870
5. Social Security: www.ssa.gov/pgm/retirement.htm

6. Center on Budget and Policy Priorities: www.cbpp.org/cms/index.cfm?fa=view&id=3261 "Policy Basics: Top Ten Facts about Social Security, 11-6-12.

7. Social Security Administration (2-2013), "Social Security is Important to Women"; SSA; Retrieved on 2-3-14 from: www.ssa.gov/pressoffice/factsheets/women.htm

8. O'Neil, W. "How to Make Money in Stocks" New York: McGraw-Hill, Inc. 1995.

9. Jones, K.A., (12-3-13) "How to Survive a Bear Market in Bonds"; Schwab.com Retrieved on (12-3-14) from:
/www.schwab.com/public/schwab/resource_center/expert_insight/schwab_investing_brief
/fed_and_bonds

10. PIMCO (no pub date) "High Yield Municipal Strategy" PIMCO.com; Retrieved on 2-3-14 from: www.pimco.com/EN/Solutions/Pages/HighYieldMuni.aspx? origin= Strategies

11. Mahn, K. (1-30-14) "Six Essential Investment Themes to Consider for Your Portfolio"; Forbes.com Retrieved on 2-3-14 from: www.forbes.com/sites/advisor/2014/01/30/six-essential-investment-themes-to-consider-for-your-portfolio/

12. Investopedia (no pub date) "Real Estate Investment Trust, Investopedia.com; Retrieved on 2-3-14 from: .investopedia.com/terms/r/reit.asp

13. REIT.com (no pub date) "REIT Attributes"; REIT.com. Retrieved on 2-3-14 from: /www.reit.com/REIT101/REITAttributes.aspx

14. Koba, M. (8-19-13); "You can't figure out your 401k? You're not alone." CNBC.com; Retrieved 2-3-14 from: www.cnbc.com/id/100965792

15. Moody's: (3-7-2012)"US Municipal Bond Defaults and Recoveries, 1970-2011"; Moody's. com; Retrieved on 2-3-14 from:
www.moodys.com/Pages/rr003_0.aspx?bd=4294966834&ed=4294966848&rd
=4294966834&tb=0&po=
0&sb=&sd=&lang=en&cy=global&searchfrom=SearchWithin&kw=1970%20-2010

16. Benz, C. (8-30-12) "A Sample Retirement Portfolio Using the Bucket Approach." News.morningstar.com: Retrieved on 2-3-14 from:
http://news.morningstar.com/articlenet/article.aspx?id=566257

17. Marquardt, K. (May 2007); "Build Your Perfect Retirement Portfolio" Kiplinter.com; Retrieved on 2-3-14 from: www.kiplinger.com/article/investing/T041-C000-S001-build-your-perfect-retirement-portfolio.html?page=3

18. Clarenbach, J. (6-13-08) "A Retirement Portfolio You Can Set and Forget" (Motley) Fool.com. Retrieved on 2-3-14 from: www.fool.com/personal-finance/retirement/2008/06/13/a-retirement-portfolio-you-can-set-and-forget.aspx?
source=isesitlnk0000001&mrr=1.00

19. Sightings, T. (1-7-2014) "4 ways women make better investors" money.msn.com. Retrieved on 2-28-2014 from: money.msn.com/how-to-invest/4-ways-women-make-better-investor

20. Garmhausen, S. (6-8-13) "Top 100 Women" Online.barrons.com. Retrieved on 4-17-14 from: /online.barrons.com/news/articles/
SB50001424052748703578204578523634164184360? mod=BOL_fa_home

Figure 1: Calculated Risk (4-5-13). Employment Graphs, crgraphs.com. Retrieved 2-3-14 from: www.crgraphs.com

Figure 2: Caveat Bettor staff (11-8-2010) "Chart of the day: US GDP growth" caveatbettor. Retrieved on 2-16-2014 from: http://caveatbettor.blogspot.com/2010/11/chart-of-day-us-gdp-growth.html

Figure 3: Yahoo finance (2-28-2014) "S & P Basic Chart" finance.yahoo.com. Retrieved on 2-28-2014 from: finance.yahoo.com/q/bc? s=%5EGSPC&t=my& l=on&z=l&q=c&c=

Figure 4: Schiller, R.J. (2006) A History of home Values Chart in "Irrational Exuberance" 2nd. www.ritholtz.com/blog. Retrieved on 2-3-14 from:
http://boingboing.net/assets_mt/2011/04/15/home-value.jpg

Figure 5: Ygraphs(12-11-11) "Business cycle phases chart" Ygraph.com. Retrieved on 2-3-14 from: http://ygraph.com/businesscycle

Figure 6: Hunkar, D. (6-25-09), "Do Americans Save Enough?"; Seekingalpha.com. Retrieved on 2-3-14 from: http://seekingalpha.com/article/145248-do-americans-save-enough

Figure 7: ObservationsAndNotes (11-17-10) "100 Years of Treasury Bond Interest Rate

History"; observationsandnotes.blogspot.com. Retrieved date 2-3-14 from:
http://observationsandnotes.blogspot.com/2010/11/100-years-of-bond-interest-rate-history.html

6 CREATIVE INCOME

Creative income is the fourth leg of retirement funding and the one you have the most control over. It's defined as income from any source other than the three legs of Social Security, pensions, and private savings. Usually it's primarily from employment, but it may also include income from alimony, inheritance, rental property, royalties, downsizing, recycling, bartering for service, selling on the Internet, being a subject in a survey, research or focus group, becoming a vendor, and more. There are endless ways to create income, and I hope you keep extending this list.

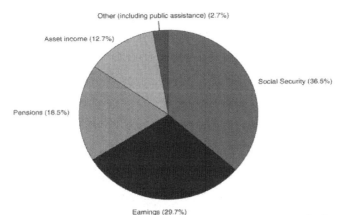

Other (including public assistance) (2.7%)

Asset income (12.7%)

Social Security (36.5%)

Pensions (18.5%)

Earnings (29.7%)

Figure 1: Sources of Retirement Income from SSA reveals that in 2008 nearly 30% of retirement revenue was created from employment.

The pie chart shows sources of income for those over 65 years old in 2008. There is no question that the earned or created income is continually evolving into a larger part of overall income. In other words, if you find that you need to supplement your income in retirement, you will be joined by millions of others.

It seems amazing today that our ancestors needed only three legs, and therefore less income, during their time. Because the Depression era program of Social Security was then intended only as a supplement to our personal savings, many of us today are still left with a shortfall. Some of us may have assumed that Social Security would take care of us, but it really is just a safety net. So, if you haven't been a disciplined saver, as few of us are, then it's critical that you establish a source of creative income.

YOUR EMPLOYMENT IDENTITY

Your individual identity is loosely defined as traits that distinguish and separate you from others. Gender, ethnicity, and religion are three common ways you may be identified. Your employment identity is the transfer of what you do at work to who you are. The longer you stay with your career, the more your work identity becomes ingrained as part of your personality. If you have been a nurse, you still describe yourself as a retired nurse despite not being employed in that area for many years. Many of us will transfer our work identity into our retirement identity.

It's no surprise that your identity or who you are becomes transformed by your career. Work is where you spend most of your time and it's what society recognizes and rewards. You have been conditioned by social and financial reinforcements to become an expert at a certain occupation. Now at retirement age, you will likely reach the point where you want to leave it behind or work part-time at something you really enjoy.

Workers who are the most deeply involved with their employment tend to experience the most identity confusion as their employment status changes, especially if the change is abrupt. Since going from full-time work to full retirement is like going from 65 miles an hour to zero, incremental adjustments make the most sense. They allow you to experience fully the feeling of some empty days without direction. Yes, expect this to happen sometimes once you retire.

Part-time work gives you a preview of what's to come and lessens the intensity of the transition to full retirement. Women tend to become less involved with their work identity and to have less difficulty re-adjusting to retirement. Their larger social networks outside work result in a smoother transition to retirement.

Transitioning from one field of work to another brings out coping and social skills that result in a wonderful exercise for the cerebral cortex. Do not shy away from such a change, as it tends to be very satisfying. You have mastered two skills or careers rather than just one, and that's a big confidence booster. Many part-time retirees fall into this "job change" category and fare very well after some initial adjustments.

But transitioning to full retirement is the biggest adjustment to your identity. This is where planning and preparation will be crucial. If you will not be doing anything that resembles work, then you will need a detailed plan to preserve your sense of purpose, as discussed in prior chapters. As retirees progress into retirement, old identities slowly transition into newfound adaptations.

You may leave your workplace behind, but your work identity is partly preserved as a sense of self. You'll experience a slow transition as you replace your work identity with other involvements, designed by you to complement your interests and needs. Consequently, your transition away from your work identity will become contingent upon your ability to navigate and adapt to your current situation.

Common Sense Conclusion: Your retirement identity is of a successful person who creatively and efficiently manages your money and lifestyle to adapt to the ever-changing economic and personal conditions of the times.

ESTABLISHING CREATIVE INCOME

Since starting a new income stream is often filled with uncertainty at first, I'll begin with a few real success stories from people I know personally. All these retirees had to go through the decision-making process before they settled on a direction. Most started out doubtful and anxious, but persistently stuck with their pursuit until they found success.

A retiree who had been a housewife all her life realized that she didn't have a clear marketable skill. She had raised a family of four children and was recently divorced. Luckily, her domestic skills were transferable to a number of different home service jobs. After months of deliberation, she decided to follow her heart and started a babysitting business out of her home.

She now has no commute to make, no work clothes to buy, and no boss to worry about. "There's fun and laughter in my house every day; I get attached to these little tykes," she explained. The fee in her area for babysitting is about $800 per child per month, and she babysits three children, so her income from this job is higher than her Social Security income. Her application of her existing skills allows her to get paid to watch children she has fallen in love with.

A 62-year-old schoolteacher was laid off in the last recession, along with many other educators. "I knew I couldn't retire then because I just didn't have the money," she complained. Teaching positions were being eliminated due to budget cutting and downsizing. Since she already had two master degrees, she didn't want or need more college education.

She decided to emphasize his communications skills in her job hunting. She eventually got hired full time doing telephone surveys. She continued to work until she qualified for the maximum Social Security benefits at 70. This schoolteacher applied her existing skills to a different field with similar criteria. "Looking back, it turned out better than I thought," she said with a smile.

A young looking 58-year-old woman and her 60-year-old husband decided to take the RV route in retirement. Because they were too young for Social Security, they had to be creative. They now reside completely in the RV, drive around the country at their leisure, and take temporary jobs where they stop. "I'm so relieved not to have a mortgage or rent," she said. When I asked about leaving all those friends behind, she said, "We stop to see friends and relatives on our route, some that we've never met before." The combination of downsizing and creative income has allowed this couple the freedom to explore and connect with family like never before.

Common Sense Conclusion: Converting existing skills and interests into a marketable product or service is the easiest and most reliable way to establish creative income.

At the local Walmart, there is an elderly gentleman who has been a greeter for many years. He told me, "I retired about 25 years ago from accounting, but I've been working here for 13 years." He was first retrained as a cashier, but decided to accept the lower paying position as a greeter because he's tired of dealing with people on that level.

Since he is still working full-time at 80 years old, I assume his other three legs of income are simply insufficient. I asked him about what he would advise others to do if they have a shortfall in retirement. He responded, "Tell them to just deal with it!" He seemed quite proud that he was successful at dealing with his own situation.

Many vendors sell their arts and crafts at summer festivals and fairs. Some crafts are handmade creations, while others are bought wholesale and marked up. One of my favorite vendors is a retiree who makes colorful handmade Mardi Gras and Carnival masks for wearing or for wall art. When I asked her how she liked the work, she said with a grin, "I'm just happy to be out of the office."

She travels to many West Coast cities for the craft fairs. She happily announced to me that she now has a website up and running. This second act allows her to be artistic and creative, travel as she wishes, meet other artists and customers, and get paid as she does it. She's following the philosophy of working part-time at what she truly enjoys.

Many retirees tend just to follow their established interests. An intelligent woman who has an MBA decided to turn her hobby into a business and sell costume jewelry on the Internet. The venture seemed straightforward at first; she had fun shopping for bargains, photographs them, lists them for sale, and ships them out. She wisely began with free ads on Craigslist and the Penny Saver. This process brought in a little business, but not the volume of customers she had hoped for.

So, she decided to upgrade to the heavily populated Amazon and Ebay websites. These websites charge a fee for a short-term listing, so her overhead increased. She also noticed that due to the increased competition, she couldn't sell the products for as much money. This unexpected development compressed her profit margins and made it impossible for her to continue her business.

It's a great advantage to be able to learn from the mistakes of others. In the above example, a business-educated person made a surprising blunder in a basic business. She knows about the importance of a business plan, but overconfidence can be distracting. The lesson from this story is always do your research before you plunge into a new business direction.

Your business plan can be extensively detailed or brief and to the point. You start with a company summary of whom you are and what you plan to do. This section often includes the details of your business along with a vision of what you want to accomplish. Your will describe your product or service and how it benefits your customers. Next you will include a market analysis for which you have researched your competitors. You will also look at market trends and try to determine future growth of your company based on past performance of similar or related businesses.

Your strategy and implementation section covers how you will benefit your target market and how you will develop a large customer base. If you are self-employed, your management section might be short. The financial plan, often last, is critical, since many businesses fail due to lack of initial funding. The financial plan includes your expected cash flow, expenses, sales forecast, and break-even analysis. Many business plan outlines and examples of completed plans are free online for your review.

Common Sense Conclusion: Before starting any type of business, no matter how small, always complete a business plan or template, with an emphasis on the financial plan.

HOME-BASED BUSINESSES

It's no secret that some home-based businesses of the past involved fraud. This usually involved working for a stranger you never met or a mail order scheme where you sent money first. There are websites set up to review and recommend businesses. Some of these are the Better Business Bureau, Department of Consumer Affairs Fraud Department, and the Department of Justice, among others. RetirementJobs.com (1) has provided a list of verified home-based businesses because "Several reputable research projects have concluded that only about 1 out of 100 work-at-home opportunities are legitimate." That's too high-risk for most retirees.

In getting more information about other business, most search engines like Yahoo and Google display store and product reviews by customers. You can also check public records for any prior lawsuits or criminal records, or question their accountant and lawyer. This process is called due diligence, and every prudent businessperson and investor must perform it before moving forward. I've always felt that being self-employed at home with your own business versus working for someone else's business gives you much more control over your life.

The Small Business Administration (SBA) website (2) seems to be a good place to start, since it offers guidelines for businesses that are home-based, women-owned, and senior-owned. The website discusses different types of financing like loans and grants. It even offers resources for finding a business mentor or consultant. Answering survey questions online to determine if a home-based business is appropriate for you is helpful and gets you thinking about the prospect.

If you've been an entrepreneur or in private practice, you can start out performing every work task yourself. You complete your business plan, rent the office, conduct your own marketing, take phone calls, make appointments, do the billing and collections, and sweep up at the end of the day. In time, you may hire office and professional staff. When you are self-employed, you have a network you work within, but don't want to be dependent on one source.

If you're home-based, it's always best if your customers pay you directly. The first step is to identify a business that you can do yourself, and then work on your business plan. No need to have regrets if you're not well suited for self-employment; a regular part-time job tends to provide more stability and reliable income anyway.

Since many of us would like to earn creative income while staying home, let us see what AARP recommends. In the article *Great Home-Based Jobs*, (3) it lists five jobs to fit the bill:

1. Translator/ Interpreter of a foreign language: This will obviously work only if you are fluent in English and a foreign language.

2. Mediator/Arbitrator of legal matters: Most practitioners have a law degree and experience in the field.

3. Graphic Designer on the Internet: A degree and experience in the field are required.

4. Grant Writer: This is technical writing for people with backgrounds in journalism or related fields.

5. Bookkeeper/Accountant: This also requires a degree in the field.

So, AARP recommendations are very specific and require specialized training. They could work for you only if you possess particular skills.

If you like to write, a blog called *My Two Dollars* (4), says: "The second biggest source of income after my day job are my two blogs. It took a long time and a lot of work to get to this point, but now they bring in enough income that I could comfortably give up my day job and still be OK." Most bloggers have expertise in a particular field that they can adapt and continue into their retirement.

"In addition to my job and running my blogs, I have also now learned enough about blogging to offer my services to other bloggers. I have two clients that pay me a percentage of their blog income each month in exchange for helping them get their blogs noticed by search engines and advertisers." He is so successful at creating a new income stream that he doesn't need his day job anymore.

In this Internet age, we all dream of starting a business that runs itself with little or no maintenance. Your site could make electronic sales by charging credit cards and sending a notice to a factory to ship the product while you sleep. We have all seen this on the big websites like Amazon, Apple, Macy's, and other retail sites. But how practical is this for the average person?

William King's article (5), *Online Business Failures--Reasons and Remedies*, confirms that a huge number of Internet business fail every year. In his opinion, the hyped stories of instant millionaires create unrealistic expectations. Just having a website doesn't mean people will swarm to it -- you have to continually market and update your site. He feels a number of online businesses fail simply because they don't offer value to the customer. People will compare you with other competitors before making their selection, so you have to be competitive.

King also feels many people do not have a unique idea and just want to cash in on the latest trend in the market. This is not bad if done correctly, but you still have to distinguish yourself in some way. The customer wants to see some advantage in buying your product. Another problem is attitude; some people are simply not interested in providing a product or service -- they just want to make money. Historically, shoppers will pay a higher price for a distinguished service even if the products are the same.

Lets take a look at King's Seven Common Causes of Business Failure:

1. Emphasis on product rather than on the market and marketing
2. Emphasis on company image

3. Undesirable or Bad Business Partnerships
4. Too complex business model
5. Attempting to pioneer a new product or industry
6. Involvement in a lawsuit or bankruptcy
7. Divorce Proceedings

King's golden rule for business is keeping overhead low, especially at the beginning of any startup. His other theme is keeping it simple and down to earth. It seems that avoiding online business failures is easier and less costly than avoiding failures in the real world. If you had to rent commercial space, furnish and decorate it, hire staff, buy insurance, pay utilities, and do collections, it would cost you much more, regardless of whether you ultimately succeed or fail.

Common Sense Conclusion: An online or home-based business is more practical and cost-effective than buying an existing business or creating any bricks-and-mortar start-up.

ALTERNATIVE MARKETPLACES

Microfinance

Microfinance is a subcategory of financial services involved in loans, savings, and insurance, designed to help the credit-challenged. Many people around the world do not meet the standards to qualify for a commercial bank loan. The microfinance business began by lending money to emerging entrepreneurs so they could start or expand a business. Some parts of this business focus on loans to poverty-identified clients while other areas focus on loans to women or agricultural businesses.

These are higher interest loans because of increased risk of repayment failure. The loan fees may be the same, but it's a higher percent of a smaller loan. There are two ways to use this system: by taking a loan or by providing a loan to collect interest. Your return on the loan will be higher than average rate for bank loans.

Since a higher risk endeavor would be counter to your purpose, why would you risk it? Two reasons: the loan size is usually a small amount, beginning at $25, and you are helping make a difference in the life of someone who is working hard to get ahead. So, it's a small money risk for a important social cause.

People still have to qualify for these loans by showing income or business development. It's designed as a business loan for those with prospects and not just to help people with low incomes. Many websites provide photos and personal information about the loan applicant. Viewing a photo of a struggling family in a third world country, along with an interesting narrative, helps you identify with them. It also provides perspective on how lucky we are compared to what life looks like elsewhere.

Over the years, *The New York Times* (7) has printed various articles on microcredit and microfinance. Since 1998, PlaNet Finance, based in France, has provided micro-financing help to over 140,000 people. They have loaned more than $80 million spread over 60 countries. They are only one of the many companies that make micro-financing a thriving business globally.

In the United States, Grameen America has five offices in New York, as well as offices in Charlotte, Omaha, and Los Angeles. They have had 18,000 borrowers and have exceeded $100 million in loans. The amount of borrowing has tripled from 2008 to 2011, rendering it a booming business. The interest rate on the micro loans is generally 15% plus, so you probably want to act as the bank to collect this rate of return.

Bartercard

According to their website (8), Bartercard is a flexible system that trades and turns merchandise, downtime, spare capacity, vacant seats or rooms into sales. Business owners are attracted to this system simply because it saves money. The old problem with bartering is that one person wants an item, but the other person doesn't need their item in trade. The solution is to convert each of these transactions into trade dollars redeemable for different barter services or products. This is a great resource if you're considering starting your own business.

This alternative marketplace seems like a good idea, but can it really get off the ground? At the time of this writing, Bartercard has over 55,000 members who barter over $60 million a month in 74 global offices. You can barter real estate, auto parts, clothes, antique cars, furniture, and even groceries. Your purchases and sales are electronically recorded and summarized in a monthly statement.

Bartercard even offers franchising opportunities for $25,000. If you've ever investigated franchising, you know how expensive it is. Bartercard provides its franchisees with a multiple revenue stream, training, an accounting system, marketing, and the potential for capital growth. Forward-looking investors like getting involved in an emerging business because of its room to grow.

Since the recession of 2008, alternative marketplaces like Microfinance, Bartercard, Craigslist, Penny Saver and other websites have quietly been expanding to provide alternative market economies. On my recent purchase from a Craigslist ad, I met a seller in a parking lot to buy a piece of furniture. I was at first uncomfortable because the transaction seemed so unorthodox, but I thought I'd give it a try. The seller informed me that there is a whole underground economy like this that avoids taxes and retail markups. Creative income sometimes requires thinking outside the box.

Common Sense Conclusion: Always consider alternative marketplaces because they could make a big financial difference when you're starting a small business.

TRAINING AND EDUCATION

But what if you don't happen to be in a profession that's in demand, or if you aren't Internet or business savvy? Even though taking college classes in retirement can be fun and interesting, you may not have the same time, determination, and stamina for a degree program as you did when you were younger. That does not mean learning new trades are out. But setting a goal of earning a college degree at this stage in life is more time-consuming and expensive than you need for the purpose of a comfortable retirement. You goal is not to start a new career, but just to supplement your income.

You may find that your existing skill set does not transfer well to a part-time job. If you're in a position where retraining could really make a difference, then it's important to be aware of your transferable skills and interests. Getting a little extra education or training could really help in terms of income and type of job.

Many well-paying trades can be learned in less than six months, and training often includes a job placement service after graduation. Below is the beginning of a list of 24 trades requiring six months or less to learn.

BUSINESS	MEDICAL	SERVICE
Paralegal	Phlebotomist	Cosmetologist
Insurance Agent	Certified Nursing Assistant	Driver
Mortgage Broker	Dental Assistant	Manicurist
Real Estate Agent	EKG Tech	Carpenter
Stock Broker	Dialysis Tech	HVAC Tech
Collections	Medical Lab Tech	Bartender
Bookkeeper	Medication Tech	Smog Tech
Loan Agent	Home Health Aide	Security Guard

If you find yourself less than excited or conflicted about retraining, take a visit to the locations where these trades are being practiced. Try to observe and talk to the workers to get a feel for the job. If you're not sure what direction to take, take an aptitude test and an interest inventory to see if your skills or interests have changed over the years. Some of these tests are free online, or you can go a junior college testing office. Many freshmen take these tests the first year in college to help narrow down a major. Part of retirement is accepting that we can be at an occupational crossroads.

This stage of reinventing yourself is tantamount to taking the bull of life by the horns. You'll need an initial burst of energy, with a determined effort to get your momentum going. Once you're in motion, all kinds of social and personal benefits will occur because of your effort. You will increase your education, update your social network, gain a sense of accomplishment, and feel that you now have new purpose and meaning in life. There are also a variety of health benefits from being employed, as previously discussed.

The Occupational Outlook Handbook and website is an indispensable tool in your employment decisions. You can look up jobs in terms of their growth rate, salary, educational level, number of new jobs expected and short-term or on-the-job-training. On the Occupational Outlook website (9), "short-term training" has 113 positions and the "on the job training" category lists 538 different positions. These numbers are constantly changing, of course. Besides offering projected job demand for each field, this guide provides many employment descriptions and salary expectations.

The amount of time and financing needed for retraining can vary widely. A stockbroker needs to be licensed to work for a firm. But only four months of stockbroker school are required to pass the exam to become a licensed stockbroker. I took this low-cost course, passed the exam, and was immediately offered a job with the sponsoring firm, though I choose to work from home instead.

At another time, I ordered a home study book to become a life and health insurance agent. I studied the book over the weekend and passed the exam Monday morning. Depending on the state where you reside, a brief period of study can transform your career or begin a new income stream for you with a minimal amount of effort.

Common Sense Conclusion: Inexpensive short-term training of six months or less, not a college degree, is all you need to enter the job market at this stage.

Self-assessment of transferable skills is a systematic process. If you are unskilled and can't or don't want training, then knowing which of your abilities are transferable is key. The housewife turned babysitter successfully transferred her existing abilities. If you are skilled, but you discover that your skill set is not easily transferable, you'll want to look for variations of that skill. The teacher who turned to telephone surveys because of her communication skills applied this concept.

If you are well educated, but find you can't transfer skills at all, then you may consider a similar or a different field. The accountant turned Walmart employee at the age of 80 is an example of this approach. We can all benefit from additional training and most likely earn a higher salary as well. But because time is more precious now, efficiency is paramount.

EMPLOYMENT AND LONGEVITY

It's not so much that employment itself increases life span; it's the type of involvement in the job and with co-workers that matters. Most studies simply attempt to correlate years worked with years lived. Their focus has been on quantity of work and not quality or type of involvement. But we know that many other factors matter as well.

On further examination, the characteristics of the work position and the stress level must be taken into account. Blue-collar workers on average die sooner than white-collar workers, but just being white- collar doesn't by itself extend your life. It's the behaviors correlated to being white- or blue-collar that make the difference.

Some volunteer workers indicate that their involvement is just as beneficial to them as employment. However, the intent of the volunteer also comes into play. If the volunteer has genuine empathy for the job, it extends his or her life. But, if the volunteer's attitude is simply to combat boredom or to try to extend his or her own life, there is no benefit. It's not an oxymoron that by genuinely helping others, you help yourself.

Some feel that life can be extended when one is in the role of caretaker, a primary role for women. This added element of genuine caring for others ties into our need to be needed and make a difference in life. Being needed by other people who we care about adds an extra social and emotional boost to our own existence. This increase in self-esteem translates to benefits in physical health. I have no doubt that this biochemical reaction in our bodies can be measured once scientific studies catch up.

A study that links longevity to relationships at work (10) involved 820 adults, ages 25 to 65, when they went to their local HMO for a check- up. They worked an average of 8.8 hours a day for 20 years. The focus of the study was on relationships at work between their boss and co-workers. 53 workers died during this period, most of who had poor social support from co-workers. Individuals who claimed they had poor social support were 2.4 times more likely to die than other subjects. The study controlled variables such as smoking, obesity and depression, in order to eliminate their possible relevance.

The office environment in this study was open, and other co-workers were accessible. Social networking sites were blocked. But many people used impersonal email rather than physical contact. The result is that technology usage was causal in creating a distant environment. People have fallen into digital communication that is counter to the "perception of emotional support" which is the key indicator of future health.

Just getting a job to pay the bills will help you financially, but the more involved you become with that job the greater will be your personal benefits. The concept of working part-time in retirement at what you love needs to be rephrased to "work at what you love to extend retirement."

Common Sense Conclusion: The more emotional investment we put into the people at our jobs, the more we can expect to enhance our quality of life and increase our longevity.

CREATURES OF HABIT

Long-term stability at our jobs can lead to long-term security in our lives. Most of us have depended on our employment for our survival. But our employment identity became attached to a place we will now need to leave behind. For some of us, evolving beyond old security bases does not come easily. If you find yourself in a position where you will be leaving your old job for something new, and are reacting negatively to the change, you're not alone.

After establishing trust and reliability with one employer, how do you know you can trust the next employer? Compounding this concern is the fact that some of us feel that we may have lost our edge; our skills are not as sharp as they were years ago. Suddenly, we are full of self-doubt and insecurity.

We may try to cling to our existing position, which could work for a while. Remaining in place helps our budget and puts off the full-time retirement adjustment. But, most of us will be evolving into a different part time position based on our passions that requires some adjustment. I consider this type of transition as a labor of love leading to greater self-actualization and social connections.

I'm currently doing pre-retirement planning with a woman who has maintained a long-term low income position in an expensive city. She is 67 years old, divorced with two grown children. She has remained in the same town she lived in as a child, and has many positive memories of it. This sense of familiarity with her surroundings has provided stability for her.

However, she acknowledges that she is unable to save any money for retirement. Her current job offers no health insurance, no sick leave, no vacation, and she must work six days a week. In discussing the two most obvious options, that of getting a higher paying job in the same town or a finding a similarly paying job in a more affordable area, she suddenly started to feel frightened. "What if I change jobs and get fired or laid off at the new one?" she asked.

In a chaotic world of unreliable people, it isn't easy to give up stability. We all get attached to that which we can trust and rely on, whether it's people or situations. We become anxious when we're uncertain about our next key step. Retirement is no different than any other major life transition. We were in a similar position when we transitioned from junior high school to high school, then to college, to work, to marriage, to parenthood, and now to retirement. We have been through major transitions before, and our successful adjustments have added to our confidence.

Adjusting to loss of job security will take time and planning. First you will need a clear plan that outlines the rationale for the change from work to retirement. If a job change is driven by your budget, it becomes a less emotional issue and is just a matter of fact. Second, you will confront emotional issues as well. When you make a written list of these issues, they appear smaller and more manageable.

Writing is a form of catharsis, or release of emotion, that helps decrease the intensity of your fears. If you lost a job when you were younger, you would automatically start looking for another one without much thought. Fortunately, this same unconscious survival instinct takes over regardless of your life stage. Additionally, some support from loved ones, which is usually the primary support for women, can go a long way. So, in times of uncertainty, you may be able to rely on your partner and your social network to help you sort through your emotions.

Since it's normal to feel some anxiety and loss when retiring, give yourself some time to get used to the idea. Build confidence by combining the memory of past success with a well worked out plan. I always feel that adding a plan B and C to the original plan offers me much greater security going forward, because then I won't be caught off guard.

Resigning from a long-term, secure position, or retiring, is a difficult emotional and financial decision. Even if it makes rational sense to move on, even if your current job situation is negative or stressful, your emotions are attached to what you've known. You may become paralyzed in this attachment and need extra help moving forward.

If you're concerned that you may have lost your edge, brush up on your skills. If you cannot trust the next employer, research the company and its employee turnover. If you still cannot move forward, go to your current boss and talk about staying with the company part-time into retirement.

If you still feel uncertain or anxious, consider some counseling or a life coach. The worst case scenario would be that you expect to stay with the your employer, who then lays you off, and you don't have another plan. You can avoid this type of panic situation with contingency planning for unexpected outcomes.

The philosophy of working part-time at what you love takes on additional importance at this point in your life. This may be the last chance that you have to really follow your passion. When you reach your final days and are looking back, you don't want to be filled with longing or regret. This is your last opportunity to make a difference, completely express yourself, or create a legacy. My personal recommendation to you is to enthusiastically seize this great opportunity to fulfill your most cherished dreams.

Common Sense Conclusion: Overcoming prior employment security takes time, planning, and social support before you can move forward.

ECONOMIZING

Economizing is a frugal attitude displayed in habitual behavior. All of us do some economizing on one level or another. If you came from modest means, then it's already in your blood. If you were spoiled as a child and got your way as an adult, then you may have a little adjusting to do. American lives are often financed by debt for homes, education, cars, boats, furniture, TVs and even vacations.

The American way of life is to buy products and services we don't need and can't afford, and most of us have fallen in love with this way of life. But with retirement, the accumulation phase of life and the emphasis on status symbols ends. We have now matured, and can focus on social cooperation.

Retirement can resemble that of college life. You're not working full time, must economize, have a loosely structured life, and are determining your future direction. Despite low income, you always managed to find something affordable to do as a student, and will now find yourself in a similar situation. If you maintained a frugal lifestyle then, you will have a successful mindset to return to.

The average American consumer spends about 28% on housing, 15% on transportation, 10% on food, 6% on utilities, and 5% on healthcare. These figures change with different age groups and different eras. Besides housing expense that I'll address in the next chapter, automobile expense is next. If you use the various online calculators to determine the "cost to own" your vehicle, you'll be quite surprised how even economy cars get expensive. Reviewing these figures will motivate you to cut your costs even if you're not retired.

I don't think the solution to high transportation costs is necessarily taking the bus. Creative compromising is trying to get by on one car as a couple or an economy car as a single woman. We certainly drive less without a job, and we need to economize, so this solution makes perfect sense. Going completely carless may be more practical if you reside in a metropolitan area where public transportation is well developed. More car sharing businesses are becoming successful alternatives to owning a vehicle. So, if you are a single or a couple, reducing transportation cost can make a big difference.

Economizing within the home can reap financial rewards as well. Remember the show "Design On A Dime," where expensive furniture was replaced by similar, but much cheaper, designs? A retiree who for years was interested in antiques started shopping at thrift stores because she noticed an overlap. After her divorce, she had to start over with very little money.

So, she decorated her entire house with thrift store acquisitions. For her wall art, she was able to find interesting masks from different cultures around the world. "People always comment on my decor; they think I travelled the world to collect all this, but I never left town," she snickers. Since the recession of 2008, she has seen more Mercedes and BMWs parked at these thrift stores.

For those items that were scratched a little, she said, "I like the distressed look; it has more character." She mentioned that many people don't know that thrift stores have new items with the tags still on them. These items are perfect for reselling on the Internet, as she has done for years. She has an eye for design and color, and applies that talent to her new situation. She has turned her passion for interior design and shopping for bargains into a creative income stream.

Frequenting the antiques shops has made her a master at another transferable skill, dickering. No matter if it's an auto repair shop, a retail outlet, a dentist office or restaurant, all prices can be negotiated. I can understand how she can negotiate a price at an auto repair shop, but I asked her how she manages to change retail prices. "You just ask for the manager and point out some small damage to the item you want," she instructed. Even more interesting is that people are happy to accommodate her.

No matter how financially successful you have been in your prior life, your success now will be based on your ability to conserve income through balanced budgeting. Remember the story of the doctor who had to return to work at age 73, after he lost over one million dollars in the stock market? He never did adjust to the fiscal conservatism demanded by the reality of retirement.

You cannot let a current large savings delude you into believing you can act carelessly. If this doctor was ten years older and in poor health, what would he do then?

The Internet affords us abundant data to compare prices and products. The major auction sites have a good assortment of product reviews that I always use if I'm buying online or not. The price comparison sites like Pricegrabber, Bizrate, Shopzilla, and Pricewatch show the surprising range of pricing for the same product. Our goal is not to be cheap; it's to find the best product or service at the best price.

Does this mean that you have to give up Macy's for Walmart? Your budget will determine the extent that you need to make cutbacks. Your acceptance of a downsized lifestyle should not affect the pride or self-esteem you enjoyed in the past. Your current self-esteem should now be based on your successful adaptation to your changing situation.

Common Sense Conclusion: Economizing becomes a skill that you need as you adapt to a fiscally limited retirement budget.

CREDIT CARDS VERSUS CASH

"Do Payment Mechanisms Change the Way Consumers Perceive Products?" (11) This article discusses a study that compares cash to credit card spending. The study found that what method you use could affect how much you spend and what you buy.

The study found we spend more when using credit cards because we apparently feel detached from our money when we don't count the amount with our hands. When we use cash, our awareness of the price increases. This technique of using greenbacks instead of plastic has proven to reduce impulse and recreational buying.

We have all experienced a credit balance that can quickly get out of hand if we pay only the minimum. But, is it prudent to toss the cards in favor of cash? Well, for everyday items and shopping at the mall, cash benefits are apparent. For larger or returnable items, credit cards do carry certain fraud and security protections that we want. It's the debit cards that lack protections if your card number is stolen or lost. The other benefits of cash are that everyone accepts it, and sometimes you get discounts with it.

Business.time.com (12) reveals the best times to use cash instead of plastic. The first instance is when you are trying to stick to a budget. There are many studies that examine spending behavior and they all come to the same result: you spend less with cash. The second instance is when you go to a farmers market or small store -- because 3% of card purchases goes to the card companies. The third instance is when you buy something at a flea market, or any place where prices are negotiable, because you get a better deal with cash. The fourth instance to use cash is when you might have something to return because you are refunded with whatever means you used to pay for it. If you used a credit card, you have to wait days for the refund to show up on your card. I disagree with this last suggestion because I believe that if you have to dispute a transaction or overcharge, you are better off if you paid with a card than with cash.

When using plastic, you can refuse to pay if you have been overcharged or mischarged—a nice protection. The final instance in which to use cash is when you leave a tip in a restaurant for the waiter. Most restaurants are not concerned with the waiter's tips, and restaurants are one of the most likely places for someone to steal your card number. When you hand your card over, you don't know if someone is copying the number by hand or machine. Paying the full bill and tip in cash protects you from this identify theft.

Common Sense Conclusion: Using cash instead of credit cards for everyday purchases automatically reduces your spending.

Here are some additional tips on how to save money on common items (13):

1. Don't pay a dime for banking privileges with free checking.
2. Reduce cable television costs by ordering only the basic package, or use antennas.
3. Shop for car insurance by comparing quotes.
4. Transfer existing debt to get special offers of zero interest.
5. Say goodbye to your land line and consider cell phone use only.
6. Skip the theater and subscribe to Netflix.
7. Increase all insurance deductibles and reduce premium payments.
8. Buy used automobiles only.
9. Ride a bike for short commutes.
10. Change driving habits so you slow down to save gas.
11. Try to fix things yourself rather than pay an expert.
12. Give up your daily Starbucks coffee and treat yourself to coffee at home.
13. Drink healthy tap water and skip bottled soft drinks.
14. Eat less red meat for better health and savings.
15. Consider buying generic brands at the store.
16. Use coupons to reduce food bills.
17. Eat out less and go out for lunch instead of dinner.
18. Grow you own fruits and vegetables in your backyard.
19. Avoid pre-packaged goods and buy in bulk.
20. Use a drying rack or clothesline to dry clothes.
21. Plant shade trees to lower your energy bill.
22. Take shorter showers and water your lawn less often.
23. Avoid buying by not browsing in retail stores.
24. Don't renew your gym membership, and start your own exercise program.

25. Color your hair at home.
26. Go to the library rather than buy books.
27. Pay off your credit card balance each month.
28. Use cash instead of credit/debit cards so you'll spend less.
29. Quit smoking for better health and savings.
30. Shop on Craigslist or Penny Saver and skip retail stores.
31. Forgo the expensive vacation for a local trip.

In summary, creative income is now averaging 30% of retirement income, and this amount is increasing. Accepting some work in retirement is critical for most of us, and enhances our health and self-esteem. If we find our skill set from work does not transfer well to a part-time job, we need to consider retraining. The amount of education we need in our final careers should be much less than in our earlier ones. Our personal involvement in our new careers rewards us with longevity. Alternative marketplaces provide additional options for creative income. Many of us will consider experimenting with cash as a budgetary tool. Innovative economizing to reduce expenditures becomes an effective and fun way to balance our budget.

Figure 1: Social Security Admin. (2008); "Income of the Aged Chartbook, 2008." Socialsecurity.gov. Retrieved on 3-17-14 from: www.socialsecurity.gov/policy/docs/chartbooks/income_aged/2008/iac08.html

1. Staff Writers(2014 copywrite) "Verified work at home opportunities." RetirementJobs.com retrieved on 2-4-14 from: http://www.retirementjobs.com/career-advice/self-employment/work-at-home/
2. www.sba.gov/content/women-owned-businesses
3. Hannon, K. (8-11-11) "Great Home-Based Jobs" AARP.org. retrieved on 2-4-14 from: www.aarp.org/work/working-after-retirement/info-08-2011/work-from-home-jobs-for-retirees.html
4. David (2010 copywrite) "My Sources of Alternative Income and how I make them work for me."; mytwodollars.com Retrieved on 2-4-14 from: mytwodollars.com/2008/02/21/how-i-make-extra-money-and-rewards-every-single-month/
5. King, Wm (4-27-2007) "Online Business Failures - Reasons and Remedies." ezinearticles.com; Retrieved on 2-4-14 from: ezinearticles.com/?Online-Business-Failures---Reasons-And-Remedies&id=542025
6. Dawber, C. (11-18-2005) "Seven Common Causes of Business Failure"; ezinearticles .com; Retrieved on 2-4-14 from: ezinearticles.com/?Seven-Common-Causes-of-Business-Failure&id=98787
7. Kristof, N. (12-28-2009) "The Role of Microfinance" nytimes.com Retrieved 2-5-2014 from: ttp://kristof.blogs.nytimes.com/2009/12/28/the-role-of-microfinance/?_php=true&_type=blogs&_r=0
8. Bartercard staff(no pub date)"Use bartercard to improve your profitability" bartercardusa.com. Rerieved 2-4-2014 from: www.bartercardusa.com/
9. OOH staff.(1-8-2014)"Jobseeker or Worker"; bls.gov. Retrieved on 2-1-2014 from: /www.bls.gov/audience/jobseekers.htm
10. Vieru, T. (5-12-2011) "Study links Longevity to Workplace Relationships"; news.softpedia.com; Retrieved on 2-5-2014 from: /news.softpedia.com/news/Study-Links-Longevity-to-Workplace-Relationships-199910.shtml

11. Chatterjee,P., Rose, R.L.(Vol. 38; 2012) "Do payment mechanisms change the way consumers perceive products; ideas.repec.org; Retrieved on 2-5-2014 from: ideas.repec.org/a/ucp/jconrs/doi10.1086-661730.html
12. White, M.C.;(9-10-2012) "When Cash is King: 5 situations in which you should pay with hard currency"; business.time.com. Retrieved on 2-5-2014 from: /business.time.com/2012/09/10/5-times-you-should-always-pay-cash/
13. Jason(6-16-2008) "75 ways to save money every month" affordableschoolsonlinne.com. Retrieved on 2-5-2014 from: affordableschoolsonline.com/75-tips-to-survive-a-down-economy/

7   GIVE ME SHELTER

"Retirement can be a great joy if you can figure out how to spend time without spending money." -- Anonymous

Downsizing is an expected adjustment in retirement and starts with your budget. The largest expense, of mortgage or rent, is always first on the chopping block. There are many different ways to adjust your bottom line here. Historically, roughly 80% to 90% of us remain in our current residence and don't downsize. I expect this number to change since we over bought for our primary home and we are not savers. So, for many of us, downsizing may not only make sense, but may be essential.

In 2010, TopRetirements.com (1) conducted a forward-looking survey:

39% of baby boomers plan to relocate out of state or country
46% plan to move out of their "current metro" area
2 % expect to stay where they are

62% are looking for an average cost of living in a new location
30% are looking for a lower cost of living in a new location
58% would relocate for a lower tax burden

51% prefer to move to the Southeast
17% prefer to move to the Southwest
17% prefer to move to the West

This survey reveals the intent of boomers and not the final statistics. But with the current real estate economy as it is, these figures seem very probable. The noticeable difference from past years is the big number of boomers who plan to relocate. The historical number of 80 to 90% remaining at home is now down to 2%. That's an amazing difference and an indication of how important downsizing has become -- the first focus for most of us. Depending on your individual situation and location, you have a number of creative options.

RENTING VERSUS OWNING PROPERTY

Renting is reported as the best possible option for extending your retirement money. Many articles compare renting to owning, and about 70% to 80% of them confirm that renting is cheaper. These articles cite the many hidden costs of owning, like insurance, taxes, maintenance, and unexpected repairs.

Owning is better if you can benefit from the mortgage tax deduction. One caveat is that if your taxes are relatively low or nonexistent, your inability to take advantage of this great deduction is costly. But if you're working full time and earning a sizeable income, you benefit from being able to deduct mortgage interest on your taxes.

If you own a home but decide to rent a place instead, you can either sell your home now, wait for it to appreciate, or rent it out to someone else when you move. If you own a home and want to stay there, you can refinance your debt, rent out a room, or list it as a vacation rental on weekends. If refinancing is complicated due to depressed values caused by the recession, you may have to be patient for values to return -- unless you qualify for one of the government-sponsored programs.

While you wait, you can generate some creative income by renting out a room or a garage. Yes, this will take some thought and adjustment, but that's why you're reading this book, because you're willing to make calculated adjustments that benefit your bottom line. If you decide to take the weekend rental option, you can avoid daily exposure to a roommate. The great benefit here is that weekend renters are paying substantially more per night for your entire house. In this case, you get to take the weekend away and get paid for it.

There is an old principal that says no one should have any debt in retirement. That principal suggests that paying off your mortgage is wise. The problem I have with this theory is that you can become house rich and cash poor. Having a half million dollars or more tied up in the home's equity is not going to produce income for you. Plus, real estate is not very liquid, and you may need money in case of an emergency.

This situation of seniors having equity, but are cash poor became so problematic that the housing industry and the federal government addressed it by offering reverse mortgages. If you have substantial equity, refinancing at a lower rate while putting money in an income-producing account makes sense. If you are wealthy, then paying off your house to eliminate debt is great, as long as you can cover your day to day budget needs.

If you are a renter and want to stay where you are, negotiate for lower rent with the owner. If you have ever been a landlord, you know how expensive it is when your tenants move. The house must be cleaned, repaired, and often painted. The yard has to be kept up during vacancy, utilities must be left on for new tenants to try them out, you must advertise, and, of course, you must continue to pay the mortgage, insurance, and taxes on the property. Estimates for the cost of tenant turnover average about $2000 for an apartment and double that for a single-family dwelling.

I recently advised someone to talk to the owner about lowering her rent before she decided to relocate. I suggested that she ask him for a larger price reduction than she really needed or expected to get. I know owners like to negotiate. She asked for $300 off her rent, so the owner gave her $200 off. This amount may not sound like much, but it made a noticeable difference in her budget. You can also negotiate price if you sublet a room or sign up for a weekend vacation rental.

If you own your home now and want to sell at some point, you can keep your equity profit tax-free on the sale of your personal residence. The first $250,000 (for single people) or $500,000 (for couples) of your sale is not taxable. To qualify you need to reside in the home any two of the last five years. This money can be a significant boost for your savings.

If you are downsizing to a smaller house, be sure to sell your first house before you buy another house since many people unwittingly get stuck with two mortgages. Even in a normal real estate market, it takes six months to sell a home. The new home should have the lowest down payment possible so you have maximum liquidity.

You probably know people who are house rich, but cash poor. Not having access to your money when you need it is not common sense retirement. If your primary house has lost value, so that selling it doesn't make sense, you will have to be patient while you wait for its value to return. You have an option to rent out your house and move to a smaller one. This is a viable option if you don't mind being a landlord.

Common Sense Conclusion: It's more cost-effective to rent rather than own property since your home equity cannot produce an income stream.

That being said, there have been a few locations (Las Vegas, Phoenix, Sacramento, Orlando) where the real estate crisis has depressed values so much that owning a home is actually cheaper than renting. Because of the large number of people who have lost their homes, increased demand has been placed on rental units, which has led to rent increases. This situation will correct itself as the economy improves.

Such places would now be ideal for real estate investment. There is certainly nothing wrong with buying distressed property and turning a profit down the line. Just be sure you are okay being a landlord and you have a good feel for real estate and employment trends in the neighborhood.

All the above scenarios assume you are relocating in the same town or city where you already live. If you live in New York City, San Francisco, Stamford, Silicon Valley, Honolulu, or any other expensive area, you are probably at least considering a relocation out of the area. Perhaps you're ready for that cute little college town, and reconnecting with the educational experience.

WHEN TO SELL YOUR HOME

If you own property, you are a real estate investor. Many of us don't see it that way, but in order to maximize our profit from this investment, we need to. Our home is usually our largest investment and can influence our budget more than any other income source. When to sell may be the most important financial decision we make for the rest of our lives. Most of us who own our home have experienced a decline in its value since the recession of 2008. The national real estate market appears to have bottomed out in 2012 and is in recovery, so that's good news for all of us.

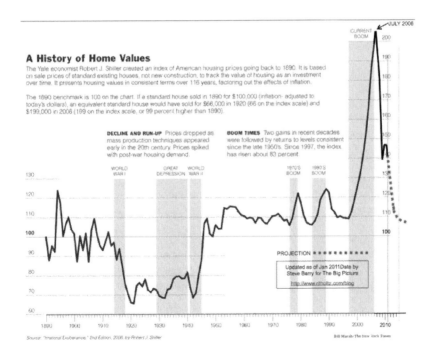

A History of Home Values

The Yale economist Robert J. Shiller created an index of American housing prices going back to 1890. It is based on sale prices of standard existing houses, not new construction, to track the value of housing as an investment over time. It presents housing values in consistent terms over 116 years, factoring out the effects of inflation.

The 1890 benchmark is 100 on the chart. If a standard house sold in 1890 for $100,000 (inflation-adjusted to today's dollars), an equivalent standard house would have sold for $66,000 in 1920 (66 on the index scale) and $199,000 in 2006 (199 on the index scale, or 99 percent higher than 1890).

Figure 1: U. S. History of real estate prices.

The Real Estate Cycle

Compared to other markets, the real estate cycle moves slowly. During WWI (grey bar), around 1914, we notice a steep decline in prices that did not return to prior levels until about 1944 -- 30 years. This recovery was especially slow due to the depression and WWII. Let's look at the length of the cycle after 1950, where we see more stability. The four down cycles lasted about seven years (ranging from 3.5 years to 11 years) and the four up cycles lasted about six years (ranging from four years to nine years.).

We can confirm that as of 2012 a new cycle of price appreciation has started. We know the up cycles have lasted four to nine years, but since we don't know how long this one will last, we focus on changes in the price curve. That is, we stay invested until we see three months of price declines and we then list our property for sale, if that's our intent. We don't know exactly when that will be because the price trends from our chart determine our decision.

That is, our intended goal is to sell our home near the top of the cycle. We want to buy near the bottom of the cycle, if we are downsizing to a smaller place. That may involve renting for a while to let the cycle fall again.

If you are a real estate buyer, then you know buying in 2012 to 2014 is close to the bottom of the market, and is an excellent time to buy, especially when combined with low interest rates. It's very important to know where you are in the cycle to determine your buy or sell decisions.

Many folks made the mistake of buying in the mid-2000s because they did not realize that the curve was over-extended far beyond the average. If you are interested in learning more about chart patterns, you can pick up a book on chart technical analysis.

Regression to the Mean

A second important concept in analyzing price movements is regression to the mean, or return to the average. Real estate historically tends to appreciate at the rate of about 4 to 5 percent a year, depending on location. From 1998 through 2005, we saw appreciation of triple to quadruple that amount, which is why this period was considered a real estate bubble. When that happens, we expect a price return to the average of increase of 4 to 5 percent. But since the market was so over extended, or so high, returning to its average would mean a significant price correction. This correction is what we saw from 2006 through 2012.

Now that the market has corrected itself, should we expect to see returns of 4 to 5 percent again? I think that is a fair assumption for the long term. In the near term, I expect the rate of price increase to be from 5 to 10 percent for the first two or three years. I expect this because the market has over-corrected and is expected to return to its historic average. After sharp declines or increases, we often see a type of sharp rebound effect in the opposite direction. As we examine the chart above again, notice how sharp increases are often followed by sharp decreases and vice versa.

We need to understand the concept of regression to the mean in order to understand the trends of the cycle. The regression of prices is not a gauge for buying or selling per se. That's because when a trend gets out of balance, it can be out of balance for many years before it returns to the average, which was the case during the Depression.

Knowing that the market is out of balance determines your buy or sell strategy going forward. Your goal is to sell near the top or buy near the bottom of the cycle, depending on your financial strategy.

Local Economic Factors

The third key factor for deciding when to sell your home is your local economy. If your area is influenced by a lucrative industry, like high tech in Silicon Valley, then your property becomes supported by local market conditions, and waiting to sell can pay off. If your city is having economic problems, like the Detroit bankruptcy, your property may not appreciate much, and waiting to sell may not pay off as much.

Real estate investors take many economic factors into consideration when pricing homes for sale. I try to downplay the national trends of inflation, unemployment, GDP, wage increases, hiring trends, and other leading economic indicators in favor of the local statistics. If you reside in California or New York, where the housing market cycles are pronounced, data based on the more stable Midwest states would not be helpful to you.

Leading economic indicators often change before the economy reflects the change. So, studying market cycles and other economic data are intended to be forward looking and semi-predictive. Currently, figures tell us that the housing market is in a slow growth recovery. Now that there's a positive trend, we can focus on price increases within the current cycle to determine our sell point.

Let's take a real world example: In 1999, I purchased a home in California, a couple of years after the bottom of the real estate cycle there. For the next five years, the market increased at a rate of about 20% per year. I checked the local newspaper for the monthly price changes in my zip code.

The prices went up year after year until the third quarter of 2005, when the first sign of a change in the trend of house prices in my zip code was noticed. When the newspaper clearly revealed falling prices for three months, I put the property up for sale. The comparable properties at that time indicated an increase of 122% from the purchase price. Within four months, the house for a profit of 114%.

How do we know that three down months of prices have signaled the end of an upward trend? Well, we never know for sure. Our decision is still determined by where we are in the cycle. The market was so far above its normal rate of 4 to 5% a year that I would expect a regression to the mean to occur. The decline in those three months was accompanied by poor economic factors like increasing unemployment and poor wage growth; both indicators help confirm a true downward economic trend.

So, in this case, the real estate cycle had been overextended for many years, a regression to the mean or a correction was overdue, economic indicators had weakened, and there were three months of price declines. It was a perfect time for real estate investors and homebuyers who knew what to look for.

As I noted earlier, the first $250,000 profit from your personal residence is not taxable for singles and the first $500,000 is not taxable for couples. These tax breaks make the decision of when to sell crucial for your future budget. After I sold near the top, I rented a home for five years to allow the price correction to take full effect. When the cycle appeared to increase for three months, I purchased another house, near the bottom of the cycle in 2011, for 56% off the original selling price.

The current economic recovery seems weaker than prior ones, and new families will be slow to buy homes due to higher unemployment for those in their 20s and 30s. So, it may be 10 years or so for real estate to regain its highest price levels. But, it's comforting to know that home values are moving in a positive direction.

Few people take the time to learn about real estate cycles and other factors that cause prices to change. A little study in this area could make a big difference when selling your home. If you bought a home near the top of the cycle, it's going to take awhile to return to normal levels, maybe not until the early 2020s. But, the positive news is that real estate will eventually return to these seemingly lofty levels.

Common Sense Conclusion: With a little awareness and patience, you can time the sale of your home to successfully maximize your profit.

Some of us plan to stay in our home until our final days, regardless of our financial situation. If you are in a financial position to accomplish this goal, then let me congratulate you. I would probably sell my home at the top of the market just to benefit the next generation. I don't become emotionally attached to a house because I see it as just bricks and mortar. It's not the fact of owning that makes a home; it's the familiar surroundings, emotional connection, stability of location, and who is in the home.

FINDING THE RIGHT LOCATION

Remember in mid-life when we wanted to relocate for a better job or environment? Many of us consulted the *Places Rated Almanac*, by David Savageau (2). In his book, he rates 343 towns and cities in the United States and Canada. The rankings are based on the following categories:

Cost of Living	Based on home prices, transportation, groceries health care, utilities, property taxes, and college tuition
Jobs increase	Based on the number created and expected
Housing	Payment amount on a 15-year mortgage
Transportation	Based on a daily commute, public transportation, highways, air and rail service
Education	Based on the number of students in the community, Of four and six year public and private colleges
Health Care	Based on family practitioners, medical specialists, surgical specialists, and hospital beds available
Crime	Based on violent and property crime rates
The Arts	Number of classic radio stations, artist's bookings, symphonies, operas, ballets, theaters, and museums
Recreation	Supply of public golf, restaurants, movies, zoos, aquariums, sports teams, and theme parks
Climate	Based on hot and cold months, freezing days, etc.

Yes, there appears to be some overlap with cost of living and housing and education. The rating may not be perfect, but the information is still a lot more useful than we had previously. If you're a renter, house prices and property taxes may not be that important to you.

For retirement purposes, the categories of health care, cost of living, climate, recreation, or arts may be your priority. It's always interesting to see where your current town ranks on each factor and total score. The important lifestyle factors in your mid-life working years are different from the factors for your retirement.

Savageau ranks places from the perspective of retirement as well, choosing six factors instead of ten. His "retirement categories" include ambiance, cost of living, climate, personal safety, services, and the economy. Ambiance includes arts and recreation. Personal safety refers to the incidence of crime. Services include medical and hospital rankings. His book includes a questionnaire to help you determine which factors are important to you. I found it interesting that the town where I live did not qualify as one of the over 200 recommended retirement choices.

In his book's "Putting It All Together" section, you can compare a town or city's individual score with its overall rank. Take your time weighing all the factors, because some unexpected correlations occur. If you are looking for a very low cost of living, you may be directed to rural, economically blighted areas, or to economically depressed cities like Detroit. You must balance the variables to determine what works best for you.

There are some noticeable contrasts in statistics from his 2004 publication and those from more current surveys. In the 2004 book, he reported that:

1. 94% of people ages 55 and 65 remain at their current residence.

2. 1 in 27 retirees sell or rent their primary home and downsize to an apartment or condominium in their town.

3. 1 in 70 older adults moves out of town, but stays in the same state.

4. 1 in 94 retirees moves to another state.

5. 1 in 432 retirees relocate abroad, and most of them return to their native country.

The 2004 survey gives us a baseline of how much we have changed in just 10 years. Since we over-bought on our primary homes and are not savers, we now embrace downsizing as a natural solution. If you are an American thinking about moving abroad, you might consider that this is the least successful of the relocations. Savageau reports that a basic rule for successful relocation is that the day-to-day attractions of a new destination must be much, much stronger than the day-to-day attractions of home.

If one of your day-to-day attractions is lower taxes, you might be considering a different state. Federal taxes are the same, but your individual state's tax structure can make a difference in your finances. The Kiplinger website (4) reported the most and least friendly states for retiree taxes.

Best States	Worst States
Alaska	Rhode Island
Wyoming	Vermont
Georgia	Connecticut
Arizona	Minnesota
Mississippi	Montana
Delaware	Oregon
Nevada	Nebraska
Louisiana	California
South Carolina	New Jersey
Florida	New York

You may have noticed many financial advisors are suggesting that, for affordability, retirees relocate out of the country. They often present this suggestion as the Holy Grail for retirees on a budget. They rarely mention the social or psychological impact of an out-of-state or out-of-country move.

It's not easy to give up your familiar surroundings, your friends and acquaintances, your family, and your whole social network. Even small things matter, like the comfort of your favorite restaurant or the tree-lined street where you take a morning stroll. I live next to a park and playground where I hear the children laugh and play everyday, and I would never want to give that experience up. Even small conveniences we take for granted add up, and we may find we sorely miss them.

I know a couple who were both college professors on the East Coast. They relocated to Phoenix, Arizona, because of its affordability, warm climate, and popularity with other retirees. They bought a large home on a desert lot with golf course views. It all sounded just perfect to me until I went to visit them. Their air-conditioning bill was over $400 per month and they kept it at an uncomfortable 80 degrees. The daytime summer temperatures averaged 106 degrees, and would cool off to only about 90 degrees at night.

They had to keep the house cool when they left it because otherwise their candles would melt and their papers would curl up! I asked them if we could go out somewhere, but they complained that it was too hot to go anywhere. If you enjoy nature and outdoor activities, being hostage to the climate like this would clearly not work for you.

They could have avoided their situation if they had planned better, and visited Phoenix during the summer months. They would have noticed that the streets were deserted by noon and that air-conditioning was a constant feature of the city. This extreme climate presents dangers for those 65 years and older, who are more prone to heat stress than younger folks. Some prescription medications also reduce the body's ability to adjust to heat. Ergo, I'm recommending against any extreme climate for retirees, no matter how affordable the area.

If you're thinking about relocating overseas, you can receive Social Security, but you will need to replace Medicare with other health insurance, either local insurance or an international policy. The money you already paid into Medicare thus becomes a net loss.

The other critical medical question concerns the quality of the hospitals and doctors, which can vary greatly depending on the country. If you have mobility problems, now or in the future, you'll find facilities for the disabled generally inadequate overseas.

Besides medical issues, establishing a new social network within a foreign culture is more difficult than you probably realize. You are now an immigrant and a minority in a strange place. Unfortunately, the fact that you are American could mean you are unwelcome. This cultural shock will likely lead to isolation, disillusionment, and a return to your home country.

Another retiree I know decided to relocate to Costa Rica because her aunt told her it's inexpensive. Her only income was about $1,050 from Social Security. She lived in an expensive city in the United States that with her reduced income had become grossly unaffordable. But rather than investigate all the options and programs available here, she followed her aunt's suggestion without much thought.

Once in Costa Rica, she discovered that there were no street signs on the roads in her town, and few buildings were numbered. At first, she wandered around trying to orient herself. She complained about insects inside her hotel room and the lack of modern conveniences. She was also caught off guard when her Medicare would not transfer overseas and realized that local policies put pressure on her budget.

Without a car, she had to walk all over town trying to find items that may not even exist there. The photo she emailed me showed her standing by herself surrounded by jungle, without a building in sight. She inadvertently isolated herself without any backup plan, and no social network at all.

Common Sense Conclusion: The more culturally different or remote the retirement relocation, the longer and more difficult the adjustment, with the least likelihood of success.

RETIREMENT COMMUNITIES AND CARE FACILITIES

Where and how this generation retires is continually changing for the better. Where and how the baby boomers die is changing more slowly. Before you pass over this section, remember that about 70% of us will see a hospital, nursing home, or long-term care facility as our final stop, unless we attempt to avoid it.

Independent Living

Senior housing, independent living, senior retirement communities, or whatever name is used in your area, may vary. Residing in your own home is independent living, of course, but let's take a look at planned communities.

This type of independent living is for those over 55 years old who are still active and able to take care of their daily living needs. The activities of daily living (ADLs) refer to the person's ability to dress, bath and groom, eat without difficulty, control bowel movements, and have reasonable mobility (walking).

Independent living arrangements can vary dramatically from staying in your own home, with an option for home health care, to facilities that provide meals, transportation, cleaning, and social activities. The larger commercial developments, like Sun City, Del Webb, Leisure World, or Four Seasons, are designed for the active senior in good health. These communities often have conveniences such as stores, beauty salons, golf and other recreation, dining, classes, theaters, and even ballrooms to encourage socializing.

Many seniors purchase homes in these communities, but renting gives you access to them as well. These communities range from the expensive to affordable senior apartments. Amenities can vary wildly, so a personal visit is always the best. Some people move directly into these communities as soon as they sell their house. They often transfer equity to the purchase of a home in their new community. In the larger developments, the number and breadth of recreational and academic activities are too numerous to list, and leave no excuse not to be socially involved.

These developments solve the problem of senior isolation even for people who are disabled. If you know people who live in these settings, you know they tend to be very happy and socially engaged. They also try to encourage all their friends to move there too. Most of us will start our final chapter with some type of independent living and remain in this situation most of our retirement years.

Assisted Living

As our age advances and our bodies show their natural decline, we may need increased care. Assisted living offers the benefits of a nursing home, but it's more personalized and has fewer restrictions. Whether you are single or part of a couple, you can have your own apartment with complete freedom of movement. Some residents even continue to work part-time or volunteer. These places usually have a sense of community with multiple units, but also provide around-the-clock medical care.

Most seniors are satisfied with the benefits of this type of care because they needn't sacrifice their independence. Their family can be satisfied knowing that their senior member is well cared for instead of being isolated somewhere. Not all long-term care insurance covers assisted living. So, you need to be sure it's included in your policy. Since the average age of someone in assisted care is 83 years old, if you're healthy you may want to wait awhile before getting this policy.

There is no stigma to living in this situation since most assisted living communities are set up like apartment complexes and visually blend into the neighborhoods quite well. Many communities encourage residents to "age in place." This means that as your need for assistance increases, you can feel secure that it will be provided. Many seniors see assisted living as the best balance between freedom and reliable care.

Adult Day Care

Adult day care is an organized program to promote social and health activities for the disabled or elderly. These programs are offered five days a week for six to eight hours a day. Services usually include lunch, support groups, education, personal care, recreational activities, mild exercise, and day trips. Some locations have nursing staff and provide transportation to and from the program. There are Adult Day Health Care programs that focus on general medical support and some that focus just on Alzheimer's patients.

The senior benefits by increasing his or her socialization, improving self-esteem, doing some exercise, and practicing healthy habits. Seniors in this kind of program are expected to perform their ADLs and not need 24-hour supervision. These programs can also be a godsend for those of us taking care of an elderly person. They provide a needed respite for the caretaker and even allow time for outside employment.

Although this is a future topic for most of us, it should be discussed well in advance of the time when decisions must be made. Most of us will resist giving into the fact that we need some help. Accepting help means admitting we are losing our abilities and independence --that's an extremely frightening prospect, and it entails some adjustment.

These programs can be for profit or nonprofit, and may be public or private, with a wide range of fees. Even though the daily cost is usually around $68, Medicare does not cover adult day care. Medicaid does pay for the many expenses incurred. Some private insurance policies provide for this option, as does long-term care, depending on your contract.

Home Health Care and Hospice

Home health care is a great option for those who need assistance while recovering from illness, injury, or surgery, since most of the medical assistance a rehab center or hospital can provide arrives at your home. Health care workers are licensed nurses and therapists employed by home health agencies, hospitals, and public health clinics that must adhere to federal regulations.

This mobile medical service allows the patient to continue to live in his or her own home through the final years. The statistical trend shows that fewer of us are passing away in hospitals and more of us in our homes. From my experience as a hospice therapist, I can certainly say most people prefer their home by far. There is usually a family member or close friend who lives there to assist them.

Medicaid and Medicare Part A and B reimburse skilled nursing care, social service counseling, physical and speech therapy, occupational services, and more. The home health company must be approved by the reimbursing agency and your doctor must verify that you are home bound.

Hospice care emphasizes palliative rather than curative treatment, with the focus on the natural dying process. To qualify for this service, the patient's life expectancy must usually be less than a year. The hospice concept is that dying is part of life, and that both the patient and the family should be comforted and emotionally supported during this process.

Hospice nurses and social workers also provide home-based treatment. Maybe you've had an opportunity to see either home health or hospice care when taking care of your parents. These options are certainly the most comfortable and desirable situations for both patient and family. It's extremely calming to pass away in your own home, with all the people and symbols of your life surrounding you.

Skilled Nursing Facilities (SNF)

Skilled nursing facilities, convalescent homes, nursing homes, and rest homes are some of the terms applied to full residential medical care. Besides seniors, they admit younger adults with physical or mental disabilities from acute-care hospitals. These patients have trouble with their ADLs and need 24-hour nursing care. Medicare Part A services cover a shared room, meals, physical and occupational therapy, social services, medications, speech therapy, and medical equipment as needed.

According to the Center for Disease Control, there are over 16,000 nursing homes, with over 1.7 million residents, at an occupancy rate of 86%. More than half the residents have no close relatives, and 46% have no children. The average age is 78, and women, due to their greater longevity, compose about 70% of all residents. Medicare and Medicaid will reimburse approved facilities.

Most of us have visited a nursing home and formed an opinion about this kind of facility. Compared to other options, it seems less favorable. As a hospice therapist, I visited many patients in different nursing homes. They provide quite a range in both appearance and service, from lower cost and minimal care, to the elegant and expensive. For many patients, it's the last stop, the place where they "knock on heaven's door." Still, without this care, the end of life would be a real nightmare.

Common Sense Conclusion: We will enjoy independent living for most of retirement, but will plan and take control of future assistance as needed.

GOVERNMENT ASSISTANCE PROGRAMS

Many middle class folks who worked most of their lives are not aware of all the social programs for seniors. Now is a good time to become familiar with services you've already funded and can benefit from.

Senior Community Service Employment Program (SCSEP)

This program is funded under Title V of the Older Americans Act that provides training for low-income people over 55 years old. If you are unemployed with poor employment prospects, you qualify for this program even if you speak English as a second language, are disabled, or homeless.

SCSEP provides job and community service training, counseling, and placement in non-profit and public facilities, including libraries, hospitals, schools, senior centers, and other government agencies. Enrollment priority is given to those over 60 years old, and to veterans and their spouses.

Seniors in this program average about 20 hours of work a week. Even though salaries begin at your state's minimum wage, workers are encouraged to venture into the private sector after they've been trained. Goodwill Industries is one of the on-the-job training sites that keeps employees after training.

At the present time, SCSEP has over 76,000 participants, of whom 87% are at or below the federal poverty level. About two-thirds of retirees receive financial subsidies for training and employment. To qualify you must not have a family income of over 125% of the federal poverty level. In 2013 this level was $11,490 for a single person and $15,510 for a married couple. The poverty level changes each year, as determined by the Department of Health and Human Services, and it's easy to find online. For more information, contact your local American Job Centers or call 1-877-872-5627 for assistance.

Housing Choice Voucher Program

Social Security and Medicare are the government assistance programs most often used by seniors. Another important program, designed to cut housing expense to 30% of total income, is the Housing Choice Voucher Program, also known as Section 8. This is a federally funded program to help elderly, disabled, and low-income people pay for safe and affordable housing.

This program was created in 1974, not as a result of substandard housing per se, but as a response to the high percent of income the poor paid for housing. Receiving Section 8 assistance does not relegate you to the poorest part of town. It can be used in public housing or for a private residence. Any landlord in any neighborhood -- even in Beverly Hills -- can accept this program.

The amount of assistance you receive depends on your family size, your income, and where you live. The program allows you to pay only 30% of your income for rent, and subsidizes any additional rent up to $2200 per month. If your Social Security checks were $1,200 per month, you would only pay $360 per month for rent. In some cases, the housing voucher can be used to purchase a modest home.

Your qualifying income should not exceed 50% of the county or city income median. So, in the application process, your zip code median income will be noted. You can then apply through your local public housing agency, which is listed on the HUD website. It is common for this program to have demand above its supply of homes. So, it's very typical for a waiting list to form in most locations.

After you reach the top of the list, the housing voucher is issued to you. You may then search for a suitable property. For additional information and applications for assistance see www.hud.gov. Each state has contact information listed on this website.

The Housing Choice Voucher Program for seniors is one of the most overlooked government assistance programs. Some middle-class seniors are resistant to accepting what they perceive as a lower socioeconomic rank. Remember, you are moving into a new economic identity where your sense of success is based on how skilled you are at adjusting to your current reality. If you live in a comfortable home in a middle-class neighborhood, only you and the owner will know your rent is subsidized.

Supplemental Nutrition Assistance Program (SNAP)

SNAP is also one of the government's most underused assistance programs for seniors. Only about a third of seniors who are eligible take advantage of it. Their primary concerns are that they will feel embarrassed if family or friends know they are receiving assistance, and they expect to get only the minimum benefit anyway. Well, it turns out that the average senior receives over $100 a month from SNAP, commonly known as the food stamp program.

Because the old paper stamps looked like Monopoly money, they immediately identified the recipient as indigent. To reduce the embarrassment resulting from the use of these food stamps, the government now allows the use of plastic cards or electronic benefit transfers. Also, you no longer have to pick up stamps every month, as they are electronically added to your card.

With a plastic card similar to a debit card that fits seamlessly into normal business practice, no one will notice that you are receiving government assistance. The awkwardness that existed before has been eliminated; affording recipients the privacy we all want.

Did you know that the food stamp program has relaxed rules for the disabled and the elderly who are over age 60? People are usually not eligible if they reside in an institution that provides their meals; however, this restriction is waived for those over 60. One is usually allowed only $2,000 in savings or resources, but the elderly are allowed up to $3,000, or up to up to $4,650 not counting auto values. The calculations include state income limits and allowable medical and shelter deductions. You can see if you are eligible online, but will have to appear in person for the full application.

Reverse Mortgage Program

This is a loan for homeowners over 62 years old who have substantial equity in their property. It is a federally designed program that allows private companies to compete with government entities. A portion of your equity is converted to monthly payments you receive. You do not have to repay the loan back unless you sell the house, relocate, or fail to follow other obligations of the lender. Lenders generally want your home to be nearly or completely paid off. Unfortunately, very few of us are in that position.

You are basically withdrawing your own money from your property for a fee. You are still required to pay insurances, taxes, and all other charges on the home. When you no longer need the home or pass away, the home ownership goes to the lender. You cannot pass the property on to your heirs, but you may be able to pass on some equity, if any remains.

Complaints focus on the high expense for this loan compared to the cost of a normal mortgage. The reverse mortgage has a hidden interest rate that accumulates for the lender's profit. Other common complaints are about manipulative firms that add thousands of dollars of extra fees. Also, if your equity falls, as many of us have experienced, your heirs may be required to pay for any shortfalls.

If you are seriously considering a reverse mortgage, you want to compare the expense and outcome to a simple refinancing of your mortgage, or to a home equity line of credit that has fewer restrictions. Signing all your hard-earned equity away could be very scary, especially if you need the money for a medical emergency.

For more information on reverse mortgages, the Federal Housing Authority and HUD websites are useful. This program is referred to as a HECM or Home Equity Conversion Mortgage, and HUD must approve the property.

Very Low Income Housing Repair Program

This U. S. Dept. of Agriculture program is designed to provide free money for the removal of health or safety hazards from your property. This program is similar to the Rural Repair and Rehabilitation Program. Funds may also be used to repair or renovate the home after removal of hazards. The funding limits at this time of writing are $7,500 per house, but you are not allowed to sell the property for three years after receiving the grant. You will need to be over 62 years old and have a current income of less than 50% of the average for your area. When applying, you'll need to itemize the improvements and their cost. The website for this program is www.usda.gov.

Meals on Wheels

Nurses gave this program its name when they used baby carriages to deliver meals to British soldiers in 1940. It wasn't until 1954 that the first American

program was developed in Philadelphia, Pennsylvania. The Older
Americans Act (OAA) provided federal funding for the program in 1972.
Now there are over 5,000 locations across the United States that serve over
one million meals a day.

Often we don't recognize mild malnutrition. You may remember that when
your parents became old and needed help, their relationship with food
changed. They lost interest in putting a lot of effort into cooking, and they
began eating less. This may be the first sign they needed a little assistance.
Malnutrition is higher in the elderly than any other age group, yet this
remains the most overlooked assistance program for senior despite the
obvious need.

The critical importance of this program is revealed in a survey conducted by
Chemung County, New York, (5) for their Meals on Wheels program:

65% of clients eat breakfast
80% save a portion for a later meal
49% eat only one or two meals a day
89% say their wheels meal is the main meal for the day
48% have trouble chewing and receive customized diets
96% say meals on wheels has improved their life
89% say their illness or weight has been more in control
90% have been able to resume physical activities with the meals.

If you take a second to examine the percentages, you'll be perplexed that
benefits are so great while the use of the program is so low. The survey
clearly reveals the potential for this to be a life saving program. You may not
need this service until you are much older or impaired in some way, but you
may know others who are not aware of, or are embarrassed by, the program,
yet need it now. I know pride gets in the way for some of us, but is it worth
going hungry to preserve it?

The best resource seems to be the Meals on Wheels Association of America
at mowaa.org. Their website lists locations that serve meals or will deliver
them. Some companies ask for a payment, which can be waived, based on
need. The organizations are staffed mostly by volunteers and are often open
to accepting more help.

**Common Sense Conclusion: Seniors need to be aware of all
government assistance programs to ensure economic stability if
necessary.**

**In summary, relocating and downsizing appear to be likely for
most of us. We need to devote careful thought to this transition,
since it's fairly complicated, with many variables to consider.
Adjusting our thought processes to accept a more constrained**

budget needs to be in the forefront of our considerations. Selling our personal residence at the best time to maximize profit can greatly benefit our budget for many years.

Places Rated Almanac helps identify appropriate relocation sites. We will enjoy independent living for most of retirement. If your income were low enough to consider overseas relocation, then you would qualify for many of the above government assistance programs. If you qualify, you would not need a dramatic relocation. This assistance could certainly improve your budget and just might determine where you live or relocate. We will investigate and take advantage of as many government assistance programs as we need in order to maintain the quality of our lives.

1. Brady, J.(6-28-2010)"Surprising new survey finds many retirees plan on moving in retirement" topretirements.com. Retrieved on 2-5-2014 from: www.topretirements.com/blog/baby-boomer-issues/surprising-new-survey-finds-many-retirees-plan-on-moving-in-retirement.html/
2. Savageau,D., Boyer, R.; New York: Prentice Hall Travel; "Places Rated Almanac"; 1993.
3. Savageau, D. New York: Frommers (6th edit.) "Retirement Places Rated"; 2004.
4. Kiplinger staff(8-2013) "10 Most tax Friendly states for Retirees." kiplinger.com. Retrieved on 2-6-2014 from: kiplinger.com/slideshow/retirement/T006-S001-10-most-tax-friendly-states-for-retirees
5. Chemung County staff(2008) "Survey results 2008" Mealsonwheelschemung.org Retriefved on 2-6-2014 from: mealsonwheelschemung.org/Survey.html

Chart 1: Schiller, R.J.(2006) A History of home Values Chart in "Irrational Exuberance" 2nd. www.ritholtz.com/blog. Reterived on 7-20-2014 from: http://graphics8.nytimes.com/images/2006/08/26/weekinreview/27leon_graph2.large.gif . Permission granted 7-28-2014 from Dr. Shiller's office.

8   VISIONS OF THE FUTURE

"I want to grow old without facelifts. I want to have the courage to be loyal to the face I've made. Sometimes I think it would be easier to avoid old age, to die young, but then you'd never complete your life, would you? You'd never wholly know you." - - Marilyn Monroe

With the arrival of the baby boom generation, retirement in America entered a state of transition. The colossal number of retirees, combined with the many years they will live, will certainly test the retirement infrastructure. I'm expecting our generation to push the envelope and reset expectations for what retirement means. We might be establishing blueprints for many generations to come.

These are the areas where needed changes may occur:

EMPLOYMENT

The number of people who wish to work is under-represented in the work force. Boomers constitute a vast population of educated and experienced people with a lot to contribute. I know many retirees who want to work on a part-time basis, but claim there is not much out there. That's because our society is oriented toward the full-time worker, with little flexibility for other possibilities. Ignoring this ballooning labor pool is a huge waste of talent, and a missed opportunity for companies and society in general.

Alternative employment structures that train and place disabled and retarded workers are expanding. There are now non-profit rehabilitation centers that take referrals from social service agencies that work with these people. One rehab program just procured the maintenance contract for the international airport in my area. Employers like these programs because they save money on salaries. This government-funded model has not been adapted to seniors because we are not designated as a group with special needs, like the disabled.

Yes, there is the Senior Community Service Employment Program (SCSEP) that I mentioned in chapter seven. However, this program is designated for people with very low incomes, and ignores the larger group of middle class retirees. What we need is:

1. Publicly or privately funded training and placement services for the retired, similar to that provided by rehab programs.
2. Specific and improved job placement geared to the elderly, which includes counseling and coaching.
3. Incentives to employers, such as lower salaries or tax deductions, for hiring seniors.
4. Incentives to employers to create more part-time jobs, job-sharing positions, and flexible hours.

SOCIALLY ORIENTED LIVING

Because so many of us will be single in retirement, we will need to develop a different social network than our previous ones. Our cultural emphasis on the nuclear or perhaps extended family often leaves us alone in retirement. This situation creates long-term problems of isolation and depression that are not being successfully addressed by governmental entities.

In our review of Retirement Communities and Care Facilities, we discussed the benefits of planned communities like Sun City, Del Webb, Leisure World, and Four Seasons. Based on the responses and the involvement of the residents, this model of social activity appears to be successful. We don't have to be wealthy to enjoy these communities if we are willing to live in (or relocate) to a modest area of the country.

Due to their popularity, I believe we'll see more of these communities from homebuilders who will emphasize affordability.

The second area for future development based on need is platonic cohabitation, such as in the TV show *The Golden Girls*. A widow on the show, Blanche, is the owner of the home she rents out to three other previously married women. We may not hear a clever punch line every two minutes, but this show is a great model for a socially supportive situation in the retirement years. There is a creative income opportunity here for those single women who can act in Blanche's role as a landlord.

GENDER ROLE REVERSALS

Women are now receiving the majority of college degrees and earn more of the household income on average. What a sea change from traditional days, when men were the breadwinners! The old model may have served a purpose during the iron and industrial ages, when physical jobs were in demand. But, this culture spilled into the home and our marriages, and created an imbalance in our personal relationships. Many of women felt an obligation to support their husband's career and patriarchal behaviors, even at the expense of personal sacrifice.

Well, the days of sacrifice are over. As we enter the information or "digital" age, different survival skills are required. These skills are now based on specific education and social intelligence. That is, education needs to have a social application for its expression. It's similar to crystallized intelligence or the ability to apply your knowledge to the environment. It's my opinion that the combination of women's superior social skills with education has created a trend that will replace men at the top.

As women become doctors, attorneys, and CEOs, the social culture around us will change. Such positions provide a great deal of respect and increased socioeconomic status. They require more education and demand more of a woman's time, so household gender roles are forced to adapt. In our relationships, some men may take the role of caretaker once they realize that their wife will earn more than they do. The future culture will change as more men take on greater domestic responsibilities and more women become the primary breadwinners.

FEMALE-ORIENTED BUSINESS

It's not news that female retirement is overlooked and underserved by society. The male oriented retirement articles that are mostly financially oriented evidence this. As the number of retirees explodes, expect business to follow this group. Business owners will be of either gender, but the focus will shift toward women since they will be the majority of retirees who live longer.

Referral services for residential placement is expected to be an area that is in demand due to the vast number of single and isolated seniors. As mentioned, this systemic problem has festered too long and is far too important to be ignored.

This trend toward women oriented businesses is already picking up steam as evidenced by the success of the website, A Place For Mom (1) and a directory of Women Owned Businesses (2). A Place For Mom is a business that provides care giving information to seniors. On their site they state, "We help seniors and families like yours make informed decisions, save time, and feel less alone as they search for senior care and housing." This business did not start until 2000, but is already the largest of its kind. The website says they help Dads too, but it's clear that their orientation is in their title. This is a free service to retirees because the care facilities reimburse the company.

I would not be surprised to witness a female-oriented investment firm that is designed for women by women as well. As I mentioned in the financial chapters, women invest differently than men. Women are not the risk takers that men are, but focus instead on sustainability of income. I envision a woman-oriented investment firm as being non-profit, with emphasis on personalized service and support. That's right, it would be a caring business driven by the passion of helping people, rather than just about making money.

This concept may be picking up steam, now that more financial advisors are marketing themselves as retirement advisors. Some firms are establishing a retirement department and providing workshops for older investors. Websites with investment advice specifically for women are becoming more common. I expect more women will become stockbrokers in their second act, and participate more actively in investments for themselves and others.

EDUCATION

Lifelong learning is emerging as one of the more common goals in retirement planning these days. Its appeal goes beyond the college educated; it has become a popular pastime for people of all educational backgrounds. I don't remember my parents taking any classes when they retired, so it may be characteristic of baby boomers. In any case, we all have to exercise our cerebral cortex, and taking classes is one of the most interesting and social ways to go about it.

Since education can be expensive, more colleges are starting a separate department for older learners. In the University of California system, for example, there is a lifelong learning institute designed for those over 50, with classes taught by ex-professors or anyone with specific knowledge. This system helps keep tuition to a fraction of normal costs, and offers students social involvement as well. I suspect that many colleges will follow this idea once they realize how popular it can be. Some of us may also find a creative opportunity to teach a class in one of these situations.

FAMILY REUNIONS

Now that you've read the Estate Planning section of this book, you know that the old method of probate causes family problems. Archaic practices have existed for many years with few questioning them. The revocable trust helps avoid court, but leaves many family issues unsettled. The rising expense that probate can create, and the unpredictability of those we appoint to carry out our wishes require a different approach.

My first suggestion was to have a family meeting to discuss your plans, rather than allow the probate process to disperse your belongings after you've departed. This approach should help reduce family fighting. If you know your offspring will disown or hate each other as a consequence of the probate process then why let that happen? You can provide your donations to those you love, including friends, while you are still around so you both can enjoy and appreciate it.

Open discussions of feelings and wishes benefit your heirs by lessening the chaos after you depart. It ensures your donations go to the right people, connects you with them, and lets you share your emotions together. I feel that this family and friends reunion will allow a deep personal connection to be confirmed before we depart. It's very satisfying to say goodbye and thank people for being our life long friend.

That's all good and fine, but how do you know when to have such a farewell reunion? You don't want to give away your belongings just to live another ten years and miss them. Of course, you can give your intended heirs a rain check to receive the items later. Or just arrange the reunion anytime you are in the mood -- but before you become too frail to manage what might become complex decisions.

Your medical condition can determine when this kind of reunion is appropriate as well. You want to have the reunion before you become seriously ill because illness brings other challenges. Try to make sure those who would come to your funeral attend your reunion first. This reunion will then be the most emotionally intimate gathering of your life, a time when you can appreciate and need it the most.

EVOLUTION OF THE FUNERAL

Funeral rituals really have not evolved much over time. My consultants inform me that everyone hates funerals unless they're in the business. Of course, many people enjoy the social gathering of distant relatives not seen for a while, or to pay their respects. But, it is clear that we attend funerals for other reasons than the funeral per se.

It appears to be this somber view of mourning the loss of life, rather than celebrating the wonder of it, that's so difficult. I may be childishly optimistic to think that this long-standing ritual will change, but I've been to funerals where music and dancing are a part of the ceremony. This kind of funeral does not involve a change of faith in any way; you just add a little music.

These funerals are called "funerals with music" or "jazz funerals." Their roots go back many years to the Cajun culture in Louisiana. The brass bands used in these processions were characteristic of the culture's colonial history, blended with spiritual practices. This spiritual practice started with African American musicians, then gained cross-cultural acceptance.

The jazz funeral begins with a gathering of all friends and family at the home of the departed. Traditionally, the casket is placed in a horse-drawn carriage that leads the way to the cemetery for burial. The funeral party follows behind, walking along as the brass band plays fairly somber music. The music becomes more upbeat as the procession continues, and some people then dance as they walk. Observers are allowed to join in this celebration of life when the procession reaches the cemetery.

I know that as a way of releasing our emotions we are supposed to mourn and cry at funerals. However, most people I know prefer to mourn or cry in privacy. I also think most of us would prefer departing on a positive note rather than a negative one. The emotion you feel after participating in a Cajun funeral is very positive, despite it being associated with death. If you ever get a chance to attend a Cajun funeral, you will probably find it surprisingly upbeat and enjoyable.

Can these Cajun or jazz funerals really become a trend for the future? Well, they've already been an accepted part of Southern culture for many years, and now occur all over this country. Exposure to "something different" like this might just lead to wider acceptance.

There is also the Irish Wake, which celebrates the life of the person who has died, and provides comfort for the living. In this tradition, the body is returned to the person's home, and not a funeral parlor. Family and friends gather in the home to say prayers. In the burial phase, the community is invited and alcohol is served. At this point the funeral turns into a party or celebration, where dancing and joking are common.

So, there are a number of positive alternatives to the traditional funeral that we might consider.

In saying farewell, I hope this book has motivated, empowered, and encouraged you to think outside the retirement box. Just because society has done things the same way for many years, that's no reason to continue doing them that way or not improve upon them. Women will be the harbingers of retirement transformations going forward, and will be more creative and humanistic in the process.

1. www.aplaceformom.com/assisted-living

2. http://www.feminist.com/market

Made in the USA
San Bernardino, CA
26 October 2016

40726716R00111